DISPOSSESSING
THE AMERICAN INDIAN

DISPOSSESSING
THE AMERICAN INDIAN
Indians and Whites
on the Colonial Frontier

By

Wilbur R. Jacobs

UNIVERSITY OF OKLAHOMA : NORMAN AND LONDON

Library of Congress Cataloging-in-Publication Data

Jacobs, Wilbur R.
  Dispossessing the American Indian.

  Bibliography: p.
  Includes index.
  1. Indians of North America—Government relations—To 1789. 2. Indians, Treat-
ment of—North America. I. Title.
E91.J3   1985   323.1′197073   84-21998
ISBN: 0-8061-1935-7

  3   4   5   6   7   8   9   10   11   12   13   14   15   16   17   18   19   20   21   22

For Priscilla
and William

WOODLAND INDIAN CONSERVATORS

The hunting and gathering which furnished the food supply of these people was by no means a hit-or-miss random search. Their dependence upon limited resources in limited territories required provision for themselves and their descendants, and they took stock of their resources. They knew in some detail what the supply of each resource was: deer, moose, beaver, fur-bearers, edible birds, berries, roots, trees, wild grasses. They knew the districts where each was to be found when wanted and, roughly, in what quantities. . . . In taking animals for food or for skin, the survivors, as breeding resources, were constantly considered, and the life thus taken was atoned for by rituals of address, apologizing in sympathetic phrases for their death. They were thanked for the sacrifice they made to man and death-rites were performed for them with rituals of thanksgiving.

Frank G. Speck
"Aboriginal Conservators"
Audubon Magazine (1938).

Contents

Maps

Illustrations

Preface to the 1985 Edition

Since *Dispossessing the American Indian* was first published in 1972, there has been a veritable explosion of publications in Indian studies, especially in Indian history and in the history of Indian-white relations. A renascence in scholarship suggesting new interpretations, new methods of investigation, and new approaches in evaluating data was responsible for setting off the burst of articles, books, and symposia at academic meetings.

During these years the renascence has made a particular impact upon scholars gathering at national meetings of the American Society for Ethnohistory. Later there were reverberations at conferences of the Western Historical Association and the American Society for Environmental History. Papers read at the meetings soon made their appearance in the scholarly journals of those societies — *Ethnohistory*, *Western Historical Quarterly*, and *Environmental Review* — along with publications sponsored by the Newberry Library's Center for the Study of the American Indian. A milestone was observed in January, 1974, when the staid *William and Mary Quarterly* printed an issue devoted to Indian-white history. Younger scholars, including a number of my former students, notably Calvin Martin, William Swagerty, and Yasu Kawashima, made significant contributions to the revisionism and reinterpretations published in these journals. Their work as well as that of other scholars is discussed in the Note on Sources.

While the renascence was still in embryo, the first edition of *Dis-*

possessing the American Indian was being written and prepared for the press. Included in the book were more than a half dozen key themes and interpretations that have since blended into the mainstream of the new American Indian history:

• Comparative frontier history of aboriginal-white relations, involving Indians of the Western Hemisphere, southern African peoples, indigenous peoples of Australia, New Guinea, and Oceana, has increasingly become a tool for investigative research.

• The *conquistador* version of frontier history has been expanded to show the impact of Europeans and Anglo-Americans from the time of the Columbian exchange to that of the Puritan assault upon New England and the later frontier expansion across the continent.

• The chain of friendship policy of the Iroquois has now been more thoroughly studied to show the complex history of a covenant chain peace diplomacy carried on through the eighteenth-century era of Iroquois restoration.

• Indian religion and Indian cultures and life-styles are increasingly recognized as a significant part of general American history.

• Research in pre-Columbian demography indicating that millions of Indians died from epidemics caused by European imported diseases is now generally accepted. This revised view of early American history suggests that colonists moved into a widowed land rather than a virgin land.

• The fur trade is gradually losing its romantic overtones and is seen more clearly as a predatory business that exhausted wildlife and Indian sources of livelihood.

• Frederick Jackson Turner and Francis Parkman, though still regarded as two of America's leading historians of the wilderness frontier, are more and more coming under academic fire for promoting exaggerated Anglo-Saxon images and for creating stereotypes of Native Americans.

• "Upstreaming"—the research technique of reevaluating historical sources from ethnographic perspectives, a cultural-historical approach to Indian history (see especially Chapter 11, "The Price of Progress")—is now firmly supported by leading ethnohistorians.

• The cultural-historical approach of tracing Indian-white relations through stages of acculturation (or contra-acculturation) is gradually being incorporated into the writing of American frontier history.

• The historic psychological basis for racism as a factor in Indian-white relations and the writing of history (see the Prologue) has gained credibility among scholars.

In a sense, *Dispossessing the American Indian* anticipated the renascence because it was a part of the churning, bubbling-over revisionism of the 1960s and 1970s. It should be noted, nonetheless, that themes, interpretations, and arguments in *Dispossessing* were controversial when the book first appeared, and though many of the viewpoints are accepted today, there is a corresponding backlash. The debate continues over the nature of the American frontier advance, the significance of Indian people, and the awareness of environmental despoliation. If anything can be said with the perspective of time, it is that the interdisciplinary field of ethnohistory has widened the perimeters of debate. There is, as a result, more widespread knowledge about the importance of Indian people in our society and about the value of their cultures as a part of the heritage that belongs to all Americans.

Additions and revisions have been made to the footnotes and to the Note on Sources. For intellectual stimulation that resulted in the first edition and revisions in the second edition, I am greatly indebted to four friends and scholars, Henry F. Dobyns, William N. Fenton, Francis Jennings, and the late Sherburne F. Cook. I am also grateful for suggestions for the 1985 edition made by my wife, Priscilla, and by Leland Carlson and by Alexander DeConde.

Santa Barbara, Calif. WILBUR R. JACOBS

Preface to the First Edition

This book, focusing on the confrontation between the eastern woodland Indians and the Anglo-American pioneers of the eighteenth century, attempts to restore highlights of a historical canvas that is not often seen clearly in our histories. A central part of that canvas was the tenacious struggle of the woodland tribes under a few great leaders such as Pontiac to preserve their landed heritage. From the white point of view, Indian resistance was expected, for the Indian represented the savage world that had to be tamed for civilization's westward march. The colonial frontier populace came to expect Indian war as a price for tapping the riches of the wilderness hinterlands. Inevitably the confrontation with the colonists was fatal for the Indians because it resulted in their defeat, their dispossession, and finally the virtual disappearance of their way of life. As Red Jacket, a Seneca orator argued in an 1805 protest against activities of a white missionary:

> "Brother": Our seats were once large, and yours were small. You have now become a great people, and we have got scarcely a place to spread our blankets. You have got our country, but you are not satisfied: you want to force your religion on us. *

We may recognize in this speech a tone of outraged protest against what might be called white cultural imperialism. Indeed, the whole process of conquering the Indian and removing him from the path of the onrushing white frontier of settlement exhibited, as we now can observe,

* W. E. Washburn, ed., *The Indian and the White Man* (Garden City, N.Y., 1964), p. 212.

the development of racist attitudes toward the Indian which, in turn, help to explain many of the injustices and irrationalities that characterized white policy. As one chapter of this book demonstrates in a comparative analysis, a number of the Indian experiences were shared by other native peoples such as the Aborigines of Australia and New Guinea who also faced waves of Europeans invading their lands.

The appearance of the Europeans brought a technological revolution and profound changes in the use of the land. A retreat of the Indians began as cattle and other domestic animals and the white man's maize fields overran the villages of the woodland Indians, who were among the first farmers of all native people in North America. As the forest gave way and the animal life in it changed, so the Indian's way of life passed into history. The days of wampum, peace pipes, gift-giving, and fur trading were soon gone. For the Indian, the white man's agricultural frontier was an ecological calamity.

The primary purpose of this book, then, is to throw more light on the ecology of the frontier and on the shadowy history of early native-white relations, particularly the relations between the woodland Indians and their adversaries, the Anglo-Americans. I also hope this volume will contribute to a better understanding of the unique culture of the woodland tribes and help to erase the blot of prejudice against the Indian that has persisted for centuries. It is in this spirit that my book is offered.

It would be impossible for me to mention all the individuals who have helped me in a work carried on for some fifteen years, during which time the majority of the following chapters were published as separate articles. For indispensable help in furnishing research and reference materials, I am indebted to the officers and librarians of the Henry E. Huntington Library, the Library of Congress Manuscripts Department, the William L. Clements Library, the Harvard College Library, the Public Archives of Canada, and the Libraries of the University of California at Santa Barbara, at Berkeley, and at Los Angeles. For assistance in probing the archival records of the early native-white contacts in Australia and New Guinea, I am grateful to the staffs of the Mitchell Library in Sydney, the State Library of Victoria in Melbourne, the Library of the University of Papua-New Guinea, the State Library of South Australia in Adelaide, the Menzies Library at Australian National University, the National Library in Canberra, and the Library of the Department of History, School of General Studies, Australian National University. I am appreciative of the courtesies extended to me by governmental officers of Australia in permitting me to visit Aborigines in Queensland at Palm Island and in reserves near Alice Springs. Domestic airline officials and Australian territorial government officers generously cooperated in making it possible for me to be a guest at interior Sepik River villages of Papua-New Guinea, where native people continue to live much as they have for thousands of years. Likewise, in the United States and in Canada I am appreciative of the kindnesses extended to me by native American Indians and governmental officers during visits I have made on a number of Indian reserves over the years. Some of them have diminished in size and in one or two cases have disappeared. I am especially grateful for the welcome extended to me by Six Nations Iroquois on their reservation near Brantford, Ontario.

With regret for the summary treatment that considerations of space entail, I acknowledge the help of individuals who have assisted me: Ray A. Billington and Mary Isabel Fry, Huntington Library; William Brandon, Monterey, California; Alexander DeConde, Jay Monaghan, and Roderick Nash, University of California, Santa Barbara; George E. Frakes and Curtis B. Solberg, Santa Barbara City College; Norris Hundley, Leo Lemay, John W. Caughey, Peter Loewenberg, Gary Nash, and Terry Ranger, University of California, Los Angeles; Joe Illick, San Francisco State College; John Hawgood, University of Birmingham, England; Carl O. Sauer and N. Scott Momaday, University of California, Berkeley; Alden T. Vaughan, Columbia University; Wilcomb B. Washburn, the Smithsonian Institution; William T. Hagen, State University of New York, Fredonia; Francis Paul Prucha, Marquette University; William N. Fenton, State University of New York, Albany; Bernard W. Sheehan, Indiana University; Howard H. Peckham, William L. Clements Library; Douglas E. Leach, Vanderbilt University; Edmund S. Morgan, Yale University; E. Gregory Crampton, University of Utah; Norman Harper, University of Melbourne; Russel Ward, University of New England, Armidale, Australia; H. Frank Wilcock, Canberra, Australia; C. Manning Clark, Australian National University; B. J. Dalton, James Cook University of North Queensland; Ken Inglis, University of Papua-New Guinea. A few of the above individuals have read chapters of my book and have given me advice; others have given me the benefit of their knowledge by conversation, by correspondence, and by their published writings. I have also profited greatly by help given me by advanced students at the University of California, Santa Barbara. Among these are Calvin L. Martin and Charles Townley who possess a wide knowledge of interdisciplinary scholarship on the American Indians. Both Jean Bonheim and Elsie Kearns have made valuable editorial suggestions, and my wife, Beth, has made a number of recommendations that have improved the book. I am indebted to Alice Kladnik for excellent typing assistance.

The Committees on Research of the American Philosophical Society, the University of California, Santa Barbara, the Committee on the International Exchange of Persons, and the Australian-American Educational Foundation provided funds that have helped to defray the costs of research and travel.

Pilot versions of chapters of this book have appeared in the *Pacific Historical Review*, the *William and Mary Quarterly*, the *Indiana Magazine of History, Michigan History*, the *Huntington Library Quarterly, Ohio History, Western Pennsylvania Historical Magazine, New York History, The Journal of Southern History, The A.H.A. Newsletter*, and in *Attitudes of the Colonial Powers Toward the American Indian* (University of Utah Press, 1969).

W. R. J.

Santa Barbara, Calif.,
February, 1972

Prologue:
Indians and Whites
An Essay on Misunderstanding

In recent years there has been increasing public interest in the history of the native American Indian. This has arisen partly because of a widespread feeling, often stressed by modern Indian writers such as Vine Deloria, that the kind of conventional American history readily available to us tends to be one-sided in its interpretations. Since most of our history is written by white writers, many have come to ask whether much that has appeared in print is biased or unreliable. A generous friend who assisted me in editing Francis Parkman's letters in the 1950s, the late Bernard DeVoto, once spoke to me about this kind of one sidedness and the arrogant manner in which some historians wrote American history as if the Indians scarcely existed. In the introductory remarks to one of his books he stated his case very well:

> A dismaying amount of our history has been written without regard to Indians, and of what has been written with regard to them much treats their diverse and always changing societies as uniform and static.

DeVoto went on to charge anthropologists with a tendency "to overvalue Indian traditions, which are among the least trustworthy of human records." [1] But it was the historians who really neglected the Indian, DeVoto argued. Since the documentary material concerning Indian-white relations was scarce and often suspect, there was a tendency to accept the axiom that "without documents there can be no history." Indeed, DeVoto went so far as to say, "there is some inherent tendency to write American history as if it were a function of white culture only." [2]

Certainly the heightened attention given Indian history is related to the growing self-consciousness of other American minorities, especially blacks. The role of all minority Americans in our history needs to be more adequately described and documented. My own interest in the American Indian has been a lifelong experience. Over the years I have written a number of essays on various aspects of Indian-white relations. Recently I gathered a number of these together and deposited them at the library of the University of California, Santa Barbara, so my students and other interested readers could consult them. The result was surprising. The American Indian's history obviously appeals enormously to undergraduate students, and my makeshift book proved popular beyond my expectations. Indeed, I had to replace the copy several times. With the hope that other readers may find this subject of interest, I have reworked these essays and brought them together for a wider audience.

I cannot say that the essays grouped here provide altogether pleasant reading. In a sense, they concern a seamier side of Indian-white relations that is often neglected in early American history. The evidence shows that the Indians were unmercifully exploited—as fur-gatherers, as fighting allies, and as landholders. Much of what is included here documents that exploitation—an exploitation, we should explain in our written American history, made possible by a transplanted European population that tolerated such excesses. The vast majority of the Anglo-American settlers knew little of Indian culture or life, yet they generally thought of Indians as savages inferior to the white man.

It would be a distortion to argue that the Indian was always treated with disregard for his well-being, that there were no humane men among the colonials or British officials who concerned themselves with the interests of the Indian. We know that contacts between Quakers and Indians were constructive and "of a special kind: they have been on the whole, nonviolent contacts. To put it more positively, they have been motivated and animated by friendship, sympathy, understanding, respect and love." [3]

Nor are the Quakers the only bright spot in this cloudy segment of American history. In fact, the treatment of the Indian varied widely from colony to colony because the imperial government found it all but impossible to enforce uniform policies and regulations on the farflung woodland Indian frontier. Among those individuals who knew the Indian best from long personal contact—Indian agents, traders, and occasional military leaders—there were men who had a very high opinion of the native Americans. Some of these men, such as Indian superintendents Edmond Atkin and William Johnson, were in a position to advocate changes in policy that could soften the clash of interests between whites and Indians.

The essays here fall into three general groups. Those in Part I sketch the background of Indian contacts with whites and the impact of the fur-trading frontier upon the land and the aboriginal way of life. Particular attention here is given to the wampum diplomacy of the woodland Indians and the phenomenon of gift-giving by which the British and French controlled a huge and sometimes hostile native population during the colonial era. Then follow essays on particular aspects of Indian-white relations: Indian superintendent Edmond Atkin's remarkable scheme for British imperial Indian control; an account of events at Fort William Henry in 1757 that have had unusual repercussions in American history and literature; and a discussion of the fascinating Indian chief Pontiac and what has been called his "conspiracy" to remove the British from North America. Despite the reluctance of the Indians to give up the hardware, textiles, and rum they had come to expect in the form of frequent subsidies or "presents," they united to drive the British into the sea in a struggle for self-determination and independence. The savagery of the war on the Indian frontier of 1763, the enormous appetite for land on the part of the colonists, and the desire of the home government to provide a solution to the Indian problem led to a unique proposal: an Appalachian Indian boundary line separating civilization from the Indian world. The last essay in this group deals in part with the question of whether the boundary line was an antecedent to the later development of a removal and reservation policy.

The essays in Part III give an overview of early native-white relations on a worldwide scale. The first of these is concerned with the particular attitudes and policies that British colonials had toward the woodland Indians bordering their frontiers. Here there is evidence of both favorable and unfavorable attitudes. Surprisingly enough there is documentation in the form of written commentary to show a factual basis for the noble savage image that has grown into part of American legend. But even this contemporary opinion seems to have become a basis of frontier mythology. The reader can draw his own conclusions after examining the case presented here. Another point scrutinized in this essay is the nature of Indian-white violence. Who, if anyone, was at fault? Did the violence have a force, a momentum of its own beyond the control of individual colonies, the imperial government, or the Indians themselves? Again, the reader may evaluate the arguments and the evidence given.

The last essay in Part III spotlights native-white relations in a world-wide scene. What happened to North American Indians and other native peoples on remote frontiers of European expansion as they confronted waves of explorers, missionaries, soldiers, and settlers? More particularly, what happened to the Aborigines as the Europeans advanced into the wildlands of Australia and New Guinea? Is there a parallel story of Indian-white contacts? This essay also attempts to answer other provoking questions: Did native cultures quickly dissolve as the acid process of dispossession and occupation began? In this time of fatal confrontation, what happened to the delicate ecological balance that natives maintained in their special culture areas?

The evidence culled from a vast reservoir of data compiled by anthropologists, historians, and others tells us that there was a violent impact that, in many cases, shattered native societies. But there were sturdy survivors among the native peoples. Indeed the author has visited reservations of such peoples as the Navajo and the Iroquois, reserves of the Australian Aborigines, and villages of the native people on the interior Sepik River of New Guinea (still unmapped today). Many of these people have managed to resist complete assimilation and to cling to portions of their ancestral lands. The story of the Australian Aborigines is a tragic one that has many similarities with that of the American Indian. In their confrontation with whites, the native indigenous people paid a dear price for progress, especially in loss of land.

Throughout these essays runs a thread of pervasive racism that illuminates a very complex but intriguing pattern of Indian-white relations. Roy Harvey Pearce in his perceptive study, *The Savages of America*, which was originally published a number of years ago, was among the first to recognize the subtle complexity of this pattern when he argued that Indians were a symbol of what the white settler must not allow himself to become. The Indian warrior was a kind of survivor, a relic of the savage past that civilized man had left behind long ago. Thus, to destroy the Indian was to destroy savagery, to control the Indian was to protect white culture from being subverted.[4] More recently, Winthrop Jordan in his award-winning study, *White Over Black, American Attitudes Toward the Negro, 1550–1812*, has explained that white attitudes toward the Negro existed at both levels of consciousness and unconsciousness and that prejudice became automatic and self-reinforcing when a cycle of debasement in servitude and prejudice of the mind had begun.[5] Jordan went on to argue that the origins of prejudice against the Indian were based on somewhat similar attitudes; although the whites developed and maintained separate attitudes toward Indians, the conclusion was reached that "the Indians were more like Negroes than like Englishmen."[6] In other words, whites acquired grotesque stereotypes of blacks and Indians very early in American history.

What were the reasons for such racial prejudice? Peter Loewenberg, a historian highly trained in psychoanalytic research techniques, has provided some answers[7] in a brilliant essay that throws a powerful search-light on the psychological aspects of racism in American history. Men of all races and times, Loewenberg argues, have held in the *unconscious*° desires that are inadmissible to the consciousness. Such desires, some-times murderous or incestuous, are often projected onto others because what is outside the individual can be denied. In other words, Loewenberg shows us that projection is seeing in others what we may deny in our-selves. When we project evil or sordid desires by perceiving them in other people, we are able to criticize or even to act against others. Throughout American history, whites, often forced to live within certain codes of conduct, have had the problem of repressing forbidden desires in attempting to conform to values of their own society. Thus, in their perspective, blacks have frequently become the personification of sloth and sexuality. So it was with the American Indians who, in the eyes of whites, became stereotyped symbols of lewdness, sloth, dirt, violence, and treachery.[8]

Projection, as a way of self-deception, a way of convincing one's self that "the evil impulses are out there, not here in me,"[9] is a convincing explanation of the psychological basis of racism, and the Indian was one of the first historic victims. He was often characterized as a lazy, danger-ous brute hostile to civilizing influences. At the same time he became an object of hate and fear. There was a tendency on the American frontier to equate the Indian with the savagery of uncontrolled violence when in fact he was, in many respects, a better peacemaker and peacekeeper than the white man. Indian hating goes back to the first violent Indian wars of the seventeenth century. Certainly the morality of such hatred over centuries of time is something for all of us to ponder.[10]

Although the last essay published here partly concerns the larger In-dian population of North America as well as other native peoples, the main thrust deals with the woodland tribes, those of the greater Appa-lachian frontier that made a final defense for eastern portions of the Great Lakes and the Mississippi Valley against the Anglo-American frontier. These Indians were courageous defenders of their homeland and perhaps the best farmers in North America. Though some of the Algonquian tribes of the western woodland fringe were seminomadic, frequently changing the locations of their villages, they, like their eastern cousins, raised maize, beans, squash, and tobacco and were skilled fisher-

° "The term *unconscious*," according to Loewenberg, "means the kind of symbolic preverbal thought that is the heritage of us all . . . it fulfills wishes for pleasure; it is timeless—condensing the past, present, and future . . . it knows no logic . . . the unconscious will hallucinate facts or objects to obtain gratification . . . "The Psy-chology of Racism," in Gary B. Nash and Richard Weise, eds., *The Great Fear, Race in the Mind of America* (New York, 1970), p. 186n.

CHRISTINAUX
or KILISTINOS

Lake Superior

TEMISCAMING

EASTERN
SIOUX

MESSESAGUES
(subdued by the Iroquois)

OUTAOUCS or OUTAWAS

SIOUX or
NADOUESSIANS

NICARIAGES
*(United with the Six
Nations making them
the seventh member
of the League)*

Lake Huron

WESTERN SIOUX

OUTAGAMIS

Ft. Toron

ANCIENT
HURONS

*Lake
St. Clair*

Lake Eri
or Oksweg

MASCOUTENS

Ft. Detroit ■

Lake Michigan

PANIS

*(The Six Nations have extended
their territories to the River
Illinois ever since the year
1672 when they subdued the
Ancient Chaouanons, the native
proprietors of these countries.)*

MIAMIS or MIAMMEES
(TWIGHTWEES)

ANCIENT ERIEZ
(extirpated by the Iroquo

*(extensive meadows
full of buffalo)*

Ft. Miami ■

MINQUAS

PICKAWILLANEES
or PICTS

OHIO INDIAN
*(A mixed tribe
Indians under th
Six Nations)*

PYANKASHEES

Pickawillany ▲

Illinois

Miami

DELAWARES

(country full of mines)

WAUWAUGHTANEES

Wabash

Ohio

LOWER SHAWNOES

OSAGES

*(A fine, level, and
fertile country
by accounts of the
Indians & our
people)*

River of the Cherakees

▲ Gr. Telliquo

Mississippi

CHERAKEE

ARKANSAS

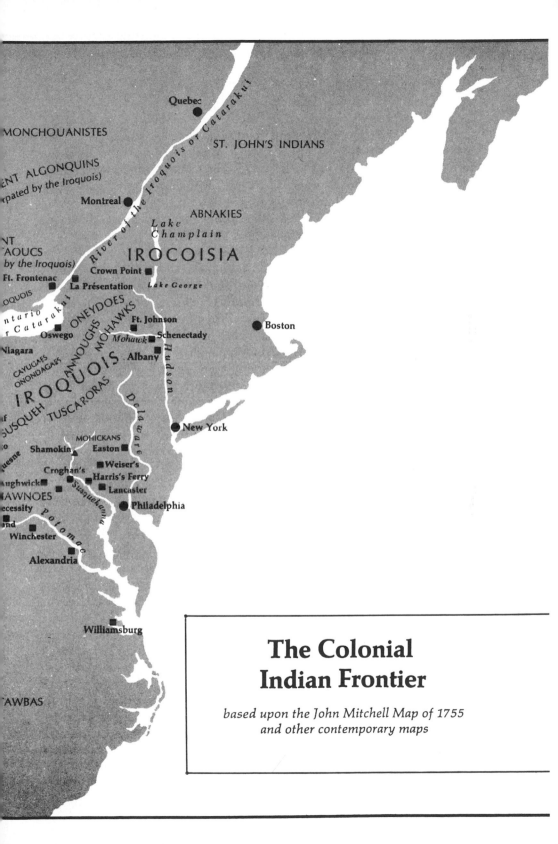

MONCHOUANISTES

ST. JOHN'S INDIANS

Quebec

RIVER ALGONQUINS
(usurpated by the Iroquois)

Montreal

ABNAKIES

Lake Champlain

AOUCS
(by the Iroquois)

IROCOISIA

Ft. Frontenac

La Présentation

Crown Point

Lake George

OQUOIS

ONEYDOES

ntario
r Catarakui

Oswego

ANNOUGHS

MOHAWKS

Ft. Johnson

Schenectady

Niagara

CAYUGAES
ONONDAGAES

Mohawk

Albany

Hudson

IROQUOIS

TUSCARORAS

Delaware

SUSQUEH

MOHICKANS

New York

Shamokin

Easton

Croghan's

Weiser's

uesne

Harris's Ferry

aughwick

Lancaster

Susquehanna

AWNOES

ecessity

Potomac

Philadelphia

Winchester

Alexandria

Williamsburg

AWBAS

The Colonial
Indian Frontier

*based upon the John Mitchell Map of 1755
and other contemporary maps*

men and hunters. Besides food harvested from their fields and fish and meat taken from the forestlands and streams, they collected a wide variety of wild fruits, berries, nuts, seeds, and mussels. They were also craftsmen skilled in chipping and in grinding stone implements. Their copper, hand pounded from nearly pure chunks found in the Lake Superior area, was made into colorful jewelry. They fought and hunted with bows, arrows, and spears, and fished with hooks, nets, and multi-pronged spears. Their buckskin breeches and skin robes closely resembled those of their more sophisticated farmer cousins in the East and South: the Iroquois, the Cherokees, and the Natchez.[11]

Among the Iroquois, the men fished and hunted in the spring (and sometimes fought) while the women had the responsibility of clearing the land, seeding, and later weeding and harvesting. The sturdy Iroquois women cultivated at least fifteen varieties of corn, sixty types of beans, and eight kinds of squash. Their tools, a digging stick and a hoe made from the shoulder blade of an animal, made possible a bounty of the basic nutritious maize-bean-squash food combination if the hunters failed to provide meat or if there was a seasonal shortage of wild plant foods, which included thirty-four fruits and about fifty types of edible roots, seeds, and leaves.[12] The bulky elm-bark canoes of the Iroquois were as serviceable as the colorfully decorated dugout canoes of the southern woodland tribes. What the whites came to admire as an engineering marvel, however, was the graceful birch-bark canoe made by the Algonquian warriors to the north. Ordinarily their canoe could be made by peeling the tree, but for large canoes a big birch was felled.[13]

Most of the great Indian tribes and confederacies populating the wilderness frontiers of the colonies were concentrated in semipermanent towns with as many as six or seven hundred people. The Iroquois log-palisaded-settlements, called "castles" by the New Yorkers, were surrounded by a huge ditch. Beyond were fields of waving maize and beans comprising several hundred acres of cultivated farmland. Longhouse buildings inside the fortifications were sometimes three hundred feet in length. Covered with elm bark they were used for civic and religious purposes, for storage, and for family apartments.[14] The cornfields, kept productive for as long as a dozen years without the chemical fertilizers or pesticides that modern farmers must use, were burned in the fall, and then planted in the spring with maize and beans. Burning released nutrients and made them available, but the most important factor increasing the Iroquois yields was the growing of beans and corn together. The importance of nitrogen fixation by bacteria in the roots of leguminous plants is known to modern scientists; with the Seneca it was a belief in the spiritual union of the two plants that gave vitality to the soil.[15]

The Mohawk "castles," connected by a web of trails that also led to the other Iroquois cantons, were a formidable barrier to the westward expansion of New England and New York. Similarly, the Iroquois "half-king" Mingos who lorded over the Ohio area villages (also populated with Delawares, Shawnees, and remnants of other tribes conquered by the Iroquois), controlled land purchases and trading privileges. Further south, the populous "Upper" and "Lower" Cherokee towns were centers of wilderness politics and deerskin trade on the inland frontiers of Virginia and the Carolinas.

Powerful Creeks and Choctaws, the latter usually allied to the French, occupied towns on strategic sites of the numerous waterways on the southwestern frontiers of Georgia. Far into the interior, north of Louisiana, were the fortified towns of the Chickasaws, staunch allies of the English. Because they harassed the interior trade between Louisiana and the Illinois country, the Chickasaws were a favorite target for French intrigue and attack. But even the French admired the valor of the Chickasaw warriors who fought on magnificent horses and whose women faced the enemy like men. The towns, fortifications, and societies of all these great woodland people were a source of wonderment to those Europeans who saw them in their pristine state before the introduction of disease, liquor, and dependence upon the white man's technology.[16]

Even before the coming of the white man, however, the societies of these woodland peoples were in a constant state of change. Cultural changes resulted from trade in copper, wampum, salt, tobacco, and other items. As one tribe came to excel in the growing of tobacco, it might become known as the Tobacco Nation and trade its surplus to other nations. What anthropologists call diffusion was the result. Surplus products were traded again and again and thus diffused throughout the Indian world.

The influx of white gifts and trade goods of hardware, textiles, and food likewise had a profound influence upon the culture of the woodland tribes. More particularly, white technology, especially the Indian trading gun (made specifically by British artisans for the Indian), brought about fundamental alterations in Indian warfare and hunting techniques. Close examination of lists of gifts and trade goods reveals a gradual change away from toys and jewelry to basic necessities such as cloth, tools, and weapons. By the 1750s there was a diffusion of the white man's trading goods throughout the whole woodland Indian world.[17]

The process began in the early 1600s after the visit of Henry Hudson, who is reputed to have given rum and biscuit to the Mahicans, river Indians. Soon afterwards New Netherland traders at Fort Orange built up such a thirst in the Indians for guns, hatchets, rum and other items that the Iroquois scoured the woods for furs to buy more. The result was a swift depletion of some fur-bearing animals, particularly beaver.[18]

The Iroquois had no alternative but to turn to another source of supply: the seemingly inexhaustible reserves of Great Lakes beaver.

It is now clear, from the evidence amassed in the last few decades, that the virtual extermination of beaver was an underlying cause for much seventeenth-century forest warfare.[19] This struggle eventually helped to bring about the long series of bloody wars between the French and the Iroquois, wars that led to the near extermination of the Hurons.* The Iroquois felt obliged to fight distant Indian peoples to maintain wide-ranging beaver hunting grounds and to maintain a position as middleman in the fur trade between the Dutch and the Great Lakes Indians. As the Iroquois sachems told Governor Thomas Dongan of New York in 1687, "wee warr with the Farr Nations of Indians, because they kill our people, & take them prisoners when wee goe a Bever hunting." Cadwallader Colden, writing forty years later in his *The History of the Five Indian Nations* explained that Iroquois beaver wars persisted because "the Five Nations have few or no Bever in their own Country, and for that Reason are obliged to hunt at a great Distance, which often occasions disputes with their Neighbors about the Property of the Bever." [20]

As early as 1640 there is evidence to show that the Dutch fur trade brought about an ecological catastrophe in the Iroquois hunting grounds. A shrewd Dutchman in that year who knew the intricacies of the lucrative Fort Orange trade argued that those "French savages" had "more furs . . . than are now bartered in all of New Netherland." [21] Busy trade in brass kettles, guns, knives, and other items had brought great wealth to the Dutch fur men. Nevertheless their hunger for furs, recorded in, for example, the purchase of some 30,000 beaver and otter skins in the single year 1633, exhausted Iroquois home hunting areas.[22] The thoroughness of the beaver and otter extermination reverberated ecologically in every corner of the Iroquois preserves and brought about new Iroquois policies of trade and war with Canadian tribes.

We can be reasonably certain that the experience of the Iroquois was shared by other woodland tribes bordering the colonies. They, too, had their lands depleted of certain kinds of fur-bearing animals with the influx of traders and their followers, the land speculators and the settlers. Increasingly all these native people were dependent upon subsidies, or presents, of food, clothing, tools, and weapons for their very livelihood. Clearly these outlays of goods became the very lifeblood of forest di-

---

* In their "Beaver Wars" the Iroquois, armed with Dutch guns, had a considerable advantage over the Hurons, who as late as the final invasion of their country (in 1648–49) had only limited firearms. F. W. Hodge, ed., *Handbook of the American Indians North of Mexico*, pt. 1, Smithsonian Institution, Bureau of American Ethnology Bulletin, no. 30 (Washington, D.C., 1907), p. 588: Alfred G. Bailey, *The Conflict of European and Eastern Algonkian Cultures, 1504–1700, A Study in Canadian Civilization*, 2d ed. (Toronto, 1969), p. 53.

plomacy as the French and English competed for Indian allegiance in the contest for empire during the whole colonial period of our history. Whites were sometimes astonished to discover how quickly Indians developed a cumulative and persistent demand for a wide variety of European goods.

There is another aspect of gift-giving to the Indians, particularly concerning land transfers, that has seldom been understood by whites, or for that matter white historians. When woodland Indian chiefs spoke of transfer of land from one people to another, they apparently referred to Indians alone. Investigators have found that almost all Algonquian and Iroquois tribes, particularly those of the Great Lakes, the Ohio Valley, and the Northeast, saw whites as strangers who could expect no land except that which was "given" to them by Indians. In return for such gifts of territory, the Indians could accept presents from whites in the form of reciprocity, but not compensation. Thus, according to authorities who have studied this question, land grants were considered gifts that should not be bought with money. There were, in short, no sales of land as we understand them, and whites were interlopers who could only receive "gifts" of land.[23] Moreover, the land rightfully belonged to the Indians because it was originally a "gift" to them:

> The Great Spirit gave this great island to his red children; he placed the whites on the other side of the big water; they were not contented with their own, but came to take ours 'from us. . . . These lands are ours: no one has the right to remove us because we were the first owners.[24]

As the cutting edge of white settlement sliced deeper and deeper into aboriginal lands, the European method of landholding, which had caused irreversible changes in the lives of native peoples throughout the world, also moved westward pushing the Indians into the interior and surrounding reserves that the tribesmen managed to keep. One of the tragedies of American history is the poignant narrative of the dispossession of the woodland tribes. Like their cousins further west, they conceived of the land in an entirely different way than the Europeans. Their enemy, the white settlers, were largely fugitives from the European landlord system. First-, second-, third-, and even fourth-generation settlers[25] were fiercely determined, Indians or no Indians, to have a piece of the great new world they could call their own, their very own piece of the rich good earth. The Indian, as we have seen, saw the land as supernaturally provided for man's use and not subject to sale or individual ownership.[26] For the tribesmen, the land, as well as the life-sustaining plant and animal life on it, was part of the bounty of Mother Earth. Though tribal and village councils often controlled garden plots or maize fields, and some Algonquian tribes seem to have developed family hunting territories[27] to conserve beaver from fur trade exploitation, the woodland Indians, as well as other North American tribesmen, had no real conception of the full meaning of individual land ownership. They regarded the land, the wilderness, and the heavens as part of a sacred, mystically conceived explanation of life.[28] Thus the whites misunderstood the woodland Indian's almost astonishing awareness of the ecological relationships between plants and animals, which was attributed to the Indian's sharper perception of such phenomena. As we now know, the awareness was due instead to an attitude of reverence toward nature, the result of a different culture than the white man's. It is this basic difference in attitude toward the land that helps to explain the clash between natives and settlers.

Misunderstanding has also arisen because the early wars between Indians and whites were so bitterly fought that even the colonials themselves disagreed about causes, results, and interpretations. For instance, there was a storm of debate over the two major New England Indian wars of the seventeenth century, the Pequot War of 1637 and King Philip's War of 1676. Such Puritan writers as Increase Mather and William Hubbard feuded with each other as they prepared histories of the Indian war of 1676 that was still in progress.[29]

There is, however, one thing the white man's accounts of these wars generally agree on (we have no respectable Indian accounts that have been preserved), and that is Indian conspiratorial tactics. Since the whites tended to justify their own actions in their histories of these conflicts, the Indians are usually cast in the role of perfidious villains, of scourges, instruments of God's anger. Even the kindly Roger Williams, who had defended Indian land rights in Massachusetts and adopted a humane policy toward the Indians at Providence, spoke darkly of Pequot negotiators who attempted to unite New England Indians against Massachusetts in 1636. Recalling his mission to prevent their alliance with the Narragansetts, Williams wrote:

> Three dayes & nights my Busines forced me to lodge & mix with the bloudie Pequt Embassadours, whose Hands & Arms (me thought) reaked with the bloud of my Countrimen murther'd & massacred by them on Conecticut Riuer, & from whome I could not but nightly looke for thejr bloudy Kniues at my owne throate allso.[30]

The Indian method of warfare, often depending upon ambush, a camouflaged surprise attack, or an unexpected assault (which Williams feared might take place) did of course help to build the image of machinations and conspirators. Thus King Philip in the period immediately before the outbreak of the war that has his name, was suspected by Plymouth authorities of heading a conspiracy. When he refused to disarm himself, he was portrayed as a leader who was in truth a perfidious scoundrel. Yet it was the English, in this long and murderous war, who caused the first blood to flow.[31]

Likewise, in early Virginia, the great chief Opechancanough, who led his people in two fiercely fought wars against the Virginians in 1622 and 1644, was often portrayed as a sly, secretive old villain who bided his time for a sneak attack on the whites. This "conspiracy" theory of the seventeenth century was reflected and projected into later Indian wars and into our modern histories.[32] Of course all Virginia Indian wars have not been portrayed as conspiracies, but in the end the Indian was beaten, as in the case of Bacon's Rebellion of 1676, an abortive revolt in Virginia against royal authority resulting from a failure of Indian policy. In the midst of the fighting, Susquehannahs and other Indians were defeated, opening up the Piedmont of Virginia for white occupation.

Further south, the remaining interior Virginia-Carolina frontier east of the Appalachians was cleared in two early eighteenth-century Indian wars. The first of these, the Tuscarora War of 1711–12 resulted in the partial decimation of these Indians whose survivors moved northward in the next decade to join their brethren the Iroquois, as the "sixth" nation. William Byrd's diary of this period in 1711 records his explanation of Indian resistance at the time: "We went to the capitol where we heard that the Indians were forming a conspiracy against the English and that a Nottoway Indian told a negro of it." [33] In the Yamasee War of 1715–1728, the Carolinians seem to have nearly exterminated a once powerful coastal tribe that today is only remembered for its skillful warrior-canoemen who paddled with a graceful "Yamasee stroke." [34] Since the Yamasee had "organized a combination against the English" in "the great conspiracy of 1715" and had allied themselves with the Spaniards, little quarter was given to these people who in 1761 were said to have only a surviving remnant of twenty.[35]

It is not surprising that the conspiracy theory of the seventeenth century persisted into the eighteenth century to explain the origins of Indian hostilities. One could scarcely expect another interpretation of history to attach itself to what has become known as "the conspiracy of Pontiac" in 1763. Probably no more pseudo-historical view of the past has been invented than the conspiracy theory of Indian war and politics, an unfortunate oversimplification of historical causation that looms behind misunderstanding and bitterness in early frontier Indian-white relations. Misunderstanding persisted despite the sympathetic understanding of many whites. Among these were a few devoted Anglo-American missionaries such as the Puritan clergymen John Eliot and Thomas Mayhew whose efforts on the eve of King Philip's War resulted in the conversion of an estimated 2,500 Indians (out of some 15,000 living in the New

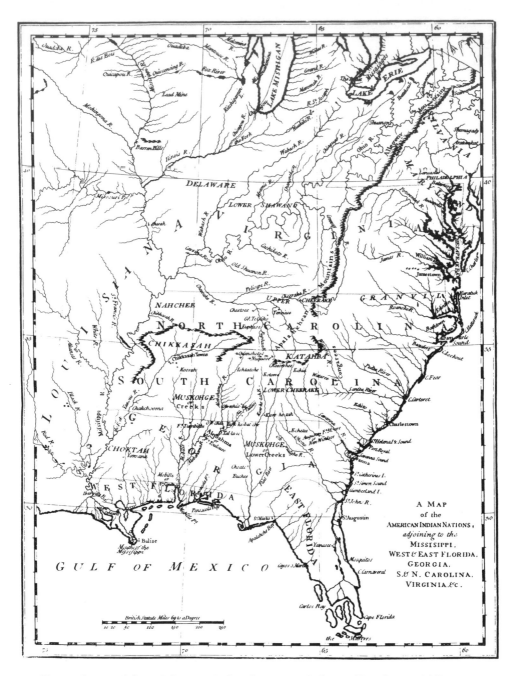

From: James Adair, *History of the American Indians* (London, 1775).
Courtesy, Huntington Library.

England forests).[36] Roger Williams, who had made a special effort to understand Indian culture and languages, seems to have established a better rapport with his Indian wards because he took no advantage of his prestige to press them into becoming professing converts.[37] But even Williams was drawn into the orbit of conflict between Indians and whites if only as a mediator. The pages that follow provide some of the details of that conflict as it expanded into the interior woodlands and reached a crescendo in the middle of the eighteenth century.[*]

*Neal Salisbury, *Manitou and Providence: Indians, Europeans, and the Making of New England, 1500-1643* (New York, 1982), pp. 203–39, describes the Indian loss of equilibrium following the European contacts and settlement; and Francis Jennings, *The Invasion of America: Indians, Colonialism, and the Cant of Conquest* (Chapel Hill, 1975), pp. 3-14, analyzes Eurocentric attitudes justifying the *conquistador* motives of New England colonists. Jennings enlarges on this theme in his account of the Iroquois "chain of friendship" alliance, or "covenant chain," in *The Ambiguous Iroquois Empire, The Covenant Chain Confederation of Indian Tribes with English Colonies from its beginnings to the Lancaster Treaty of 1744* (New York, 1984), pp. 84, 112, 367-74.

PART I

INDIAN-WHITE CONTACT: BACKGROUND

The niggardliness of our history, our stupidity, sluggishness of spirit, the falseness of our historical notes, the complete missing of the point. Addressed to the wrong head, the tenacity with which the fear still inspires laws, customs—the suppression of the superb corn dance of the Chippewas, since it symbolizes the generative processes—as if morals have but one character . . . till, in the confusion, almost nothing remains of the great American New World but a memory of the Indian.

William Carlos Williams
In the American Grain

The White Man's Frontier in American History: The Impact upon the Land and the Indian

In writing their histories of this country they have so hastily disposed of this refuse of humanity [the Indians] . . . which littered and defiled the shore and the interior. . . . It frequently happens that the historian, though he professes more humanity than the trapper, mountain man, or gold digger, who shoots one as a wild beast, really exhibits and practices a similar inhumanity to him, wielding a pen instead of a rifle.

Henry D. Thoreau*

We read in recent news reports that our fish and wildlife are being slaughtered by the thousands. Conservationists warn that many types of birds and animals are in danger of extinction here and abroad as expanding human population relentlessly squeezes them out of wilderness sanctuaries. Even breathing is difficult in air dangerously polluted by millions of automobiles and a huge industrial complex. Many of our lakes and rivers are contaminated, and even our beaches are blackened by sludge washed in from the polluted sea.[1]

* Henry D. Thoreau, *The Journal of Henry D. Thoreau,* ed. Bradford Torrey and Francis H. Allen (Cambridge, 1949), 11: 437–38. I am indebted to William Brandon for calling my attention to this passage and for criticism of an early draft of this essay.

19

The destruction of our natural environment is usually viewed as a great modern problem, the implication being that only in the twentieth century has the onslaught taken place. There is a growing realization, however, that from the beginning of our history we Americans have been both destructive and wasteful of natural resources and that the American Indian was an early victim. It is actually the scale of the damage instead of its newness that forces us, though still reluctantly, to confront the problem today.

We must bear some responsibility for the lateness of our awakening, for we really have not done our homework. We have avoided, and in most cases ignored, the complicated series of historical phenomena that brought about our dilemma. Our histories, particularly our frontier-sectional or "western" histories, tend to give us a glowing get-rich-quick chronicle of the conquest of the continent. As Frederick Jackson Turner wrote in his influential essay of 1893:

> . . . the Indian trade pioneered the way for civilization . . . the trails widened into roads, and the roads into turnpikes, and these in turn were transformed into railroads. . . . In this progress from savage conditions lie topics for the evolutionist.[2]

The Turnerean theme of "progress" of American civilization has generally reflected itself in American social attitudes toward the wilderness. The Indian is viewed as a "consolidating influence" on frontiersmen who banded together for defense. When the tribesman is brought into the story, he is depicted as a kind of obstacle to the westward movement. The Indian's respect for animal life and reverence for the land, when mentioned, are usually dismissed as superstition.* On the other hand, the white man, with his Judeo-Christian ethic stressing man's dominance over nature, had no religious scruples about exploiting the wilderness. From the beginning, fur traders, who had rum to encourage warriors to hunt, were often frustrated by the reluctance of natives to busy themselves in the useful activity of scouring the woods for furs and skins.† Modern American social attitudes toward wild animals show a persistence of the fur trader's point of view. Unless a species can be fitted into a category of being particularly "useful" in a commercial sense, there is public apathy about its survival. A good illustration is the general acceptance of an extensive government poisoning project designed to exterminate coyotes in several western states, a project so indiscriminately and carelessly administered that serious damage is being done to the so-called non-target species as well. The foolish bounty system, which ignores

* See Chapter 11.
† See Chapter 2.

basic ecological principles (and in many cases is economically unsound) was in force in thirty-three states and ten Canadian provinces as late as 1963. Bounties are often based upon hearsay about "bad animals" or those of exaggerated ferocity that are no longer serious predators. Alaska still pays bounties for killing certain types of seals; and many states or counties offer bounties for crows, bluejays, blackbirds, hawks, owls, ground squirrels, woodchucks, raccoons, and other animals.[3]

This strictly utilitarian attitude toward wilderness life, though widespread in American society, has been partially balanced by a counter-theme of wilderness appreciation and respect for the Indian by such writers as Francis Parkman, Henry David Thoreau, John Muir, Willa Cather, and Aldo Leopold. They identified wild country with Indians, with wild animals, and with genuine human freedom. If we have no free-roaming wildlife in wild country, they argued, then we eliminate space for that remaining wild thing, the irrepressible human spirit. These writers particularly felt a kinship for the natural simplicity of the Indian life style that embraced an intuitive understanding of nature's ways. They could appreciate the Indian's deep attachment to lakes, mountains, valleys, and rivers and his ear-to-the-land attitude that is recognized today as the rudiments of ecological awareness. Thoreau in particular could readily sympathize with the "Old People" among the woodland tribes who revered the Mother Earth who had nurtured her people. It was understandable that these agricultural woodland Indians would shun a steel plow that would tear at her body, when it should be gently caressed with a stick or a hoe.[4]

But the white man's farming and industrial frontiers were based on other principles entirely, bringing about massive alterations in the land. At what point in American history can we say that such carving of the land began to cause ecological changes that would result in permanent damage and hardship for future generations? Do we have an obligation in our histories to criticize harmful white social attitudes about the environment that run contrary to the best interests of the nation at large? Such questions as these have plagued the consciences of some of our best writers including Francis Parkman and Frederick Jackson Turner.[5] Certainly historians have no responsibility for what has happened in the past, but there are historic records showing what earlier generations did or failed to do. Therefore, the public and students can expect writings undistorted by patriotism, prejudice, sentiment, ignorance, or lopsided research. But such a presentation of the American past is, in certain areas of history, not always the rule. This criticism can be applied particularly to specific topics in "frontier" or "westward movement" history.

Historians of the American frontier, for instance, have failed to impress

Frederick Jackson Turner, historian of the frontier, "On the Trail" with his daughter in 1904. Turner often backpacked into the wilderness and in 1915 visited mountain highlands in California on an outdoor trip sponsored by the Sierra Club. Courtesy, Dr. and Mrs. James G. Edinger.

their readers with the utterly destructive impact that the fur trade had upon the North American continent and the American Indian. There are no investigations of the role the fur men had in killing off certain types of wildlife, which in turn had a permanent effect upon the land and upon native and white societies. The traders and their followers, the fur trading companies, are usually depicted as positive benefactors in the development of American civilization as it moved westward from the Appalachians to the Pacific Coast. The rugged individualistic traits of fur men are praised, in contrast to Indian communal ways in which the hunter killed for his clan or community and not for himself. Indeed, the story of the fur trade is almost always (and perhaps unconsciously) told with a laissez-faire bias. The historian usually expresses a businessman's outlook in describing the development and expansion of this mercantile enterprise. If the fur trade contributed to the rapid economic growth of the country, and it unquestionably did, then the implication is the fur trade was a good thing for all Americans.[6] Free furs and skins, free land, free minerals—it was all part of the great westward trek and the development of American society,[7] according to Turner and his followers. The self-made man, the heroic figure who conquered the wilderness was the free trapper, the mountain man. Because the history of trading does not naturally attract the reader's interest, historians of the frontier have often gilded their flawed lily with a bit of spurious romanticism. The bear and bison hunter becomes the courageous tamer of the wilderness.

The basic question of interpretation here is: who is the real varmint, the bear or the trapper who killed him? Aside from the fact that bears are sometimes noted for anti-social behavior, our frontier historians have not had a problem in answering such a question because their interpretations have been conditioned by a society steeped in a businessman's ideology. Our view of progress—one that permeates all groups of society and leads us to accept without question the need for an expanding economy—is that progress consists in exploitation and growth, which in turn depends on the commercialization and the conquest of nature. In our histories we have treated the land more as a commodity than as a resource. We have here in a nutshell the *conquistador* mentality that has so long dominated much written American history and relegated the Indian to historical insignificance.

Until recently historians have ignored the ecological challenge. Yet truthful, interesting American history, double-barreled and difficult to write, is in part the revolting story of how we managed to commercialize all that we could harness and control with our technical skills. It is, in its unvarnished state, an unpleasant narrative of the reckless exploitation of America's Indian people, along with minerals, waterways, soil, timber,

wildlife, and wilderness, a part of a larger story of the white man's rape
of nature over centuries. Can we ignore the fact that today all Americans
can no longer afford such cruelty and wastefulness? Is there an obligation to help teach the art of frugality in husbanding our resources? If historians hope to foster an awareness of the dangers of further greedy
exploitation of the land, our history must be reexamined in detail to see
what has led up to our present situation.

Among the earliest exploiters of the American continent, those who
tampered seriously with the ecological balance that had existed for centuries were the colonial traders and trappers. (The aboriginal tribes,
such as the Iroquois who depended upon an economy closely governed
by the ecology of the northeastern forest, had left the natural balance
relatively undisturbed.)[8] Their successors, the American trapper-frontiers-
men, have been blown up into heroes in our histories. Turner in his 1893
essay helped to shape the myth; his enthusiasm for pioneer types proved
to be so infectious that we have tended to accept his interpretations, ignoring the fact that men of the trapper-trader fraternity were often unscrupulous, lawless, and hungry for personal gain. These rascals and
pleasure hunters destroyed without scruple countless beavers, otters, large
and small carnivores, and the great bison herds that once lived on our
grasslands and woodlands. Even Turner in later years reached the conclusion that pioneers were "wasteful and seeking quick results rather
than conservation and permanence." [9]

Can modern Americans stand back and look at the historic western
migration as a huge page in social history? Can we see how the white
man's frontier advance is also the story of the looting and the misuse of
land? The traders who led the procession of pioneers through the Cumberland Gap and the South Pass were the vanguard of those who slaughtered
wapiti, beaver, buffalo, and antelope and thus reduced the Indian tribes
facing the frontier to a state of semi-starvation, making them easy victims for sporadic white military campaigns. Ironically the individual fur
men, miners, and cattle raisers were, in many cases, ruined by powerful
combines devoted to large-scale commercialization of the natural resources of the West. Because of our exaggerated respect for the entrepreneur (or the pioneer or frontiersman, as we have often called him), we
have failed in our histories to condemn this early rape of the land, just
as today—and for the same reasons—there is no visible unity behind the
condemnation of industrial pollution or the sacrifice of the priceless
American wilderness heritage that belongs to all generations of citizens.

How can one assess the historical damage brought about by allowing
commercial interests to override our true national interests? A beginning
might be an attempt to gauge the effects of the substitution within a half
century of hundreds of thousands of horses and domestic cattle for wild

hoofed animals that existed in the huge area of the Louisiana Purchase. What effect did this have on the fertility of the land and the ecological balance? Can historians join scientists in calling attention to the important principle that the earth's productivity largely depends upon an organic cycle, an order of nature in which organic material taken from the earth must be returned to it? The ignorance of this principle by white Americans in the eighteenth and nineteenth centuries was responsible for the destruction of the ecosystems of a great virgin wilderness. In this destruction the substitution of annual grasses for the life-sustaining primordial prairie sod of middle America is one of the more momentous happenings in American history, but the subject is something less than a favorite with historians of the frontier. We know, for example, that in Texas huge prairie grasslands have been converted into a mesquite jungle resulting from overgrazing and fencing a land that had once been burned periodically by Indians and by some stockmen who followed their example. Today, only along railroad rights of way is there preserved the ancient prairie flora that has survived many burnings.[10] We may soon learn to appreciate the fact that the Indian is closely tied to the ecological history of the American nation and opposition to the pioneer's changing the face of the land.

Those who hope to write about such significant historical events (and their far-reaching consequences) will need a sort of knowledge not ordinarily possessed by historians. To study the impact of the fur trade upon America and her native people, for instance, there must be more than a beginning acquaintance with ethnology, plant and animal ecology, paleoecology, and indeed much of the physical sciences. In addition, there is a sophisticated body of thought about the value of the wilderness to Americans that should be studied. Better knowledge of Indian cultures will help us to understand that there is often a difference between what wilderness is and what we *think* it is.[11] Francis Parkman, perhaps our greatest historian despite his faults, trained himself to write about the Indian, the American forest, and early American civilization. At one time a professor of horticulture, he understood and loved the American forest; he could grasp, therefore, the respect for nature among the Indians. Parkman is a rare example of a historian who took the trouble to educate himself so that he could "manage," as he said, "to tell things as they really happened." [12]

But the writers who followed Parkman did not follow his methods or his example. Those historians who dominated later frontier historical writing were in many respects unsympathetic to the Indians, the land, the wilderness, and animal life. The historiography of the fur trade is a kind of case study of the larger problem of rewriting the history of the American frontier. The old guard of the fur trade history— Hiram M. Chittenden, Harold A. Innis, Douglas MacKay, Reuben Gold

Thwaites, Wayne E. Stevens, Frederick Jackson Turner (and some of his pupils and disciples, especially Louise P. Kellogg, Albert T. Volwiler, and Robert Glass Cleland)—have left us with a one-sided view of the fur trade in American history. Though Chittenden, Turner, and Cleland loved the wilderness and spoke against the despoliation of nature, all bear a responsibility for the romanticizing of the traders. Cleland's approach to the mountain trappers as a "reckless breed of men" conferred on them a spurious glamor as well as a scholarly stamp of approval. It is in the mountain man of the Rockies in the heyday of the fur trade that we find an archetypal hero emerging, an adventurous figure—bold, violent (often an Indian fighter), colorful, aggressive—a representative figure found in virtually every nationalist account of western man's contact with the undeveloped world.[13]

This particular view of the mountain man prevails today in influential monographs and textbooks and indicates that perhaps it is time to make a revaluation of such "pathfinders" as George Croghan, Manual Lisa, Jedediah Smith, William Ashley, James Ohio Pattie, David Jackson, Bill Williams, and the Sublette brothers, who were among the significant figures in white civilization's war against wildlife and native people on the American continent. If an overdue revaluation of these men fits them into the classification of some of the "varmints" they cleaned out, then there are others who might be reclassified for recognition among the heroes of American history. We might even want to take a second look at Daniel Boone, Kit Carson, and Jim Bridger, or the great entrepreneur, John Jacob Astor. By about 1840, ten years before California became a state, the traders had all but exterminated the Rocky Mountain beaver. As Kit Carson complained: "Beaver was getting very scarce, and finding that [,] it was necessary to try our hand at something else." [14]

It can be argued that we cannot morally condemn our pioneers for exploitation. They acted in a manner consistent with their circumstances, within their concepts of territorial rights, justice, and morality. Their actions were governed by needs and impulses that differed in about as many ways from those of their neighbors in the frontier behind them as from those of their Indian foes in the wild land before them. When the sky was darkened by thousands of pigeons, the normal expected reaction was to kill them off wastefully. What we can blame is the continuation of such attitudes into an era of scarcity. We should understand our pioneers, perhaps, rather than blaming them for what they did.

It can be further argued that the pioneers, who were quite as mercenary as the leaders of large companies and early corporations,[15] did not understand the long-range consequences of what they were doing to the land. There were few individuals among the farmers, the hydraulic strip and dredge miners, the loggers, or the sheep and cattle men—or for

The White Man Transforms the Wilderness Frontier in the 1760s. Engraved by James Peake from a painting by Paul Sandby. From: *Six Remarkable Views in the Provinces of New-York, New Jersey, and Pennsylvania in North America Sketched on the Spot by his Excellency Governor Pownall.* (London, 1761). Courtesy, Huntington Library.

that matter, the fur companies and the railroad tycoons—who had any
real conception of the vital importance of the resources they were
destroying. They did not grasp the significance of muddy streams (caused
by the clear-cutting of forests) that had once run deep and clear. Nor did
they appreciate the importance of the vital prairie grasses that were
plowed under in a few decades. They were often unaware that precious
minerals quickly and forever disappeared from our streams and mountains. Indeed, what nineteenth century conservationists complained
about the railroads destroying the ecological balance of the Great Plains?

Yet it is not entirely true that the pioneers, the miners, the fur men,
and the western entrepreneurs were ignorant of the consequences of
their acts. The pioneer's question, "Why should I look after my descendants?" and his answer, "They ain't done nothin' for me," go back generations in American history.[16] Nor were the Indians allowed to stand in
the way when there were valuable land assets to be developed by white
frontier society. In California, for example, the manner and thoroughness
in which California's wildlife and groups of aboriginal people were
killed or exploited is a mark against all Americans. The Spaniards and
Mexicans of California were evidently able to live with wildlife without
destroying it. But the forty-niners of California's golden age and their
followers were wildly wasteful of elk, antelope, bighorns, bears, small
fur-bearing animals, grouse, geese, and shorebirds. Thousands of dollars
were made by selling game meat to miners. In California alone a great
faunal shift took place in the years 1850–1910, duplicated only by prehistoric postglacial terminations of certain species.[17] The California
grizzly was pursued until none at all survive today. Here we have a historic example of the dismal story of mass slaughter of wildlife. Alaska
faces a somewhat similar crisis today as the oil industry makes powerful
efforts to exploit the northern slope and native rights to ownership of
land and minerals.

The attempt to protect the wilderness resources left to us surely deserves the support of historians. The old fur trade history was lopsided
—unsympathetic to the Indian and land, glorifying the hunter and the
trapper. It should be rejected by the coming critical generation of American historians. To a degree, the same kind of criticism can be leveled at
conventional "frontier" expansion histories of Indian-white relations,
cattle men, mining, lumbering, agriculture, business, transportation, oil
exploration, drilling, and industry. The assessment will certainly be made;
and the sooner it begins, the better. The tunneled frontiersman vision of
our past that has engendered a *conquistador* attitude toward native
people and the land will be revised. Our history will surely have new
heroes and a new category of destructive varmints. When we come to understand the full implications of the destructive impact of the white fron-

tier throughout the centuries of America's history, we will then come to have an increased appreciation of the significance of the American Indian in this complex story.

Henry David Thoreau, as much as any other writer of the nineteenth century, perceived that the white man misunderstood the woodland Indian. Our histories, Thoreau was convinced, were full of prejudice and misconceptions. Writing in his journal in 1859 he argued that the portrayal of "the Indians, as a race possessing so little skill and wit, so low in the scale of humanity, and so brutish that they hardly deserved to be remembered," did primitive men an injustice. "It frequently happens that the historian," commented Thoreau, "though he professes more humanity than the trapper . . . [who] shoots one as a wild beast, really exhibits and practices a similar inhumanity to him, wielding a pen instead of a rifle." [18] Thoreau believed that when the history of primitive peoples is written by men convinced of the superiority of their own race, then it is no history at all, for it deprives us of a knowledge of what kind of men the natives were and how they lived, "their relation to nature, their arts and their customs, their fancies and superstitions . . . beliefs connected with the sea and forest which," he argued, "concern us quite as much as the fables of oriental nations do." Thoreau recognized almost instinctively that primitive peoples the world over have much in common, especially in their closeness to nature and their remarkable ability to adapt their lives to their physical environment. "The thought of a so-called savage tribe," he concluded, "is generally far more just than that of a single civilized man." [19] Our most recent scholars of the American Indian would find it hard to disagree.

White America may not wish to acknowledge it, but a part of our modern ecological awareness can certainly be traced to the historic land wisdom of the Indian, a heritage of all Americans. If our "progress" has all but overwhelmed the Indian, it can be seen in the litter, paint spray, and aluminum cans that today decorate portions of what was once a pristine Navajo land. Willa Cather some fifty years ago recorded for posterity the ancient Navajo practice of "leave no trace" on the land in her novel *Death Comes for the Archbishop*:

> When they left the rock or tree or sand dune that had sheltered them for the night, the Navajo was careful to obliterate every trace of their temporary occupation. He buried the embers of the fire and the remnants of food, unpiled any stones he had piled together, filled up the holes he had scooped in the sand. Since this was Jacinto's procedure, Father Latour judged that, just as it was the white man's way to assert himself in any landscape, to change it, make it over a little (at least to leave some mark or memorial of his sojourn), it was the Indian's way to pass through a country without disturbing anything; to pass and leave no trace, like fish through the water, or birds through the air. It was the Indian manner

to vanish into the landscape, not to stand out against it. . . . [Indians]
seemed to have none of the European's desire to "master" nature, to ar-
range and recreate. They spent their ingenuity in another direction; in
accommodating themselves to the scene in which they found themselves.[20]

The white man could never adapt himself to the idea that he would
"vanish into the landscape," as the Indian quietly did.* Where does the
balance lie, and how may modern U.S. society evaluate the Indian's
unique contribution to the American historical perspective? Surely the
non-Indian may learn much from Indian cultural affinity with nature just
as the Indian has profited from some scientific advances of white technology. Today it is abundantly evident that our history is barren in the
sense that it needs to bolster itself with more about Indians (as well as
other minorities) and their way of life. Modern America, the swirling
product of a long historical development, is increasingly mechanized,
polluted, and depersonalized and has a disturbing tendency toward bee-
hive regimentation. Can such a society help but profit from having better
understanding of the Indian's historic reverence for the land and his
humane lifestyle? In fact, isn't it almost self-evident that we desperately
need the native American Indian and his culture? Perhaps when our histories at last reconcile the white man's great accomplishments with a true
appreciation of what the Indian considered the virtues of Mother Earth,
we may then have redirected our priorities toward an unpolluted, pluralistic society that will prosper "as long as the rivers shall run and the
grass shall grow." [21] Like the Indian we may learn that it is almost impossible to separate the materialistic side of conservation from the spiritual and subjective aspects of life itself.[22] Perhaps the tragedy coming out
of our frontier-*conquistador* myth is the general acceptance of the idea
that our pioneering civilization, with its great Judaic-Christian heritage
(GOOD), conquered a wilderness peopled by savage, pagan Indians
(EVIL). Our Christian pioneers who revered their spirits in a trinity
rather than in rocks, plants, and beasts, came to regard their conquered
opponents as nonpersons. In dehumanizing the Indian, however, they
almost unavoidably dehumanized themselves as they chopped, hunted,
tilled, and mined on a virgin land that had once belonged to a native
people.[23]

*See W. R. Jacobs, "Indians as Ecologists and Other Environmental Themes in American
Frontier History," in Christoper Vecsey and Robert W. Venables, eds., *American Indian Environments, Ecological Issues in Native American History* (Syracuse, N.Y., 1980), pp. 46-64.

CHAPTER 2

Unsavory Sidelights on Colonial Trade

From the Lake Ontario outpost at old Fort Oswego ranging along a farflung frontier to the inland fort at Augusta, Georgia, the eighteenth-century fur traders of colonial America advanced into the wilderness market. With them they carried a wide variety of articles: special Indian blankets made for the trade out of old woolen rags (strouds and halfthicks), hardware, jewelry, toys, and rum. From Pennsylvania and Virginia they climbed the shadowy heights of the Alleghenies, plunged through the thickets and forests of the Ohio country where they often waded through streams of the Old West. Their pack horses carried merchandise where no wagon wheels had ever been.[1]

Men who followed this trade were known to be a bold, rough breed. In the words of a Scotch colonial governor, the Indian traders were a "set of abandoned Wretches." Often they were as wild and dangerous as the fiercest Iroquois warrior on the attack, but substantial numbers of them were also shrewd business men—men who were largely unscrupulous about means as long as they achieved their ends, profit. In the colonial wilderness there was no recourse to law. Drunken brawls, murder, and robbery usually went unpunished. To be sure, not all the traders were scoundrels. At any rate the well-known licensed traders did not often commit outrages at the expense of the Indians or their rivals—rather it was their subordinates or unlicensed competitors. Even those who enjoyed the confidence of leading colonials like Indian superintendent William Johnson or Virginia's Governor Robert Dinwiddie, had their critics. Most traders seemed to have accepted the premise that the Indian trade permitted ethical standards other than those used in transactions with whites.

The tribesmen who eagerly awaited the arrival of the traders in their wilderness villages or towns seemed to European eyes an uncivilized people whose chief interests (according to white men) were "Hunting and War." [2] However, the Indian warrior tended to be fiercely independent, abhorring restraint of any kind and rejecting foreign authority. The taboos and mores of his tribe controlled, to a large extent, his behavior. In a letter written to a British scientist Sir William Johnson commented:

> On their haunts, as on all other occasions, they are strict observers of meum and tuum; and this from principle, holding theft in contempt; so that they are rarely guilty of it, though tempted by articles of much value. Neither do the strong attempt to seize the prey of the weak; and I must do them the justice to say that, unless heated by liquor, or inflamed by revenge, their ideas of right and wrong and their practices in consequence of them, would, if more known, do them much honour.[3]

The reluctance of the Indian to adapt himself to colonial civilization was a source of keen disappointment to those wishing to exploit his hunting prowess. It soon became evident that the desire for manufactured goods would not always cause the natives to leave their elm bark huts or birch wigwams and search the woods for skins. "It was the English alone that taught them first to put a value on their Skins and Furs, and to make a Trade of them."

> For the Indian when he finds himself possessed of his usual Clothing and provisions enough to satisfy his hunger, will pitch his Tent with his family and continue in it sleeping and smoking his pipe by turns, for whole days, and sometimes, even whole weeks together, in the most supine Indolence and inaction, and never leaves it to return to his Hunting till a fresh call of hunger obliges him to it.[4]

The Indian believed that

> . . . their Manitou or good spirit gave them the beasts of the woods for their support, to feed and Cloth themselves withal; that it was therefore lawful to kill them for those purposes—but that it was highly criminal to kill them for any other.[5]

To spur the natives on to greater activity and possibly to overcome any religious scruples that might interfere with the fur trade, many traders established semipermanent quarters in the native villages. Here in their makeshift huts they lived like Indians and often took their wives from the tribe. The attractive display of hawks, bells, mirrors, hatchets, strouds, and other "pretties" or "nonsopretties" (decorative braid or tape) encouraged the warriors and even women and children to exert themselves in the search for game.

The warriors and their families soon regarded the trader's goods as necessities. No longer could the warrior hunt without a gun and ammunition. He demanded, and received, the services of a blacksmith from the provinces to repair his weapons,* and his womenfolk were constantly clamoring for needles, scissors, knives, and a hundred other articles carried by the traders. Once the Indians had used these things they were unable to do without them.

Rum had even more fatal results. The tribesmen pleaded with colonial governors to exclude the rum traders from their midst; yet they also requested that they be allowed to taste this evil beverage. Perhaps they wanted to experience the dangerous intoxicant firsthand! Not infrequently, bodies of native warriors who had died of alcohol poisoning were found in the forest.[6] Rum could transform a sensible young tribesman into an insane devil capable of the most horrible abominations.† The Indians knew the danger of liquor, but they were unable to resist it. They left their cornfields and homes and traversed miles of wilderness in their eager quest for rum.

Rum was in fact one of the main reasons for the trader's success with the Indians. Since negotiations for the sale of furs were often made in the heart of the forests (a practice the famous Hudson's Bay Company tried to avoid by having the tribesmen bring their furs to certain trading posts or forts),[7] the trader could easily induce his warriors to have a free "dram" of rum before the business of barter began. This was the fatal step for the Indian. One dram called for another, and before long the tribesmen were thoroughly drunk. The trader could then literally steal the skins and furs, slipping off into the night with his prizes. The trader who wished to carry on a long-term business with the tribesmen did not resort to

---

* The Indian superintendents employed resident blacksmiths in many of the important Indian villages. These men also acted as interpreters when their services were needed. For a discussion of the importance of these smiths, see Archibald Kennedy, *The Importance of Gaining and Preserving the Friendship of the Indians Considered* (New York, 1751), p. 14.

† It would almost seem as if the Indian traders had conspired to drive the whole Indian population into a state of intoxication. When a large store of liquors was confiscated at Fort Niagara in 1762 the traders found they had lost over 2,600 gallons. See *Papers of Sir William Johnson*, 3:719.

such tactics, however. Indians were unlikely to be deceived twice in this way, and they were prone to seek revenge. For one breach of justice many traders might be made to suffer. The sachems, chiefs, and their warriors had good memories*: they did not forget a true friend, nor did they often forgive an injustice.

The shrewd merchant kept a careful account of the credit he extended; his aim was to keep his Indian customers in a perpetual state of debt. But in order to extract the greatest number of skins from his victims, the trader had first to cajole and beguile his key warriors with kind words and flattery.[8] Though the Indians enjoyed the colorful rhetoric of campfire diplomacy, they did not allow themselves to be totally carried away by it. They examined with some care the unspoken intentions of the speaker. Nevertheless, no trader could afford to ignore the art of campfire speech-making, for it was an important factor in winning the allegiance of the tribesmen.

The trader of the 1760s who visited an inland confederacy such as the Ottawa for the first time was likely to open his visit by distributing presents—goods of the kind that would later be used in barter. The Indians, who had probably never before encountered many of the articles presented to them, might give a few skins in return. The custom of exchanging presents was not new: in the seventeenth century Virginia Indians had received silver medallions from whites,[9] and the usage, common to almost all North American tribes, went far back into prehistory.

Once the gifts were used, broken, or lost, the tribesmen, like children, clamored for more. This time only a few gifts were given to important tribesmen, and all the rest were told that they must hunt and exchange furs for new merchandise. Thus a cycle was set in motion. With the help of rum, which frequently had to be watered to control the staggering hunters, the traders won the goodwill of entire tribes. A few traders were clever enough to cheat the Indians over long periods of time, but most traders had to give the tribesmen what they considered a reasonably just exchange in barter.

Of course the isolated tribe, separated from the colonies by miles of unbroken forests, could not know what was a just compensation for a beaver pelt or buckskin. Most of the inland tribes during the 1750s and

* Europeans were continually surprised by the ability of Indian chiefs to remember the terms of ancient treaties. During conferences the chiefs also exhibited their amazing memory by replying point by point to lengthy proposals made by the white Indian commissioners. Examples of Indian treaties and conferences are found in almost all of the volumes of the *Minutes of the Provincial Council of Pennsylvania*. See also Carl Van Doren and Julian P. Boyd, eds., *Indian Treaties Printed by Benjamin Franklin, 1736–1762; Their Literary, Historical and Bibliographical Significance* (Philadelphia, 1938).

1760s had some experience in barter with the French. Their first contacts with Anglo-American traders, who had cut a way through the forests to their villages, revealed surprising differences in rates of exchange. The tribesmen were delighted at the generous prices offered by the British traders, much to the anger of the commandants of the French forts—and indeed Anglo-French rivalry in the fur trade was an important cause of the French and Indian War. Once the Indians had enjoyed the favorable rates offered by Anglo-American traders they were no longer satisfied with the prices that had prevailed under French monopoly.[10]

Although the bargaining position of the Indian was improved by Anglo-French rivalry, more important for his well-being was the appointment of a competent and honest interpreter and agent. One such individual, who served the colony of Pennsylvania and the Indians for many years, was Conrad Weiser; but men of Weiser's caliber were rare. Even George Croghan, "prince of the Pennsylvania traders," had a certain stigma attached to his name.[11] Thomas Cresap, the aggressive Maryland frontiersman, was called the "Maryland Monster" and the "Rattlesnake Colonel," [12] and Robert Rogers, the famous frontier ranger leader, was involved in speculating with funds earmarked for Indian goods.[13] Charges of double-dealing were leveled against even the greatest British-Indian diplomat of Colonial times, Sir William Johnson, who had won the love and devotion of the Mohawks, but who had also acquired a number of large tracts of Indian lands.[14]

Sir William, who became a wealthy and powerful man through his association with the Six Nations Iroquois, was a constant thorn in the side of traders who sought to enrich themselves by speculating in the fur trade and in native lands. Johnson's record is, on the whole, a clean one, despite the many accusations against him. He was adored by the Indians and respected by most of his fellow provincials. After he became Indian superintendent for the northern tribes in 1755, he sought to curb the illegal activities of the Dutch traders at Albany and Schenectady and criticized the underhanded proceedings at Fort Oswego. He argued in favor of imperial control over the entire frontier to supplant the inadequate existing regulations whereby each colony granted its own licenses or none at all; he supported his case with a number of examples illustrating the curious trading practices along the New York frontiers.[15]

Toward the end of the French and Indian War a few of the Great Lakes Ottawa warriors began to bring their furs to the British outpost at Oswego on Lake Ontario. The cheap prices of British goods prompted these tribesmen to avoid the French posts where they claimed they had been cheated. Hearing of the remarkable bargains in trade goods at Oswego, an influential Ottawa chief (who may have been Pontiac himself—Sir William does not identify him) brought a large packet of valuable furs to the fort. Immediately after his arrival the chief was taken into a separate room away from the main exchange counter in the post. Here, in private, the trader told a sad tale to explain the very high prices of strouds, blankets, and other merchandise. The cause, he explained to the amazed Indian, was the "severity of dutys." Then with seeming generosity he told his customer to select the goods he wished to have, but the astonished Indian found that his skins produced only a fraction of what he had expected. The trader had not only manipulated the rate of barter, but had calculated the furs at only one-third of their actual weight. Not wanting to return to his village with such a niggardly assortment of goods, the chief begged for a small quantity of rum, and as a "high favor" was presented with a tiny keg. When the chief and his warriors opened the keg on their homeward journey they discovered it to be full of water! Sir William leaves the reader to guess the reaction of the great Ottawa to this discovery.[16]

Johnson told another story about an Ottawa chief who brought a large quantity of skins to Fort Niagara, hoping to barter them for rum for an Indian feast. He was given what seemed to be more than a fair exchange—no less than thirty kegs of rum. The chief and his men shouldered their heavy burden and began a long journey homeward. However the temptation to sample part of their alcoholic burden proved too strong, and the chief decided to open one of the kegs. To his intense disappointment water, not rum, touched his lips. Opening each keg in turn, the warriors and their chief found not one drop of liquor. The Indians were quite naturally furious and, says Sir William, became "implacable enemies of the British." [17] While deploring the duplicity of the Niagara trader, the superintendent was apparently little concerned over the effects of the rum, and indeed found its sale to Indians an absolute necessity. Johnson commented on a provision in a proposed plan suggested by the Board of Trade to abolish rum in the Indian trade: ". . . the Trade will never be so extensive without it . . . the Indians will be universally discontented without it." [18]

Johnson also told of a Schenectady merchant who defrauded a powerful Seneca chief. The Indian leader had been a loyal supporter of the French during the early period of the French and Indian War. Finally in 1756 Sir William's diplomatic efforts proved successful. The Seneca chief and his tribesmen renounced the French and embraced the Cross of St. George. When the chief announced to Johnson that he wished to dispose of a number of his "Furrs," the superintendent recommended a Schenectady merchant who was privately instructed to "use them [the chief and his warriors] very kindly." To the dismay of Johnson, the tribesmen were

. . . imposed upon . . . in the grossest manner; it appearing from their
own account, & his [the merchant's] own confession, since, that as they
were strangers, he had doubled the prices of his goods and allowed them
but half the weight in peltry. . . .

Sir William later received by courier a sinister message on a wampum
belt with additional particulars listed on the handle of a tomahawk, indicating that the Indians would be revenged for such treatment. Moreover, the chief made good his threat; in a few days he and his men attacked a British settlement. For many months afterwards the chief remained a most violent enemy of the British.[19]

The New York traders, and indeed all traders along the colonial
frontier, did not confine themselves to swindling the Indians out of their
furs; they also duped intoxicated tribesmen into selling large areas of
land. Sir William complained that one of the most noted Seneca sachems
had in this way turned over a valuable parcel of Pennsylvania land to
a group of Albany traders. Naturally the sachem was deeply resentful,
and the swindle was condemned by the entire Iroquois confederacy.[20]
The drunken Indian had signed away the land of his fellow-tribesmen
shortly before the outbreak of hostilities between the French and the
English in 1754; Johnson noted that this kind of landgrabbing almost
cost the English the support of the Iroquois during the latter part of the
war. The sachem who sold the land spoke so harshly of the British in
tribal councils that he was forced to "fly to the French for protection"
from his own people when they decided to give all-out support to the
British armies in 1759.[21]

Historical records of the colonial fur trade emphasize the activities of
the unscrupulous fur traders, so that one almost believes that all the
traders engaged in such practices. Of course there were honest fur traders,
but the expansion of the fur trade led to a growth in double-dealing.
Tribesmen were frequently defrauded over a period of years, and the
correspondence of Henry Bouquet, commander of Fort Pitt, makes clear
that trading abuses were one of the major causes of Pontiac's uprising.[22]

The British home government was not blind to the gigantic problem
of fur-trade regulation and the sufferings of the Indians. Since 1755 the
Board of Trade had been seriously considering various schemes submitted by leading colonial officials.[23] Finally in 1764 a plan was put into
effect. Like the Proclamation of 1763, the "Plan of 1764" was an attempt
to deal with the problem by means of extensive regulation.[24] Under this
plan a cumbersome organization was set up—blacksmiths, interpreters,
deputies, and other assistants under the general supervision of the northern and southern Indian superintendents. As in the case of the Proclamation of 1763, the "Plan of 1764" was a dismal failure. The high cost of
supervision, the involved license system, and the many loopholes in the

law made enforcement impossible.[25] Controlling the unruly traders was almost as difficult as holding back the onrushing tide of western settlement. Although both superintendents reported initial success, they eventually found that honest traders were at a disadvantage compared with those who circumvented the regulations.[26] Resentment created by British attempts to regulate the fur trade undoubtedly contributed to the revolutionary sentiment in the West during the "decade of discontent."

The problem was aired in a contemporary drama attributed to Robert Rogers, *Ponteach: Or the Savages of America, A Tragedy*. The drama is at times ribald and blasphemous, but what it tells us of the ethics governing much of the Indian fur trade agrees with what we learn from other contemporary sources. As Francis Parkman commented, "The author of this tragedy was evidently a person well acquainted with Indian affairs and Indian character.[27]

Only a portion of the first act is given here. The scene opens in an Indian trading house.

M'DOLE. So, Murphey, you are come to try your Fortune
Among the Savages in this wild Desart?
    MURPHEY. Ay, any thing to get an honest Living,
Which, faith, I find it hard enough to do;
Times are so dull, and Traders are so plenty,
That Gains are small, and Profits come but slow.
    M'DOLE. Are you experienced in this kind of Trade?
Know you the Principles by which it prospers,
And how to make it lucrative and safe?
If not, you're like a Ship without a Rudder,
That drives at random, and must surely sink.
    MURPHEY. I'm unacquainted with your Indian Commerce
And gladly would I learn the arts from you,
Who're old, and practis'd in them many Years.
    M'DOLE. That is the curst Misfortune of our Traders;
A thousand Fools attempt to live this Way,
Who might as well turn Ministers of State.
But, as you are a Friend, I will inform you
Of all the secret Arts by which we thrive,
Which if all practis'd, we might all grow rich,
Nor circumvent each other in our Gains.
What have you got to part with to the Indians?
    MURPHEY. I've Rum and Blankets, Wampum, Powder, Bells,
And such like Trifles as they're wont to prize.
    M'DOLE. 'Tis very well: your Articles are good:
But now the Thing's to make a Profit from them,
Worth all your Toil and Pains of coming hither.
Our fundamental Maxim then is this,

That it's no Crime to cheat and gull an Indian.
   MURPHEY. How! Not a Sin to cheat an Indian, say you?
Are they not Men? Hav'nt they a Right to Justice
As well as we, though savage in their Manners?
   M'DOLE. Ah! If you boggle here, I say no more;
This is the very Quintessence of Trade,
And ev'ry Hope of Gain depends upon it;
None who neglect it ever did grow rich,
Or ever will, or can by Indian Commerce.
By this old Ogden built his stately House,
Purchased Estates, and grew a little King.
He, like an honest Man, bought all by weight,
And made the ign'rant Savages believe
That his Right Foot exactly weighed a Pound.
By this for many years he bought their Furs,
And died in Quiet like an honest Dealer.[28]

What may we conclude from such accounts of traders' misconduct in the fur trade? Old Ogden's duplicity in this drama has of course an element of dry humor, but the story is basically true in that there are many accounts of trader trickery in confusing the Indians with various types of weights and measures. It is also true that the Indians in the long run were deeply embittered by such white duplicity. If the Indian learned to respect the white man's skill in cheating him in trade, in land transactions, and in treaty making, he would have taken a step forward in protecting himself from exploitation.[29] But the Indian unfortunately learned something else in his fur trade contacts with the whites, and that was how to get drunk. As the Indian retreated ever westward and the fur trade followed the inland retreat of wildlife, we read increasing accounts of wild drinking on the part of the traders that the Indians observed first hand. The Indian soon learned that one could literally get away with murder if one was drunk or pretended to be drunk.[30] It was with astonishment that the interior tribes saw the incredible transformation that liquor produced in the white trader. Certainly one important legacy of the unsavory side of the fur trade is that the Indian saw and imitated a model of drunken behavior that in the long run had an evil influence upon Indian societies. There is modern evidence to suggest that the Indian eventually adopted drunkenness as a form of social protest.[31]

The fact that powerful trading interests and unscrupulous traders often managed to evade the law, and, indeed, sometimes had the law arranged so that they could profit from special fur trade rates of exchange with cheap rum, made it possible for liquor almost to run in wilderness streams when there was a rich prize in furs to be had. In the early 1700s, for example, Savannah Town was a trading headquarters for Creeks and Cherokees where the warriors got cheap prices for goods and plenty of rum, which was actually prohibited at other posts on the southern Indian frontier.[32]

Those who knew the Indians and had their welfare at heart always believed in limiting the amount of liquor that should be made available to Indians. And so it was that colonial Indian superintendent Edmond Atkin in his plan of 1755 to reform the Indian administration called for liquor control. Traders, he said, should carry "limited" amounts of rum and other spirits "for their own private use, and to give their Friends among the Indians now and then a Dram. But, Atkin warned, the traders should "incur a penalty for any Indian getting Drunk with such Liquor, that being the only Cause of almost every mischief they do; & the greatest Destruction of their Numbers." [33]

The rum trade went on despite the admonitions of men like Atkin. Near the beginning of the eighteenth century John Lawson, an early contemporary of Atkin's, calculated that only one-sixth as many tribesmen survived in a two-hundred-mile area of North Carolina adjacent to white settlements as had lived in the identical area fifty years earlier. He had already calculated that the white man's impact with "gifts" of rum and smallpox* had almost depopulated the whole Carolina coastal frontier.[34]

---

*The best and most recent assessment of Indian depopulation resulting from smallpox and other diseases is Henry F. Dobyns, *Their Number Become Thinned, Native American Population Dynamics in Eastern North America* (Knoxville, Tenn., 1983), pp. 7-28, 297-343. Disastrous ecological impacts of the fur trade upon Indian people are documented in David J. Wishart, *The Fur Trade and the American West* (Lincoln, Nebr., 1979), pp. 23-37, 205-17.

CHAPTER 3

Wampum and the Protocol of Treaty-Making

The word *wampum* constantly punctuates records relating to Indians on the colonial American frontier; again and again the word appears in the correspondence of frontiersmen and British soldiers, the reports of the Indian superintendents, and in other manuscripts of the period. The history of wampum as a form of money has not been neglected, but little attention has been given to its place in colonial Indian diplomacy despite its sometimes decisive role in Indian-white relations.

In native diplomacy wampum was important partly because it was a common medium of exchange. It also had certain mystic qualities never fully understood by Europeans. Beads, often called grains, had a definite value in terms of beaver pelts, deerskins, or even English coin.[1] But more important, wampum also served as an effective method of communication between the tribesmen of colonial America. Learned sachems could read wampum belts, and most Indian chiefs understood a great deal about wampum beads. When the war-hatchet was thrown upon the ground and the war belt was handed to a chief, the significance of the belt was clear. Pon-

tiac, it is believed, organized his attacking warriors by sending ambassadors through the forest carrying the message of the "conspiracy" on
wampum belts.[2] Unfortunately for the Indians, George Croghan, deputy
Indian superintendent, and Captain Donald Campbell of Fort Detroit
were aware of the existence of these belts.[3]

Both white and dark wampum beads were used by the tribesmen.
White wampum was worked out of the inside of the conch, a large
spiral univalve marine shell. The dark wampum, usually purple or blue
inclining to black, was taken from the quahog, or quahaug, a thick-
shelled American clam.[4] Since no record has been found for the source
of black wampum, it was probably erroneously called black because of
its resemblance to dark purple.[*] The size of the grains varied. Grains
from Delaware Indian "Penn Wampum Belts," obtained from the Indians by the Penn family, were approximately one-fourth of an inch wide
and three-eighths to one-half inch in depth. According to X-ray repro-
ductions, the perforations were between one-eighth and one-sixteenth
of an inch in diameter.[5] The grains were laced together with native fiber
and deerskin, cut into narrow strips, and made into necklaces, bracelets,
strings, belts, girdles, and collars.[6] Each grain had its known value, the
black or purple being worth twice as much as the white. The dark
wampum was sometimes "distingsh'd by the name of *Wampom Peak*."[7]

Making of wampum beads was difficult. For one thing, before the
natives obtained awls from Europe, they had to bore out the shell currency with sharp stones.[8] The English, observing the value placed on
wampum beads, made imitation porcelain beads, which were sold to
the Indians at what was probably a handsome profit.

Since wampum was made near the seashore, inland tribes traveled as
many as six hundred miles to trade skins and pelts for this precious
commodity.[9] Wampum was popular enough to be carried as far west as
the Dakota Indians.[10] Certainly the Atlantic coast tribes' possession of
the raw materials for making wampum was an advantage to them. Powerful inland confederacies, however, were sometimes able to exact back-
breaking tribute in the form of wampum.

In diplomacy wampum was used in many forms. Various kinds of
girdles and collars were made, particularly by such inland tribes as the
Miamis, but elaborate belts and strings were more common. Occasion-

[*] According to Daniel Gookin (1612–1687), an early Indian agent appointed superintendent of the Indians of Massachusetts in 1656, "wompom," or "wompompeague,"
was "made principally by the Narragansit blackislanders [a possible reference to
Block Island] and Long Island Indians." It was on the "sandy flats and shores of
those coasts," Gookin wrote, "the wilk shells are found." Gookin undoubtedly refers
to the whelk mollusk shell. See Daniel Gookin, *Historical Collections of the Indians
of New England*, (Towtaid [Mass.], 1970): 18 a reprint of the *Collections* of the
Massachusetts Historical Society for the year 1792.

ally these Indians used the ornate ceramic "calumet" pipe, presenting it with a blanket or with wampum. In such cases the calumet and the wampum were regarded as tokens of peace. Although the Iroquois and the Ohio Indians acknowledged the calumet as a symbol of peace, they depended upon belts and strings of wampum almost exclusively in their diplomatic negotiations. The calumet was used between the Six Nations and the Twightwees.* The Twightwees—and not the Six Nations—kept the calumet. The latter declared that they were glad that the pipe had been kept safe, for this signified the careful observance of friendship.[11]

The more widely accepted wampum strings consisted of a group of strung beads (called strands) about three feet in length and tied together at one end. These were strung with beads of various colors superimposed upon white and purple beads to signify war, peace, friendship, or whatever the occasion demanded.[12] Red was most popular and was used in both strings and belts. The strings were used for minor occasions, the belts for major. The belt designs were based upon the pattern of leather strips, which ran horizontally and vertically. Particular events often warranted the construction of large belts some six feet in length.[13] The greater the size of the belt or string the more valuable it was and the more emphatic it made any speech it accompanied. In such cases the string or the belt served as a "word" or even a complete statement.

As superintendent of the northern department of Indian affairs, Sir William Johnson needed a large supply of wampum to carry on diplomatic relations with the Six Nations and their allies. Johnson met constantly with the head tribesmen among the northern Indians in an effort to win their friendship, and wampum was used at all such conferences. Moreover, without wampum and goods and presents for trade, the British could not expect to compete successfully with the growing army of French Catholic emissaries who, with missionary zeal, had penetrated the strongholds of the Iroquois.[14] Fortunately Johnson recognized the importance of wampum. His accounts of Indian expenses show that he bought wampum in large allotments of three thousand grains and over.[15] The grains were ordered with leather and thread, the latter for easy use as lacing for the beads. In addition to purchasing the beads, he had to pay for the labor of making belts. The cost of the labor in making two large belts, over six feet in length, amounted to two pounds, eight shillings. Sometimes belts were purchased from native women who procured the necessary beads and leather for the belts themselves.[16] Johnson's large wampum belts, six feet in length, contained almost seven thousand beads.

In negotiations with Ohio Indians, Conrad Weiser, the provincial inter-

---

* The English name for the Miami.

preter of Pennsylvania, used smaller belts than those used by Johnson. Weiser's accounts list two thousand grains in one belt; but the average belts used by the interpreter contained about nine hundred grains. Weiser's large belts were entirely of black grains while his smaller belts were either all white or contained a few black grains. His strings ranged from 185 to 600 grains, and were either all white or contained only a few black grains.[17]

Designs on belts carried a special meaning. After a meeting in 1748 with the Wyandots,* Conrad Weiser described a very interesting pattern: a belt 25 grains wide and 265 grains long, in all containing almost 7,000 grains. In the design were seven Indians holding each other by the hand. The first figure represented the governor of New York (who had presented the belt to the Wyandots) or his superior, the King of Great Britain. The next five figures represented the Five Nations; and the seventh, the Wyandots.[18] Beneath the Indian figures were two rows of black wampum beads signifying a road running from Albany through the territory of the Five Nations to the Wyandots. The tribesmen told Weiser that they had received their belt from the governor of New York over fifty years before. The Indians asserted that this alliance with the English had been renewed when they sent the belt to Albany, accompanied by deputies, six years before the time of the meeting with Weiser.

Figures such as those on the Wyandots' belt were frequently worked into belts. Sir William Johnson describes this motif in a letter of 1771:

> Their belts are mostly black Wampum, painted Red when they denote war they describe Castles [tribes] sometimes upon them as figures of White Wampum, & in Alliances Human figures holding a Chain of Friendship, each figure represent[g] [sic] a nation, an ax is also sometimes described. . . .[19]

The chain of friendship motif was based on a legend concerning the Six Nations and the British that was repeated at many treaties. Culled from numerous accounts, the gist of the story is as follows: Many moons ago, when the English first came to Albany, the Indians and their white brethren became friends. The Six Nations came to love their brethren, the English, so much that they tied their ship to a bush so that it would not float away. Realizing that the bush would not hold the ship, the Indians then tied the ship to a great tree with a strong rope. But in time the rope might rot. Since they wished to make their friends more secure, the Indians chained the ship to the distant mountains. The chain of silver was to represent what was to be everlasting friendship.[20]

The legend of the chain was perpetuated by the designs made upon

---

* Ohio Hurons, also called Wondats, Owandaets, and Owandats.

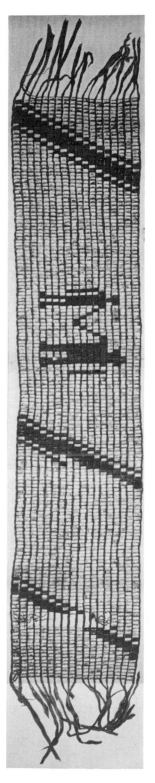

Penn Wampum Belt. Given to the Historical Society of Pennsylvania in 1857 by Granville John Penn, great-grandson of William Penn. This belt is believed to have been the belt representing the treaty of peace held under the Treaty Tree at Kensington (or Shackamaxon—the same place) in 1683 or 1684. *Memoirs of the Historical Society of Pennsylvania*, volume VI, *Contributions to American History* (Philadelphia, 1858). From: the Historical Society of Pennsylvania.

wampum belts, and significantly this remarkable chain needed to be
brightened or polished periodically with gifts. The colonies spent thousands of pounds for this purpose during the eighteenth century. The
Quaker colony in particular drew heavily on the provincial treasury to
"brighten the chain of friendship," [21] for each so-called "brightening"
strengthened an alliance.

Rows of black or white wampum on belts generally represented paths
to specific places. These open paths connoted friendship since they could
not be used freely in time of war. Several of the "Penn Wampum Belts"
are still preserved in the Museum of the American Indian, Heye Foundation, New York.[22] In 1925 authorities of the museum called upon surviving members of the Onondaga and Seneca tribes to interpret the
meaning of these belts. One example of their interpretations was the
"Freedom Belt." This belt had a white background with purple beads
running in a rectangular pattern across the length of the belt. It represented the idea of freedom: the Indian reserved the perpetual right to
traverse, whenever necessary, lands previously sold to the whites.[23]

It was normal for wampum belts to be displayed as a record and evidence of previous treaties, as in the case of the belt shown Conrad Weiser
by the Wyandots. Since the Indians preserved no written record of public
meetings, their archives were in the form of wampum. The preservation
and safeguarding of wampum belts was a sacred duty that devolved
upon a special officer of the tribe, usually a sachem. The Indians never
fully accepted the "Pen and Ink Work" of the whites. One chief did tire
of the vagaries of wampum treaty records. Teedyuscung, the great Delaware leader, demanded—and received—a clerk for his legal records
during the Easton conferences with Pennsylvania between 1756 and
1758. Although he lacked wampum belts, deeds, or legal papers to back
up his statements, Teedyuscung, showing a remarkable memory for details, pointed out exact areas in the Susquehanna and Wyoming valleys
that he claimed had been taken by fraud. When asked what he meant
by fraud, the Delaware leader replied that the land had been taken by
means of forged deeds and by trickery in using the compass.[24]

Wampum strings, although not used as a record of previous treaties,
nevertheless played their part at Indian conferences. George Croghan,
Sir William Johnson's deputy Indian superintendent, greeted the Shawnees and other visiting Indians in this fashion:

> Brethren,
>   With this String I wipe the Sweat & dust off Your Bodies Pick the
>   bryars out of Your feet & clean Your eyes that You may see Your
>   Brethren's faces and look cheerfull—
>
>   Gave a String

Brethren,
> With this String I clear Your hearts & Minds that You may Speak per-
> fectly free and open to us—

Gave a String

Brethren,
> With this String I wipe the Blood from off the Council Seats, that your
> Cloaths may be not Stained nor Your minds disturbed—

Gave a String[25]

The presentation of belts and strings usually occurred in council meetings. The main participants, who were elected by their tribes, were called
speakers. Holding a belt or string in his hand, the speaker would rise and
begin his talk. At its conclusion, he would give the wampum to the group
of persons just addressed.[26] When a belt was presented, the Indians
usually gave a shout to indicate their approval.[27] Belts, being more valuable than strings, were used for greater emphasis during these formal
talks at treaties.

Records of Indian treaties occasionally contain these words: "Shew'd
a String & retook it." [28] The return of a belt or string indicated that the
party addressed did not comply with the request. This frequently happened when the war-hatchet was presented but not accepted; in that
case, the speaker took back the hatchet.[29] The war belt, employed for
the same purposes as the tomahawk or hatchet, was equally important in
connection with the declaration of war. Thus at a conference at Mount
Johnson in 1755 * William Johnson threw down the war belt in General
Braddock's name. The belt was picked up by an Oneida sachem; and
Arent Stevens, interpreter, began the war dance while the sachems sang
the conventional song.[30]

Wampum was used by the Ohio Company of Virginia at the important
Treaty of Logstown, which in 1752 successfully secured a clear title to
a large area of land centering around the forks of the Ohio River. James
Patton,[31] one of the three Indian commissioners for the Ohio Company,
had to obtain the wampum needed for the treaty-making. He got it from
the colorful Maryland trader Thomas Cresap,[32] a member of the company, who had plenty of black and white beads to be used in his dealings with the tribesmen.

Wampum was a necessity in almost all native diplomacy.† Belts were
used in making alliances, preventing disputes,[33] cementing friendships, and
assuring future fidelity[34]—and also in identifying messengers. Collars and
girdles as well as belts seem to have served as credentials at public meet-

* Sir William Johnson's home on the Mohawk River.
† Occasionally tobacco was used instead of wampum.

ings. A belt was used by the Mohawks to request that a fort be built for the Oneidas. There was no confusion because the belt holder was identified as the official messenger. As Sir William Johnson said, the belt was a "Sacred Engagement" among the Indians.[35]

Among the Iroquois, the eloquent sachems often used wampum in dramatic diplomatic confrontations at treaties to emphasize or signal an official statement of policy. Speaking for the league at a conference in 1742 the powerful sachem Canassatego, with a rain of wampum beads, chastized the Delawares for daring to negotiate land transactions without Iroquois approval:

> Let this Belt of Wampum serve to Chastize You; You ought to be taken by the Hair of the Head and shak'd severely till you recover your Senses and become Sober. . . . Don't deliberate, but remove away and take this Belt of Wampum. . . . This String of Wampum serves to forbid You, Your Children and Grand Children, to the latest Posterity, for ever medling in Land Affairs, neither you nor any who shall descend from You are ever hereafter to presume to sell any Land, for which purpose you are to Preserve this string in Memory of what your Uncles have this Day given You in Charge.[36]

The eminent sachems of the Iroquois were "Uncles" who thought they could order generations of Delawares to behave according to pronouncements laid down with wampum belts and beads. But wampum was necessary even when the Iroquois themselves agreed to a land transaction. As Canassatego described Iroquois customs, the civil chiefs, or sachems, had to give official consent to an agreement with an exchange of wampum. In explaining this procedure to the governor of Pennsylvania in an oration of July 2, 1742 Canassatego said:

> Our people who pretended to sell the Land demanded a Belt of Wampum of the Buyers to carry to their Chiefs, and on their declaring they had no Wampum, Our Warriours said they would not Answer that their Chiefs would confirm this Bargain, since they never did any thing of this Nature without Wampum.[37]

One would suppose that the subject of wampum beads now belongs to the limbo of history. To be sure wampum should be mentioned, as we have seen, in any discussion of Indian politics relating to treaty making, and even anthropologists such as Harold E. Driver are willing to give it several page references in a large book on North American Indians.[38] And most financial histories of the United States have a few pages on wampum as a form of currency in New Netherland and New England in the seventeenth century. The traveling Anglican clergyman, the Reverend Andrew Burnaby, mentioned seeing the beads made as late as 1760 on Staten Island, but wampum seems to have largely passed out of the mainstream of history after that time.[39] At least it is seldom mentioned.

Or is it? Edmond Wilson in his *Apologies to the Iroquois* discusses some of the main grievances modern Iroquois have against the state of New York. In addition to cheating the Iroquois so that only seventy-eight thousand acres of their original eighteen million are in Indian hands, the New Yorkers have also collected in their state museum sacred Indian objects, great wampum belts, and painted wooden masks, or false faces. Why are the Indians so angry about the loss of their belts? Wilson consulted anthropologist William N. Fenton who told him that the Indians are haunted by the idea that their sacred wampum and masks are imprisoned in the white man's museums.[40] Governor Nelson A. Rockefeller was besieged with Onondaga demands that the wampum belts be returned to their rightful owners.* What did the governor do? Among the alternatives he considered was to revive the ancient chain of friendship ceremony.[41] Yes, why not revive the legend and the ceremony that first bound the great Iroquoian confederacy to the early settlers of New York. Recently he and the state legislature tentatively provided for the return of five belts owned by the state, but even this gesture will not relieve existing tensions between the Iroquois and their neighbors. Other acts to brighten the chain of friendship on the part of New York State can do much to improve the lot of the Iroquois in a modern white society.†

* The controversy is discussed in a learned essay by W. N. Fenton, the New York State Wampum Collection: "the Case for the Integrity of Cultural Treasures," *Proceedings of the American Philosophical Society*, 115, (Dec. 30, 1971) pp. 430–71 and in a series of articles and resolutions in *The Indian Historian* III, (spring, 1970), pp. 4–18, 50.

†Richard Aquila, *The Iroquois Restoration, Iroquois Diplomacy on the Colonial Frontier, 1701-1754* (Detroit, 1983), traces the emergence of a policy of neutrality in Iroquois wampum diplomacy. See especially pp. 85-156.

CHAPTER 4

White Gift-Giving: French Skills in Managing the Indians

Clark Wissler, one of the leading writers of the past generation on the North American Indians, tells us that the Europeans gave the Indians "three strange gifts," the gun, the horse, and liquor.[1] For better or for worse, the Indians were never the same again. Wissler might have added a fourth "gift," epidemic diseases that, according to a recent investigator, Henry F. Dobyns, reduced the North American Indian population by millions from a high point of almost ten million at the time of discovery.[2]

The French traders in North America in their eager search for furs found that the Indians would do almost anything to get enough brandy. And indeed brandy was one of the most sought after "gifts" that the Canadian Indians prized, despite its evil influences.[3] Canadian missionaries, traders, soldiers, and agents had found that Indians had a long-established custom of exchanging presents. At public meetings there were traditional ceremonies for the exchange of such articles as calumet pipes, wampum (sometimes called "strings" of porcelain), clothing, and beaver pelts. When the French sought to win over a key group of Indian warriors for a special

50

purpose they resorted to enormous expenditures of gifts because the Indians expected them. So it was when the Marquis de Duquesne, governor general of Canada, issued instructions to his new commander of forces in the Ohio River area in 1754; he sent special gifts to the Indians of the region to be distributed in the name of the King of France.[4] Anxious to win Indian allegiance because of rivalry with England for control of the fur trade and for the possession of North America, the French were willing to go all out in giving presents even if the economy of New France was jeopardized by extraordinary expenditures for gifts. An army to police the vast inland empire would have been enormously expensive. Besides, the French found that the alternative of gift-giving was so much a part of the warp and woof of Indian life that no business could be transacted with Indians without suitable gifts. Thus, early Canadian historical records are filled with accounts of giving presents to the Indians. Everybody, it seemed, was involved in gift-giving, government agents, explorers, missionaries, and the governor himself. All kinds of Indians of all tribes received gifts, and these included war chiefs, sachems, warriors, and women. Indian children were an object of particular solicitude by Frenchmen who wanted to make a special impression on Indians, for it was well known on the inland frontiers that the Indians had great love for their offspring.[5]

From the earliest times in Canadian history the Jesuit missionaries and the French explorers emphasized the special importance of giving appropriate gifts to the Indians. A particularly significant present was the calumet pipe.° The bestowal of this pipe (with its long stem occasionally wrapped with strands of wampum beads) could even lead to the cessation of hostilities among tribes that had been at war. The Algonquian Indians had such a veneration for the pipe that a violation of the "law of the calumet" was considered an unpardonable offense.[6] The French, like other Europeans experienced in dealing with the woodland tribes, used wampum at treaty conferences and accepted it as a token of alliance.

Tobacco was the most popular of the many "gifts" that the Indians gave the French and other Europeans, and it was eagerly accepted. The Europeans proved to be as fascinated with the fragrant weed as the Indian was with the white man's liquor.

Among the far-western Canadian Indians, especially those of the Pacific Coast, marathon gift-giving contests, or potlatch ceremonies, occupied key tribesmen who sought to give away a lifetime of wealth to outdo a competitor. Literally thousands of blankets, bracelets, and other articles

° The remarkable influence of the calumet is discussed in W. N. Fenton, *The Iroquois Eagle Dance, an Offshoot of the Calumet Dance,* Bureau of American Ethnology Bulletin 156, (Washington, 1953).

were presented as gifts, and as many as fifty seals were eaten in an accompanying feast.[7]

There are records of such contests on a smaller scale among the woodland Indians east of the Mississippi. Among the Iroquois and the Algonquian tribes of the Great Lakes gifts were exchanged in a whole series of ceremonies that marked the average Indian's progress through life: at the time of his birth, when he was initiated into the tribe as an adult warrior, when he was married, and finally at the time of his death.[8]

Scalps, hatchets, blankets, and food were other types of presents given by the natives (both to whites and to each other), each of which had a definite purpose. Among the Algonquian Indians, for example, the calumet served as a record of previous agreements, while wampum was used for the same purpose in the Iroquoian confederacy. All tribes appear to have regarded the hatchet or ax as a present to be used in the declaration of war. To "bury the hatchet," especially in the "bottomless pit," was one way of making peace.[9]

The Canadian Indians also gave and received goods that had been manufactured by whites. The *Aouapou* was a native word used by the Canadians "to denote the complete suit of clothing that one must give to a savage." [10] This outfit consisted of a blanket, a shirt, leggings, shoes, a breechcloth, and sometimes a capote. A similar set of clothing was given to the native women, but a short skirt (machicotté) was substituted for the breechcloth. In winter the native allies had to be supplied with what the Canadians called the *Apichmont*. This included a bearskin, snowshoes, and leggings.[11] The quality of these outfits varied; the finer types were given to influential natives, while the poorer quality were doled out to ordinary warriors. Beautiful scarlet coats decorated with silver buttons and lace were presented to the sachems, and the older villagers who could no longer hunt or fight were also clothed, for these old warriors played an important part in determining the policy of the various confederacies.

The stroud, a cheap woolen cloth made of rags, was almost an English monopoly, but the French used it for blankets and certain items of clothing. The tribesmen received a number of other textiles and articles of clothing: gaily colored calicoes, hats laced with tinsel and trimmed with large colored feathers, ruffled and plain shirts, handkerchiefs, stockings, shoes, and waistcoats.[12] Purple and white French ratteen, a woolen fabric used for linings and stockings, was a coveted item that Sir William Johnson wanted very much for his native wards. He even confiscated French blankets captured by British warships because he considered the French blankets to be superior to those made in England.[13] Despite the popularity of certain French goods, however, French cloth used for gifts was often poorly dyed and of an inferior grade.

Medals, brass kettles of assorted sizes, iron wire, axes, scissors, combs, paints of different colors, especially vermillion, thread, needles, "steels" for striking fire, looking glasses, and a hundred other articles were repeatedly distributed among the natives by both the English and the French.[14] Some were designed to satisfy the vanity of the warrior, others were mere toys to amuse native children. Of course such items as needles, thread, and scissors were soon regarded almost as necessities by Indians, especially native women.

Among the more essential gifts demanded by the Indians from the French, were guns, powder, knives, bullets, and hatchets—items ostensibly intended for hunting but all too often used in warfare. In exchange for these gifts some of the more hardened French administrators received scalps or even heads of enemy tribesmen.[15]

The various Indian confederacies who were the recipients of French gifts had for centuries lived in vast forest lands of eastern North America. Those Algonquian people who lived in or near what is now Maine were called Abnaki, a term derived from the Algonquian words "east-land." [16] This name, however, was also (and more generally) used to refer to the Algonquians who lived along the eastern seaboard including the Delaware of the Ohio Valley. It was the Algonquian warriors who traveled hundreds of miles from the remote parts of Canada and the Mississippi Valley to aid the French and collect their rewards of presents and plunder. These people—among them the Chippewas,* the Sauks,† the Foxes, the Ottawas, the Hurons‡ the Illinois, and the Miamis[17]—were the most frequent recipients of French gifts. On one occasion the Marquis de Montcalm had as native auxiliaries more than three thousand warriors representing thirty-three different "nations." [18] The Miami and Ottawa confederacies with their scattered settlements throughout the Great Lakes region could boast the greatest number of warriors.

Other beneficiaries of French presents were the members of the Six Nations Iroquois, located within the present boundaries of the state of New York. The Senecas in western New York were in most frequent contact with the French. Although their number had been decimated by disease and liquor they could in 1763 still muster 1,050 warriors, while the Mohawks, the recipients of British gifts, had dwindled to only 160 fighting men.[19] Along the Ohio frontier there were some 789 warriors who were presented gifts by both the French and the English between 1748 and 1763. According to Conrad Weiser, these tribes consisted of the Delawares, the Shawnees, the Wyandots, the Mohigans, and the Ohio Iroquois (these latter sometimes called Mingo).[20] The French also made

* Often called the Chippeway, or the Ojibwas.
† Sometimes referred to as the Sacs, Sacks, or Sackis.
‡ Of the Iroquois linguistic family.

it a practice to give large outlays of gifts to their allies among the south-eastern tribes, especially the Choctaws.[21]

Throughout the seventeenth century the French followed a policy of pacifying their closest and most dangerous neighbors, the Iroquois, with gifts. If subsidies did not keep the Iroquois at bay, then French governors actually punished the closest tribes, usually the Senecas, by leading small armies of French soldiers into the Iroquois cantons and destroying their towns and stores. From time to time French officials considered a policy of exterminating the Iroquois, but armed with Anglo-Dutch guns and hatchets, the Iroquois defended themselves successfully, and actually embarked on several occasions on an extended offensive against the Canadian settlements. Following depletion of the Iroquois fur resources about 1640, these aggressive tribesmen carried on far-flung hunting and trading expeditions.[22]

After the treaty of Aix-la-Chapelle in 1748 the French and British began in earnest to compete for the vitally important friendship of the Indian. During King George's War and in the period of peace that followed it, the Joncaire brothers,[23] Philip Thomas and Chabert, were sent to distribute presents among the Ohio tribes and the Seneca in western New York. They were William Johnson's most important rivals for the control of the Six Nations, and they were also in sharp competition with agents from the Quaker colony of Pennsylvania, George Croghan, Conrad Weiser, and the half-caste interpreter Andrew Montour. At Logstown on the Ohio in 1749 Céleron de Blainville,[24] with Philip Thomas as his interpreter, found that his gifts were not attractive enough to lure key Indians away from the English. Nor was he successful in winning the rebellious Miami leader La Demoiselle (known as Old Briton to the English) from the Pennsylvania traders who came to the Miami town of Pickawillany and plied the natives with wampum belts and other presents. Between 1748 and 1752 La Demoiselle consummated an alliance with the province of Pennsylvania through the exchange of calumets, wampum, and other goods, and made himself the center of an alliance against the French; the Wea, the Potawatomi, the Kickapoo, the Piankashaw, the Ottawa, and the other allies of the Miami also turned against the French. When conciliatory presents failed to quell the secret alliance, the French saw no alternative but to destroy Pickawillany. This they did in June 1752. The old chief was boiled and eaten before the very eyes of his confederates by the savage allies of the French officer Charles Langlade,* leader of the assault.[25]

* Langlade had a long and varied career on the frontier, participating in almost every major battle between the French and the English including Braddock's defeat. His influence with the Indians made him almost indispensable on military campaigns. He had a son by an Ottawa woman and this son served the British for many years in Canadian outposts.

This show of power, plus the French occupation of the Ohio Valley in 1754, succeeded in enhancing French prestige among the northwestern Indians. British land purchases in the Ohio region in 1752 and 1754 also caused the tribesmen to go over to the side of the French.[26] It was no longer necessary for the French to ply the natives continually with presents, for their services could sometimes be bought with mere promises of plunder.[27] The 650 French Indians who fought against Braddock in 1755 found themselves all but overwhelmed with loot left by the British and could not be prevented from returning immediately to their villages, laden with plunder.[28] The British did not fare so well. As a result of their failure to provide adequate presents and supplies for the Cherokee and Ohio Indians who were to fight for Braddock, the British were left with only eight native guides, certainly no match for the French Indians.[29]

The Marquis de Montcalm, who succeeded the Baron Dieskau, "had the report spread throughout all the Indian nations that there would be plunder for those who would come and fight. . . ."[30] The victories at Oswego in August 1756 and Fort William Henry in August 1757 afforded the Indian allies of the French ample opportunity for plunder of weapons and goods and gave them a harvest of scalps.

Although the French had in early years played the Indians against each other and on occasion had gone so far as "to foment and excite wars" among dangerous tribes in order to weaken them,[31] policy changed as New France gradually strengthened her defenses and took the offense against her enemies. By 1755, when Pierre Rigaud· de Vaudreuil * became governor and lieutenant general of New France,[32] the French had adopted the rôle of "protectors and pacificators."[33] It had become French policy to maintain peace between the confederacies that were friendly to New France. Presents and other concessions were the means used to win those natives who leaned toward the English. If these methods failed, the offending tribesmen were to be punished as those at Pickawillany had been.

As long as hardware, textiles, and other Indian goods could be purchased, presents were considered normal expenses of the French government. Extraordinary expenditures were made for available Indian merchandise during time of war and other emergencies. François Bigot,†

---

* Pierre Rigaud de Vaudreuil de Cavagnal served as governor of Louisiana from 1743 to 1753. In the latter year he returned to France and was appointed governor general of New France in 1755. After the capitulation of Montreal, he again returned to France where he died in 1778. He is to be distinguished from his brother, Pierre François or François Pierre Rigaud de Vaudreuil who was made governor of Montreal in 1757.

* François Bigot was Intendant for New France from 1748 to 1760. He was noted for his extravagance, for pilfering public funds, and he was later punished. Regarding Bigot's gambling, Montcalm complained that "hazard has been played to excess in the Intendant's house. . . ." See M. de Montcalm to M. de Paulmy, Quebec, Feb-

the Intendent, complained that in 1759, near the end of the French and Indian War, he laid out a total of four hundred million francs for Indian goods.[34] Even in peace time the governor of New France spent one hundred and fifty thousand francs yearly to purchase presents for the tribesmen of Canada.[35]

The presents that were doled out annually by the French were a tremendous burden on the government—in times of peace as well as war. Vaudreuil, writing to France in 1756, declared that goods for the Indians were as important in carrying on the war as were munitions. Thus the Abnaki and their allies had to be supplied with ample provisions before they could be persuaded to ravage the British colonial frontier.

At no time between 1748 and 1763 (during a period of increasing competition with the British) did the French have adequate supplies of Indian presents or other necessities from France. The shortage of goods became most acute in the latter part of the French and Indian War, when British men-of-war caused many French vessels either to turn back or be captured. In 1757, for example, only three out of an expected seventeen ships arrived in Canada.[36] Vaudreuil, Montcalm, Bigot, and other French officials were continually complaining about the scarcity of Indian merchandise and the high prices that resulted from that scarcity, for by 1759 Indian goods and military supplies had skyrocketed in price.[37] As the French had neither goods nor munitions to give their native allies, the Indians either tried to distance themselves from the conflict or joined the winning side; presents and plunder were rewards for joining the British.

Indian presents passed through the trading posts. Since few Canadian officials hesitated to cheat their government, the loss to the government in fur trade goods and gifts was considerable, six hundred thousand francs yearly.[38] Large quantities of goods earmarked as presents for the Indians never reached the natives. One official complained that "certificates of presents pretended to have been made to the Indians, are accepted without any examination. . . ."[39] Men who had monopolies on trading posts, usually army officers, purchased the king's stores and charged their expenses to the government, thereby causing the king to buy Indian goods twice, once in France and once again in Canada.

This situation was further complicated because (with the help of alcohol) the presents were sometimes won away from the tribesmen and resold to the government. In this way the king's expenditure on gifts was again increased. Montcalm thought that the immense profits made by "officers, storekeepers, [and] commissaries" would "impoverish" New France.[40] Indeed, it is not unreasonable to assume that one of the reasons

---

ruary 19, 1758, in E. B. O'Callaghan, *et al.*, eds., *Documents Relative to the Colonial History of the State of New York* (Albany, 1853–87), 10:685.

for the downfall of New France was excessive expenditure for Indian goods that all but plunged the colony into bankruptcy.

By 1760 most of the Canadian Indians had been brought over to the British side. The military successes achieved by James Wolfe and Jeffery Amherst and the latter's huge expenditures for gifts were partly responsible for this shift in loyalty. But after the conquest of Canada, Amherst decided that the Indians should once again hunt and earn their livelihood, and so between 1760 and 1763 he drastically pared the money available for gifts,[41] thus causing much discontent among the western and northern confederacies.[42] After the long wars the western Indians were practically destitute of goods and supplies, especially powder and arms for hunting purposes; yet it was these very goods that the British withheld from them. When the tribes asked for a beer to quench their thirst, Amherst replied that the Indians should learn to make their own brew by soaking spruce branches in water. With the flow of goods from both the French and the British stopped, Pontiac did not find it difficult to mobilize native discontent for a war against the British.[43] Gifts had been used by both the French and British to subsidize the Indian as a military ally. Now that the war between the European powers was over, the Indian was expected to shift for himself.[*]

[*] Early French policies and attitudes toward the Indians are reevaluated by Cornelius J. Jaenen in *Friend and Foe, Aspects of French-Amerindian Cultural Contact in the Sixteenth and Seventeenth Centuries* (New York, 1976), pp. 190-97. Later French-Indian relations are discussed in a series of ethnohistorical essays in Bruce G. Trigger, ed., *Handbook of North American Indians*, vol. 15, *Northeast*, (Washington, 1978), pp. 4, 6, 81, 94-95, 111, 344-46, 506-507ff.

PART II

INDIAN-WHITE CONTACT: FRONTIER CONFLICTS

Long and dismal are the complaints which the Indians make of European ingratitude and injustice. Often I have listened to these descriptions of their hard sufferings until I felt ashamed of being a **white man**. . . .

They begin with the Virginians, whom they call the **long knives**. . . . "It was we," say the Lenape, Mohicans, and their kindred tribes, "who so kindly received them on their first arrival into our country. We took them by the hand, and bid them welcome to sit down by our side, and live with us as brothers; but how did they requite our kindness? They at first asked only for a little land on which to raise bread for themselves and their families, and pasture for their cattle, which we freely gave them. They soon wanted more, which we also gave them. They saw the game in the woods, which the Great Spirit had given us for our subsistence, and they wanted that too. They penetrated into the woods in quest of game; they discovered spots of land which pleased them; that land they also wanted, and because we were loth to part with it, as we saw they had already more than they had need of, they took it from us by force, and drove us to a great distance from our ancient homes."

The Reverend John Heckewelder, Moravian clergyman, writing of his experiences with the Indians beginning about 1760, *History, Manners, and the Customs of the Indian Nations Who Once Inhabited Pennsylvania and the Neighboring States.*

CHAPTER 5

British Indian-White Relations: Edmond Atkin's Scheme for Imperial Control

In 1755 a destructive war raged along the British western frontier. A powerful British army had been defeated by a force of 600 Indian warriors and 220 French soldiers.[1] The British were left with a dying general and a routed army. The leadership fell upon young George Washington, who was not fully recovered from a serious illness. Worse was to come: most of the Indians had joined the enemy who were about to unleash a major attack upon the whole northern frontier. The campaign that followed brought with it its full share of the atrocities characteristic of the French and Indian wars.

Confusion and maladministration of Indian affairs were partly responsible for the British misfortunes. Luckily Edward Braddock had appointed William Johnson superintendent of Indian affairs for the north before the disaster on the Monongahela. Indeed in the period immediately after Braddock's defeat, most of Johnson's efforts were devoted to keeping the majority of the Six Nations neutral and preventing them from joining Montcalm,[2] thus saving the northern colonies from almost certain military calamity.

But in the south the Cherokees, the Chickasaws, and the Creeks were planning to join the French.

Such was the state of affairs when Charleston merchant Edmond Atkin submitted his scheme for the management of Indian-white relations to the Board of Trade, the governing body for the colonies. Atkin's plan won him a reputation in his own day as a leading provincial figure and led to his appointment as southern superintendent of the Indians in 1756. Although he later negotiated, with the aid of the Maryland frontiersman Christopher Gist, a number of successful treaties with the southern Indian nations and provided Indian warriors for Washington in 1757 and for General John Forbes in 1758,[3] Atkin's work was soon forgotten by his contemporaries; his career has usually been judged a failure.

The superintendent was much criticized by his contemporaries. In a letter to William Pitt in 1760 he complained that he had carried on his duties for four years without a "Shilling of the King's Money," but that his enemies had "hatcheted" his reputation worse than an Indian warrior had disfigured his body.[4]

The criticisms of Atkin were not simply the result of malice among his contemporaries. In fact his personality made him unsuited for the job he had undertaken. He lacked tact and discretion, and quarreled with Sir William Johnson's deputies and the colonial governors.[5] He worked slowly and meticulously, so that matters of importance were frequently left undone. The tribesmen deeply resented this pompous and overbearing man. A warrior named Tobacco Eater became so angry during an Indian conference that he almost scalped the superintendent.[6] Atkin's worst faults were all too apparent to the Indians and his fellow provincials.

Edmond Atkin had been born in England in 1707,[7] and had lived in South Carolina ever since his boyhood.[8] During the 1730s he and one John Atkin, probably a close relative, established a trading concern in Charleston. This venture was so successful that by 1738 Edmond had been appointed to the governor's council of South Carolina.[9]

During his eighteen years on the council, Atkin became acquainted with many of the headmen of the southern Indian nations, and according to his own account, took a deep interest in native diplomacy.[10] He learned much about the Indians, their problems, the abuses of the fur trade, and the rivalry between the French and the English for the friendship of the Indians.[11] In short, Atkin was an expert on Indian-white relations, especially on the great southern colonial frontier.

In October of 1750 he mysteriously gave up his business and sailed for England where he remained for six years, preparing documents to establish his reputation as an expert on Indian-white affairs for the imperial government. He did not give up his seat in the South Carolina governor's council, however. This peculiar situation caused the Board of Trade in 1754 to inquire if he ever intended to return to South Carolina. He replied that he was recuperating from an illness and that in addition some "particular affairs" had delayed his return to America. He also claimed that he had been occupied in "Public Service" in England, probably referring to the writings on Indian affairs that he composed in London between 1750 and 1754.[12]

Atkin produced two important documents during his stay in England. The first was a detailed history (thirty thousand words) of the bloody Choctaw revolt of 1746, and the second was his plan for managing Indian-white affairs. The paper on the Choctaw revolt tells of the intrigues surrounding the activities of Red Shoes, a Choctaw war chief who carried a large part of his people over to the British because of dissatisfaction with the French in the fur and skin trade.[13] The French governor of Louisiana, Pierre François Rigaud, Marquis de Vaudreuil, demanded the head of Red Shoes as a propitiation from the Choctaw. The subsequent assassination of the war chief led to civil war among the Choctaw and the eventual defeat of the English faction.

Atkin's essay tells how the Choctaw revolt was exploited by three South Carolinians: James Adair, fur trader and author of a history of the Indians; Charles McNaire, a Charleston trader; and James Glen, governor of South Carolina. All three received a sound scolding for promoting the civil war and then leaving their Indian allies with nothing to fight with except glass beads to be used as bullets.[14]

The essay on the Choctaw revolt is packed with information relating to the colonial fur and skin trade. But Atkin's long report to the Board of Trade outlining his plan for managing Indian-white affairs by creating the superintendencies is an even more interesting work, one that is both informative and clearly argued.[15] It was, in addition, the first complete plan for the management of Indian-white affairs to be submitted to the Board of Trade.

Atkin begins his essay by thanking the Lords of Trade for the opportunity to express his opinions on Indian affairs. He then goes on to point out that relations between whites and Indians are on a "wretched footing throughout all of America"; a general plan of management is necessary lest the Indians in disgust turn their allegiance entirely to the French.[16] It is imperative that the English support and protect the Indians, since the tribesmen are the strongest barrier against French encroachment. The French, Atkin points out, have been remarkably successful in winning the friendship of key tribes among the nations that border the British provinces. Even the Cherokee and the Six Nations, he complains, are turning away from the British.

Atkin then discusses the grounds for the growing French influence in the native settlements west of the Appalachians. Contrary to popular belief, the source of French power does not lie in French fortifications, for the Indian can be won by friendship but not by fear. Such small fortifications could be easily overwhelmed by the savage hordes that surround them. Rather, the Indians consider the French as benefactors, Atkin declares, suppliers of ammunition, guns, and many other presents. Moreover, the French provide gunsmiths to sharpen native hatchets and to mend broken weapons.[17] Atkin argues that the French, with their understanding of the savage mind, know that a warrior treasures a repaired weapon more than any new weapon that might be given to him, even though it be an outright present. Thus the French preserve the friendship of their Indian allies by the judicious use of presents and gunsmiths under the direction of a centralized Indian administration that tolerates no injustice to the Indian, even from the French traders.

Atkin follows his lavish praise of French methods of Indian control with a critical discussion of Indian management and Indian commerce throughout the British colonies. The chief target for his censure is South Carolina, his own province. What is true in South Carolina, Atkin maintains, is true to some degree in all the colonies. Mismanagement and chaos in Indian-white affairs will, he says, in time bring about the alienation of all the Indian nations:

> . . . we neither build Forts for their Protection, nor mend their Guns and Hatchets for them, as they [the French] do . . . we set no Account by any of them, but [as] Hunters for the sake of Skins; And . . . our Traders Cheat and impose upon them.[18]

Every faction within the colonies that had anything to do with the Indians considered their own private interests rather than the general good. The result was confusion; the Indians did not know whom to believe when rival trading interests lied about each other.

Worse than the lack of a wisely conceived, unified colonial Indian policy were the machinations of the rum traders, who caused what Atkin terms "scandal," "alarm," and "uneasiness" by their contemptible dealings. He neglects, however, to mention the ten thousand gallons of rum that, earlier in his career, he imported during a six-month period, supposedly for the colony of Georgia.[19]

One of the most significant parts of Atkin's essay is the section he entitled "The Character of the Indians." Here he discusses each of the major woodland confederacies bordering the British colonies from Massachusetts to Georgia. Atkin's insight into the Indian mind is such that many of his introductory statements might have been written by Sir William Johnson, or at a later date by Lewis H. Morgan. Atkin masterfully sweeps away misconceptions about the Indians that most whites had harbored for generations. He makes the reader understand what love the

Indians had for their homeland, what "glory" meant in Indian warfare, and what truthful, honest bargainers the Indians were in treaty making. Here is the noble savage at his best, portrayed by a man who knew him well:

> No people in the World understand and pursue their true national Interest, better than the Indians. How sanguinary soever they are towards their Enemies, from a misguided Passion of Heroism, and a love of their country; yet they are otherways truly humane, hospitable, and equitable. And how fraudulent soever they have been reputed, from the Appearance of their military Actions, in which, according to their method of War, Glory cannot be acquired without Cunning and Stratagem; Yet in their publick Treaties no People on earth are more open, explicit, and Direct. Nor are they [the Indians] excelled by any [people] in the observance of them [treaties].[20]

The remarkable assertion made here, that Indians actually observed treaties, was true and could easily be proved, as Atkin argued, by examining the treaties made by the Iroquois with the Dutch and later with the English.* Of course the point is a good one to stress if one wanted to point out the need of a superintendent (such as Atkin himself) who could negotiate more treaties to improve Indian-white relations.

Atkin's essay goes on to treat the history of major tribes surrounding the British colonies with special emphasis upon the southern confederacies.† Atkin gives the exact location of major tribal towns and provides a list of the number of warriors in the various tribes. His figures tally closely with the later estimates of John Stuart, Atkin's successor, and Sir William Johnson.[21] Atkin must have had extensive notes and even copies of the journals of the South Carolina council at his disposal, for such a detailed work could hardly have been written from memory.

The last section of the essay is devoted entirely to Atkin's scheme for the reorganization of the management of Indian-white affairs in North America. Obviously Atkin was not aware that William Johnson had already been appointed northern superintendent, for he writes as though nothing had been done to improve the situation.†

His plan is designed to correct the evils of maladministration outlined in the first part of the manuscript. Indian alliances were to be revived by "brightening the chain of friendship," and a uniform regulation of Indian commerce was to be put into effect. These measures would help to defeat "the designs of the French." Most important of all, two imperial super-

---

* Atkin, however, ignores early French-Iroquois relations which show evidence of bad faith on both sides.
† James Adair's *History of the American Indians,* a book written shortly after Atkin's report, contains a description of Indian customs, which he uses as a basis of an argument to show similarities between the Indians and the ten lost tribes of Israel.

intendents were to be appointed; these should be vested by Parliament with full authority and be provided with the financial resources necessary for carrying out their duties. The northern superintendent was to have jurisdiction over the Iroquoian confederacy and its allies, and his southern counterpart was to govern British relations with the southern tribes, the Cherokee and their Muskhogean brothers.

One of the first duties of the superintendents would be to negotiate a series of treaties with all the principal Indian nations that would bind them to the British. The Indians were to agree to trade only with the English, and new trade regulations were to be established by law to protect the natives from abuses. Indian commerce was to follow a regular procedure with licensed traders, fixed prices, and standard weights and measures. In addition, heavy penalties were to be imposed on any trader who allowed Indians to become drunk. All spirits given to the warriors had to be "temper'd" with water.

Atkin's scheme also provided for an extensive system of forts and block-houses to be erected by British army engineers. The purpose of these forts was to "protect" the Indians from the French, to provide a storage place for the presents and goods used in Indian commerce, and to garrison soldiers. What the future superintendent was in fact advocating was a duplication of the French system of fortifications where (at least in theory) all contacts between the Indians and government agents, licensed traders, and interpreters took place. Private individuals were to be allowed no dealings with the Indians, especially in connection with land purchases. All Indian affairs were to be under the general direction of the superintendent.

The superintendent was to be supported by a variety of assistants; S.P.G. missionaries,* frontier rangers, secretaries, gunsmiths, interpreters, and commissioners are mentioned. These helpers would aid in the distribution of presents and would frequently visit the tribesmen.[22]

Such a program would obviously cost a great deal. Atkin suggested, therefore, that part of the funds be provided by the colonies. The money could be raised by a poll tax to be leveled upon every British male subject, by a "small" duty upon wines imported from the West Indies and an "easy" duty upon foreign sugar, molasses, and rum, or by the establishment of a system of post offices throughout all of North America, which he believed would "under good regulation bring in a large sum."

Edmond Atkin was not the first to suggest an Indian superintendency system. But his was the first really practical plan for Indian management to be submitted to the British authorities.[23] His scheme gathered together into one coherent plan all earlier ideas on Indian administration.

---

* Missionaries from the Society for the Propagation of the Gospel in Foreign Parts.

Atkin's work was recognized by his appointment to the newly-established office of southern Indian superintendent, but his reputation rested on what the late John Carl Parish described as "a historical narrative and description of the southern Indians . . . unequaled in his time.[24]

Certainly this Carolina merchant of the Indian trade also gave the British empire a far-sighted and intelligently conceived scheme for controlling Indian-white relations that would have reached a high point in administrative development had not the American Revolution destroyed it. Furthermore, the superintendency system that was established in the North American British colonies after the acceptance of Atkin's proposals had significant later repercussions in nineteenth-century America, in Canada, and in Australia.[25] For instance, under the first U.S. Commissioner of Indian Affairs appointed in 1834 (as head of the Bureau of Indian Affairs), territorial governors acted as superintendents of Indian relations. They were assisted by agents and subagents who had duties very similar to those of colonial deputy superintendents. Gift-giving by the government eventually evolved into annuity giving and helped to reduce the Indians to a humiliating dependence upon federal appropriations.*

Of course Atkin never envisioned the kind of malpractices that characterized the work of many later American Indian agents. And none of these later governmental plans to control native-white relations achieved the beneficial results that Atkin had hoped for in protecting both the best interests of whites and Indians. Indeed, later commissioners, agents, and subagents (especially those in nineteenth-century American history) presided over an administrative system that dispossessed the Indian, and in some cases (as in California) actually on occasion permitted his virtual extermination from the face of the land.†

* The U.S. government also followed the custom (established by the French and the English in the colonial period) of awarding favored chiefs with special types of medals. See Francis Paul Prucha, Discussion on "Peace Medals" in *Indian Peace Medals in American History* (Madison, Wisc., 1971), pp. 3–70.

† Sherburne F. Cook, *The Population of the California Indians, 1769-1970* (Berkeley, 1976), pp. 104-141, gives vital statistics on California Indian mortality.

CHAPTER 6

A Message to Fort William Henry: Drama of Siege and Indian Savagery

On Thursday, August 4, 1757, at Fort Edward, overlooking the "Great Carrying place" on the Hudson about fifty miles north of Albany, New York, a nervous British captain scribbled out a hurried message on behalf of his commander. It was 12:00 noon. The uneasy officer, Captain George Bartman, aide-de-camp of Brigadier General Daniel Webb who was in charge of British forces on the New York frontiers, probably heard the distant boom of cannon as he wrote. The letter was directed to Lieutenant Colonel George Monro of the Thirty-fifth Regiment, commander of Fort William Henry at Lake George, almost twenty miles to the north, besieged by the French and Indians. A Connecticut sergeant, undoubtedly one of the colonial rangers who had been keeping communication open between the two forts, was handed the scrap of paper.[1] He carefully folded the paper until it was scarcely larger than a postage stamp, hid it in his vest, and set out on the journey that was to end in his death.[2]

On the southern bank of Lake George, surrounded by forest, stood Fort William Henry, a rugged structure, built under the supervision of Major William Eyre, one of the most capable of

the British army engineers.[3] Its heavy log ramparts were reinforced with
gravel and earth; contemporary diagrams show it to have been an irregular square, approximately three hundred feet along the sides and bas-
tioned at the corners for cross-fire protection.[4] Mortars, howitzers, and
cannon were mounted at strategic points. The lake on the north and a
large marsh on the east provided security. Wide ditches with *chevaux-de-
frise* protected the ramparts on the south and west. The fort was thus
built to ward off anything but an all-out siege by a powerful enemy possessing strong artillery support. Indeed, in the spring of 1757 the garrison
had beaten off an assault by the French, who had carried three hundred
scaling ladders.[5]

Before the spring attack on Fort William Henry the Earl of Loudoun,
commander of the British forces in the colonies, had moved most of the
regular troops out of the New York area to fight against the French at
Louisburg. When Colonel Monro took command of Fort William Henry
in the summer of 1757 he alerted his men for a possible counterattack by
the French. Situated near the northern border, his fort was both a threat
and an irritant to New France. Using the fort as a supply base, Robert
Rogers and his rangers spread terror along the lower Canadian frontier.
Meanwhile the French, who had received intelligence of Loudoun's plans,
prepared their attack on Fort William Henry.

By the first of August the situation at Fort William Henry was very
tense. Monro kept in close touch with Fort Edward through the colonial
ranger messenger system. He had some 2,300 men[6] and additional support
had been promised from Fort Edward.* At dawn on August 3, just as
the surface of Lake George became visible in the morning mist, British
scouts discerned moving floats, bateaux, and bark canoes forming a line
that reached almost across the sheet of water. The enemy, under the
Marquis de Montcalm, soon opened fire. By nine o'clock in the morning
the entire invading army of over 7,600 regulars, Candians, and Indians
had disembarked.[7] The siege had begun.

Yelping, whooping tribesmen from thirty-two different nations had
pledged their allegiance to the French by accepting a mighty wampum
belt made of six thousand beads.[8] Many of these warriors from the remote
wilderness of New France had not lost their taste for human flesh. Others
such as the Hurons from Detroit and Lorette and the Abnakis from St.
Francis, the mission tribesmen, bore a thin veneer of adopted culture
that hardly concealed their pent up warlike frenzy. Keeping these tem-

---

* Webb visited Fort William Henry in June 1757, and after he received news from
Captain Israel Putnam of the French preparations at Fort Ticonderoga, he hastily
left for Fort Edward, much alarmed. He was ready and willing to send aid when
he had the "whole join'd together." See Loudoun Papers, no. 4041. In his correspondence with Monro, Webb constantly exaggerates Montcalm's forces (11,000), and
maintains he needs more information in order to act.

pestuous allies under control was more than even the most capable French military leaders could manage. Of all the French officers, Montcalm had the most influence over them. *

By eleven o'clock the French unmasked their first land batteries. When the splinters of wood began to fly from the log ramparts, the Indians gave loud whoops of joy at the power of the "big guns." Two hours later the salvos stopped. All was silent. Then an emissary from French headquarters bearing a truce flag and a communication from the French general was sent to Monro. "Sir," began Montcalm's note,

> I have this morning invested your place with a numerous Army and superior Artillery, and all the savages from the higher parts of the Country, the Cruelty of which, a Detachement of your Garrison have Lately too much experienced.†
> I am obligated, in Humanity, to desire you to Surrender your Fort: I have it yet in my Power to restrain the Savages, and oblige them to observe a Capitulation, as hitherto none of them have been killed. . . . I demand a decisive answer immediately. . . .[9]

Monro retorted that he had only one reply: ". . . I am determined, to defend the Fort, to the last, And I believe it is the resolution, of every Man, under my Command." [10]

From the bastions the defenders continued their "warm" bombardment of French positions. This constant firing had disastrous results; mortars and cannon soon were honeycombed and burst at the muzzles. Nevertheless, desperate hope for reinforcements from the south caused Monro and his men to hold on from the third to the seventh of August. They could not believe that General Webb would abandon them to Montcalm and his warrior allies. Yet without help defeat seemed inevitable.[11]

Meanwhile the continual dull roar of the cannonading could be heard at Fort Edward. Fearing that Montcalm would attack, Webb sent frantic

* Concerning Montcalm's ascendency over the Indians, Bougainville, his aide-de-camp, wrote:

> They themselves observed that he was acquainted with their customs and manners as if he had been reared in the midst of their cabins, and what is almost unprecedented, he has succeeded in managing them, throughout this entire expedition, without giving them either brandy or wine, or even an outfit of which they stood in greatest need, but the army lacked. He did, indeed, take the greatest care of their sick and wounded, and he gave up his supplies to them. . . .

E. B. O'Callaghan, et al., Documents Relative to the Colonial History of the State of New York (Albany, 1853–87), 10:613 (hereafter cited as New York Col. Docs.).
† Two of Monro's boats, scouting the lake about four miles from the fort, had encountered the French on August 2. A skirmish followed, from which only five of the thirteen men in the scouting party emerged alive. LO, no. 6660. Parkman maintains that a prominent Nipissing chief was killed in this battle. Parkman, Montcalm and Wolfe (Boston, 1893), 1:493. The Indians made much of the death of their chief and held an elaborate funeral ceremony. The French commander must have been aware of this incident.

appeals for help to the colonial militia.[12] On several occasions rangers from the embattled fort had managed to evade the surrounding French and Indians and carry Monro's urgent appeals for aid to Webb. However, Indian warriors under the leadership of M. de la Corne St. Luc were guarding the road to Fort Edward and the nearby forest. While La Corne's men ranged the woods, Canadian workmen dug and enlarged the *boyaux*, or trenches. Some of the trenches were large enough to accommodate the cannon that were being moved closer to the target.

The ranger who carried Webb's message of August 4 had but a small chance of reaching his goal. He could hear the noise of battle as he reached the Lake George area. On Friday, August 5, probably in the afternoon, he was intercepted by one of La Corne's Indian scouts and killed. The sergeant's body was stripped, left in the forest, and his clothing carried to a French officer. Carefully folded in the vest was Webb's letter. It soon reached the hands of Montcalm, who must have read it with some satisfaction:

Sir   Fort Edward August 4th 12 o'clock at Noon
I am directed by General Webb to acknowledge the receipt of three of your Letters, two bearing [the] Date about nine yesterday morning, and one about six in the Evening by two Rangers, which are the only men that have got in here, except two yesterday morning with your first acquainting him of the enemy being in sight. He [General Webb] has order'd me to acquaint you he does not think it prudent (as you know his strength at this place) to attempt a Junction or to assist you till reinforc'd by the Militie [sic] of the Colonies, for the immediate march of which Expresses have been sent. One of our Scouts brought in a Canadian Pris[r] last night from the investing Party which is very large, and have possess'd all the Grounds five miles on this side of Fort W[m] Henry. The number of the Enemy is very considerable, the Pris[r] says eleven Thousand and have a large Train of Artillery with Mortars and were to open their Batteries this day. The General thought proper to give you this Intelligence, that in case he should be so unfortunate from the delays of the Militia not to have it in his power to give you timely assistance, you might be able to make the best Terms were left in your power. The Bearer is a Serg't of the Connecticut Forces and if he is happy enough to get in will bring advices from you. We keep continual Scouts going to endeavor to get in, or bring intelligence from you.

I am Sir with the heartiest and most anxious wishes for your welfare your most Obedient Humble Servant

G. Bartman
Aid de Camp

L[t] Col: Monro or Officer
Commanding at Fort W[m] Henry.[13]

Montcalm realized that this letter could be used to convince Monro to give up the unequal fight. He delayed carrying out his plan immedi-

The August 4, 1757 Message to Fort William Henry. From: Loudoun Papers, no. 4050. Courtesy, Huntington Library.

ately, but discussed his tactics with his Indian chiefs who demanded that the letter be delivered to Monro.[14] All day Saturday his batteries pounded the fort. New trenches were opened up near the ditches of the fort and the bordering camp gardens. Crawling among the cabbages and beans, the Indians watched for an unwary Englishman to appear.

The French cannon kept up its barrage on Sunday morning, August 7, until at about ten o'clock a truce flag appeared in the French trenches. The aide, Bougainville, appeared, bearing Webb's captured message and a note from Montcalm. It was a dramatic gesture and also a shrewd move on the part of the Marquis. He allowed Webb's timorous message to speak for itself; there was no demand for capitulation in Montcalm's words: •

> The 7th of August in the morning
>
> Sir
>
> One of my reconnaissance parties returned last night with prisoners and obtained the letter which I am sending to you under escort because of the generosity I profess toward those against whom I am obliged to wage war. Monsieur de Bougainville, one of my aides-de-camp, shall return after having delivered this letter to you. I expect you will wait until he has returned to the trenches before giving the command to fire. This will be announced to you by the first salvo of my batteries.
>
> I am Sir Your very Humble and very Obedient Servant
>
> Montcalm[15]

It is not difficult to imagine the dismay of Monro and his men upon reading Webb's disappointing letter. Smallpox was raging in the casemates, the wounded were in need of medical attention, and most of the heavy cannon, the thirty-two pounders, were now useless. The official recorder of the siege recounts that in spite of all this "not a man was daunted." [16] French sources declare that Monro thanked Montcalm for his chivalrous conduct. For two more days the unequal contest continued. By Monday, August 8, French batteries were only one hundred yards from the west wall. All was in readiness for the grand assault and subsequent butchery by the Indians. The defenders had reached the end of their resources, however, and on Tuesday, August 9, after a council of war, a capitulation was signed.[17]

The massacre of the prisoners that followed, carried out by drunken warriors eager for the kill, was in crass violation of the articles of the agreement. Montcalm "ran thither immediately" and did everything in his power to put an end to the butchery: "prayers, threats, caresses, consultations with chiefs, interposition of the officers and interpreters, who have some authority over these savages. . . ." [18]

The survivors, including Monro, eventually reached Fort Edward; others were later purchased from the Indians in Canada. The prisoners saved only a portion of their personal belongings from the ravages of the Indians, but the French allowed Monro to keep his official papers.* Among these papers was the letter of August 4 and Montcalm's communication to Monro. Eventually these manuscripts came into the hands of

* Monro was promoted to full colonel in 1758, but he died that same year. *New York Col. Docs.*, 10:603. According to Article I of the terms of capitulation, the officers and soldiers could keep their "Baggage," and possibly Monro concealed his official papers there. He was also accorded a six-pounder salute because of his honorable defense of the fort.

the Earl of Loudoun, and they remained in the possession of the Loudoun family until 1923 when they were placed upon the open market.[19] The message to Fort William Henry, now at the Huntington Library, still bears the creases made by a colonial soldier who was killed by a French Indian in the Lake George area over two hundred years ago.

This manuscript is one of those historical gems that occasionally shine among the numerous insignificant documents found in every great manuscript collection. This Webb letter of August 4 to Colonel Monro has been copied and summarized a number of times.[20]

The first accurate account of the letter, however, was given by Francis Parkman, in his *Montcalm and Wolfe*.[21] He probably first read about it in James Fenimore Cooper's *The Last of the Mohicans*, a novel built around the fall of Fort William Henry.* As a young man Parkman was a great admirer of Cooper, and though he was later highly critical of the novelist, his own works show a clear Leather-Stocking influence.[22] He almost certainly knew about the letter of August 4, even before he started collecting documents for the writing of his great history.

The folds in the original message show how small the original paper was folded for purposes of concealment, and the hasty scrawl and abbreviations give evidence of the extreme tension at Fort Edward. Certainly the original message stands out from the great mass of manuscripts surviving from this period. It is one of the few that reveal the reality of those tragic events in the great forests of North America when the Indian was still a savage foe in wilderness fighting. Moreover, the massacre of prisoners at Fort William Henry by Indians clearly showed that the courtly methods of eighteenth-century warfare could be vastly altered when pent-up warriors, excited by liquor, were exposed to unarmed white prisoners of war.

---

*[James] Fenimore Cooper, *The Last of the Mohicans* (New York, 1826), p. 207. In this work Cooper brings Montcalm together with Monro at Fort William Henry on August 7, 1757. When the French general hands Monro Webb's letter, Monro exclaims, "The man has betrayed me . . . he has brought dishonor to the door of one where disgrace was never before known to dwell, and shame has he heaped heavily on my gray hairs." Literary historians argue convincingly that Cooper provided realistic accounts of historical incidents because he read extensively in missionary records, government reports, and in histories. See Lee Clark Mitchell, *Witnesses to a Vanishing America, the Nineteenth Century Response* (Princeton, N.J., 1981), pp. 44–45ff.

CHAPTER 7

Gift-Giving
and Pontiac's Uprising

The Indian war of 1763, now known as Pontiac's Uprising, was the culmination of Indian-white hostility that had its origins in the beginnings of white settlement. Most of the Indian grievances, that is, the underlying reasons for hatred of whites, could be traced back to the time of seventeenth-century Indian-white contacts in North America. Almost any instance of good will, especially in the exchange of gifts, had its counterpart in atrocities. As we have seen, the trader's hunger for profits often resulted in the exploitation of the Indian. When this was combined with the loss of his lands, there was an inevitable reduction in the tribesmen's store of good will. If the Indian responded with violence, he also took the initiative in seeking peaceful solutions to his disputes with the white man.[1]

Early American history is punctuated with hundreds of treaty conferences in which the Indians attempted to find a reasonable way of solving the never-ending series of disputes with the whites. Throughout these conferences the Indians insisted on the exchange of gifts, the smoking of peace pipes, and a ceremonial series of speeches, punctuated with presents "to brighten the chain of friendship." Often the whites, in the process of loading the Indians down with merchandise to help forget their grievances, attempted to use the "gifts" to purchase lands. Later, at the end of the eighteenth century, they attempted to use money, but the Indians, as the following excerpt from a speech of the confederated Indians of the Northeast illustrates, refused money and instead proposed that funds be used to help destitute pioneer families:

> Money to us, is of no value, and to most of us unknown, and as no consideration whatever can induce us to sell the lands on which we get sustenance for our women and children, we hope we may be allowed to point out a mode by which your settlers may be easily removed and peace thereby obtained.
>
> We know that these settlers are poor, or they would never have ventured to live in a country which has been in continual trouble ever since they crossed the Ohio. Divide, therefore, this large sum of money which you have offered to us among these people; give to each also a proportion of what you say you would give us annually, over and above this very large sum of money; and we are persuaded they would most readily accept it in lieu of the lands you sold them. If you add also, the great sums you must spend in raising and paying armies with a view to force us to yield our country, you will certainly have more sufficient for the purpose of repaying these settlers for all their labor and improvements.[2]

A half century earlier, the Six Nations sachem Canessatego, speaking in 1742, argued that even the goods given the Indians for lands was worthless: "We know our Lands are now become more Valuable," he argued,

> the white People think we don't know their Value, but we are sensible that the Land is Everlasting, and the few Goods we receive for it are soon Worn out and Gone. . . . It is Customary with Us to make a Present of Skins whenever we renew our Treaties. We are ashamed to Offer our Brethren so few, but your Horses and Cows have eat the Grass our Deer used to feed on . . . we are really poor. . . .[3]

We see here that the northeastern woodland Indians were anticipating the possibility of becoming landless and homeless as early as the 1740's. Merchandise given in exchange for lands had no permanent value, and the pioneers were ruining their hunting grounds.

It is nevertheless true that the Indians became more and more dependent upon the white man's goods whether or not the goods were presented as subsidies or as a form of compensation for land. Examination of the historical record of native-white relations in the British colonies shows that by the middle of the eighteenth century the Indians had adopted many of the Anglo-American's tools and ideas, even his religion, but there is no evidence that the woodland Indians had the intention of becoming Europeans. They were willing to accept gifts—in fact they demanded them—but they were also determined to fight for independence. What is equally important, the Indians were willing to use what they had borrowed and learned in making a stand for self-determination. Anglo-Americans of the eighteenth century tended to mistakenly assume that as the Indians became more and more dependent upon the white man's goods (in the period before they lost their political independence, what certain writers have called a period of permissive acculturation), the Indians would become eventually assimilated, phasing out their own culture.[4] This was not the case.

Yet there is no question that the woodland Indians chose to adopt experimentally a great deal of what the whites had to offer in presents and trade. More and more Indians, men, women, chiefs, warriors, and even children became accustomed to the use of the white man's tools, weapons, clothing, toys, and liquor. At the same time that the Indians were accepting new values and new goods there were those influential Indians who valued the old customs and came to understand that the whole Indian way of life was threatened by the white man's culture (including Christianity). The choice left the Indians, then, was repudiation of white civilization. It was ironic that the Indians, by the time of Pontiac's uprising in 1763, had become so dependent upon certain tools, weapons, and textiles, that they felt a vital need for them even to continue in the old way of life. It was the gradual decimation of wildlife, especially fur-bearing animals, that made most Indians living adjacent to frontiers of settlement dependent upon whites for commodities that they felt they could not do without.

During the French and Indian War the British were able to recruit thousands of native fighting men through tremendous outlays of gifts made by such outstanding Indian agents as Sir William Johnson,[5] Conrad Weiser,[6] and George Croghan.[7] British presents and British victories brought about a loss of French prestige. The conquest of Canada in 1760, however, ushered in a new British policy with respect to presents. Intent upon economizing, the British abruptly stopped their liberal subsidies to the natives, leaving them in a desperate state—and one that could easily erupt into a rebellion against the English.

Jeffery Amherst, British commander-in-chief, had reluctantly signed warrants for presents during the period of hostilities with the French;* but after the war his frugal nature gained the upper hand.[8] He scruti-

---

* Jeffery Amherst (1717–97) was made a Knight of the Bath after the conquest of Canada. See Jane Sullivan et al., ed., Papers of Sir William Johnson (Albany, N.Y., 1921–), 3:580–82. He had seen service in Europe at an earlier date. In America in 1758 he brought about the capitulation of Louisburg. His later military accomplishments include the capture of Ticonderoga and Crown Point in 1759 and the conquest of Montreal in 1760. He was made a baron in 1776 and a field marshal in 1796. Amherst's first name according to his signature is spelled Jeffery and not Jeffrey.

nized the accounts of all persons who were responsible for distributing merchandise to the natives and frequently reprimanded subordinates for carelessness in handling government funds allotted for Indian goods.[9]

Although Amherst acknowledged the fact that Sir William Johnson, long experienced in Indian affairs, possessed a unique knowledge of the Indians, he nevertheless treated the natives in a manner completely opposed to that advocated by the superintendent. Sir Jeffery declared in no uncertain terms that the Indians should be occupied in bringing in skins for trade; otherwise they might "hatch mischief." He directed the commanding officers of the larger frontier posts to carefully control the handing out of presents so that a count could be taken of those warriors who had already received goods.[10] The officers were told to give the natives some clothing and a little powder for hunting purposes, but that was all.[11] The self-reliancy of the Indians was to be encouraged.*

A trading schedule was set up at Fort Pitt and other posts;[12] the Indians were informed that they could no longer get stroud for nothing, but had to pay two good beaver pelts or three buckskins for it. Prices for other items were listed accordingly. In short, the British held that "the Indians should live by their Hunting & not think that they are always to be receiving presents."[13]

Naturally the tribesmen disliked this policy, but Amherst felt that they would adjust to it. Between July and September 1761, Sir William Johnson carried the news of the new policy to the western tribes congregating at Niagara and Detroit.[14] He found that this new thriftiness was causing rising hostility to the British. Indeed, at times the superintendent's very life was in danger.

Because Johnson was unable to offer the poverty-stricken yet powerful western Indians goods to relieve their sufferings after the long war, he lost an excellent opportunity to gain their friendship. He had no alternative but to deliver Amherst's message: the Ottawa warriors would have to support their families by an "Industrious way of life" without other assistance.[15]

Even the former Indian allies of the British were beginning to feel the pinch of their over-frugal masters. Reports drifted in that the people of the Miami confederacy were "all naked and in want of everything. . . ."[16] George Croghan, working under Colonel Henry Bouquet at Fort Pitt, reported that the Indians there missed the frequent distributions of free goods and were extremely dissatisfied. As early as May 1762 the Indians cornered Croghan and inquired about gifts. The Pennsylvania

---

* It is only fair to point out that Amherst approved funds for schoolmasters and ministers for the Indians and did everything in his power to suppress the custom of giving rum to the natives.

trader wrote to Johnson in his usual imperfect English saying that the Indians asked "ye reason that we allways was Calling them to Council During ye War & Giveing them presents & Now Take No Notice of them." The Indians said that "ye French was butt a poor pople butt they always Cloathed any Indians that was poor or Naked when they Come to see them." [17]

The British home government was aware of the grievances of the Indians. In November 1761 the Board of Trade had stated that the "open violation" of land contracts was a grave injustice to the Indians,[18] but unfortunately no immediate action was taken.

At Fort Pitt, meanwhile, Colonel Henry Bouquet sought to quell Indian dissatisfaction by issuing a proclamation on October 13, 1761, against "outlaws" who were occupying Indian lands west of the mountains.[19] When the lieutenant governor of Virginia, Francis Fauquier, complained to Amherst regarding Bouquet's actions, the bewildered frontier commander retorted that he did not know which he was supposed to "oppress," the settlers or the Indians.[20] If he protected the Indians he offended the settlers, and vice versa. Such was the state of indecision in 1761–1762 regarding native lands.

It was becoming increasingly evident that presents from the British to "brighten the chain of friendship" were not to be expected. Throughout the remainder of 1762 rumors of war were constantly being circulated, and abuses by the whites brought retaliations from the Indians. In the spring of 1763 Sir Jeffery Amherst sat in his comfortable quarters in New York checking over old warrants for Indian expenses; at the same time in Pennsylvania George Croghan sacrificed a year's salary to pay for supplies to tribesmen who had been refused gifts by the commanding officer at Fort Pitt.[21]

In his correspondence Croghan pointed out that many Indian leaders were angry that so much of America had been ceded to Great Britain at the Treaty of Paris. The tribesmen living in the region of Detroit maintained that the French had no right to "give away their country"; they had never been conquered by any nation.[22]

John Stuart, who succeeded Edmond Atkin as southern superintendent in 1762, was able to carry out his duties with little interference from the military. Had Sir William Johnson been equally free from military interference the story of the Indian frontier of 1763 might have been considerably different. Although Johnson disagreed with Amherst's policy of frugality, he was obliged to carry out the orders of his commander-in-chief. Stuart, on the other hand, was able to act more independently of Sir Jeffery, and in June 1763 invited all the southern tribes to a great conference at Augusta, Georgia, at which expensive presents were distributed to the southern warriors. Representatives of almost all the southern tribes responded to Stuart's invitation. Even the truculent Creek warriors were represented, despite the intrigues of an able Upper Creek chieftain called "The Mortar," [23] which had put many of the warriors in an ugly mood.[24]

This change in British Indian policy can be traced to the secretary of state for the southern department, Lord Egremont.[25] He sponsored Amherst's program for economy in the North, but at the same time ordered Stuart, with the support of the southern governors, to hold the Augusta congress. The idea for this gathering originated not with Egremont, but with the astute Governor Henry Ellis of Georgia who according to the late Clarence W. Alvord exerted a considerable influence upon the secretary of state in determining Indian policy.[26]

The Indian congress at Augusta was a success. The fears of the tribesmen concerning English occupation of their lands were quelled by promises to the contrary and a tremendous outlay of beef, rum, and assorted presents.[27] The Cherokees, led by the amiable Attakullakulla,* agreed to an arrangement for controlling Indian trade, and the Chickasaws and their new-found friends the Choctaws appeared pleased with their share of barley-corn beads, calicoes, and "prettys." The loyal Catawbas† received reassurance that their small reservation would not be invaded by settlers, and even the lower Creeks who attended the meeting indicated their desire to "hear the truth" despite the fact that they had "heard bad talks" concerning the English.* John Stuart won over the Creek leaders to such an extent that they accepted the suggestion of the superintendent that the boundary line for white settlement be set at the frontier of Georgia. This action on Stuart's part anticipated the proclamation of October 7, 1763, and the exact delineation of the Augusta treaty line can be seen on the map later drawn by Joseph Purcell under Stuart's direction for the Board of Trade.[28]

Colonel Henry Bouquet, commanding officer at Fort Pitt, had suggested in the spring of 1763 that it would be wise to call a general conference of all the northern and western Indians to calm their fears. Amherst rebelled at the needless expense, but Bouquet argued that a few presents would restore the wavering allegiance of the Indians. The con-

* Attakullakulla's (Little Carpenter's) friendship stemmed from his visit to the royal court in London in 1730. Verner Crane indicates that Attakullakulla was referred to at that time as Ukwaneequa. See his account of the Cherokee embassy in *The Southern Frontier, 1670–1732* (Ann Arbor, 1956), pp. 279–80, 295–302.
† The Catawba tribe, which could muster about three hundred fighting men, was traditionally warm in their friendship for the British. The leaders of this small tribe espoused the prudent doctrine "that all Indians who have their supplies from, and are Friends of the English should be Friends also of each other." Edmond Atkin to the Board of Trade, May 10, 1755, Huntington Library, Loudoun Papers, no. 578.

ference could be held at Fort Pitt, and the natives taking part could spread the message of British good will to the more remote tribes of the interior.[29] Sir Jeffery, however, who was indifferent to the opinions of the Indians, declared that they should behave properly; then they would be assured of the king's protection.[30] The commander-in-chief seemingly had little conception of Indian diplomacy and the importance of presents.

The sachems in the North soon realized that they could expect no favors from the officers who commanded the British posts. Their situation was desperate. The war had prevented the Indians from caring for their crops; tools were needed; clothing was scarce; additional blacksmiths from the Indian superintendent's office were needed to repair broken guns; and powder was difficult to obtain. If the opportunity presented itself, fierce young warriors would not hesitate to slaughter a garrison to plunder its supplies.[31] Uneasy officers, aware of Indian hostility, complained that delays in building Great Lakes supply vessels had caused delays in refurbishing the forts. Indeed, alarmed British officers wrote that the isolated fortifications, badly in need of reinforcements, were easy prey in an Indian attack.[32]

Certainly there were many Indians who resented the presence of British forts in their country. Basically, however, the influential chiefs were angered at what they considered to be British encroachment on their hunting territories, and the forts gave every appearance of an attempt to occupy their homeland. Threats of retaliation were heard from the Seneca and their neighbors the Delaware, and even Christian Oneida Indians demanded that these forts be "pull'd down, & kick'd out of the way."[33] As if to focus attention on the Indian discontent, British officers were told not to give Indians powder and lead for hunting purposes, and Indians who came to trading posts were turned away empty handed unless they had ample furs for trading. A new schedule of prices for such items as woolen strouds was so high that the Indians were outraged; nor could the Indians, in their time of need, ask for renewal of the old credit system. Amherst, who had little sympathy with the Indians' plight and later suggested that they be infected with smallpox blankets[34] or hunted down with large dogs, did not anticipate the violent impact of Indian rebellion and did nothing to anticipate its outbreak. What Amherst did not understand was that the failure of the British imperial administration to supply the western Indians with goods could give rebellious chiefs a chance to mobilize native discontent. The lack of goods, together with the encroachment upon Indian lands, had shaken the faith of some of the most loyal native friends of the British.

Although it has not been proved, there is a story (more truthful in spirit than in fact) that has come down through generations of woodland history and literature dramatically illustrating the complete frustration

of the Indians, even with their staunch friend Sir William Johnson.
According to the story, now regarded as one of the myths concerning Sir
William, he manipulated an exchange of gifts with an Iroquois sachem
who, in the year 1760,

> being on a visit to his house, told him one morning a dream, which he
> had the preceding night. This was no other than that Sir William had
> given him a rich suit of clothes. Sir William knowing it was Indian cus-
> tom to give to a friend whatever present he claimed in this manner, gave
> him the clothes. Some time after the Sachem was at his house again. Sir
> William observed to him that he also had had a dream. The Sachem
> asked him what. He answered, he dreamed that the Sachem had given
> him a tract of land. The Sachem replied, "You have the land; we no
> dream again." [35]

Some authors have maintained that through the dream technique Sir
William outwitted a friendly leader of the Mohawks out of some one
hundred thousand acres; yet one of the superintendent's earliest biog-
raphers, well acquainted with the sources, stated that the story was "pure
fiction." [36] Fiction or not, Sir William as well as many of the rest of his
contemporaries became large landholders at the expense of frustrated
Indians who were left with gifts that soon lost their value.* It was Pontiac
who made the most of the situation by capitalizing on native anger and
disillusionment.

---

*Dorothy Jones, *License for Empire, Colonialism by Treaty in Early America* (Chicago, 1983),
pp. 93-186, traces the gift-giving, treaty system, and fraudulent takeover of Indian lands
through the American Revolution. An earlier valuable account of Iroquois dispossession is
Georgiana C. Nammack, *Fraud, Politics, and the Dispossession of the Indians: The Iroquois
Land Frontier in the Colonial Period* (Norman, Okla., 1969).

CHAPTER 8

Pontiac's War
—a Conspiracy?

Ever since Francis Parkman wrote his classic account of the Indian war of 1763, historians have questioned whether the "conspiracy" described by Parkman really deserved the name of conspiracy. Contemporary documents make clear that the abuses suffered by the Indians at the hands of the whites were sufficient to cause a rebellion. Did the indignation of the tribesmen lead to a concerted attack upon the British outposts in the summer of 1763? Or was the great Pontiac the driving force behind a simultaneous outbreak of fury by the Indian nations?

The title of Parkman's work, *The Conspiracy of Pontiac*, indicates that the author regarded the Ottawa leader as the mastermind behind the attacks. In 1762 Pontiac, according to Parkman,

sent ambassadors to the different nations. They visited the country of the Ohio and its tributaries, passed northward to the region of the upper lakes, and the borders of the river Ottawa; and far southward towards the mouth of the Mississippi. Bearing with them the war-belt of wampum, broad and long, as the importance of the message demanded, and the tomahawk stained red, in token of war, they went from camp to camp and village to village.[1]

Parkman's authority for this statement is a letter written by a Sieur d'Abbadie, the newly appointed *Ordonnateur* of Louisiana, dated simply "1764," which, however, nobody has succeeded in locating since Parkman's time. D'Abbadie arrived in Louisiana from France on June 29, 1763, and was hardly in a position to give accurate information on Pontiac's sending of war belts in the year 1762.[2] It is odd that Parkman should rely chiefly upon a letter written in 1764, two years after Pontiac had sent his wampum ambassadors "from camp to camp and village to village." Since this is a major source used to confirm his thesis of the "conspiracy," Parkman might well have given a complete description of the letter.

Howard H. Peckham in his book on Pontiac's war maintains that "there was no grand conspiracy or preconcerted plan on his [Pontiac's] part embracing all the western tribes."[3] Peckham contends that the uprising was a war for Indian independence with a local conspiracy at Detroit. According to this interpretation Pontiac did attempt to bring about a more general uprising, but only after the failure of his first campaign against the British. It was during the second campaign that the British almost lost their most important frontier posts.

The source materials on which to base an evaluation of these opposing points of view are meager. Parkman's depiction of the character and personality of Pontiac and of the manner in which the conspiracy was planned is convincing; nevertheless, the historical basis on which Parkman built was not very solid.[4] The Pontiac manuscript that Parkman skillfully used in his narrative was the work of an unknown author, presumably a French priest. In justifying the use of this document Parkman declared that the details closely paralleled events described in other sources, and that "this very minuteness affords strong internal evidence of its authenticity." The unidentified author was supposed to have learned about Pontiac's speeches and the secret negotiations preceding the attack on Detroit from French Canadians who were present at certain Indian council meetings.[5]

Howard H. Peckham used this same manuscript, which has since been attributed to Robert Navarre, a Canadian. He also secured much material from the collections of the William L. Clements Library.[6] Parkman, of course, had no opportunity to use these collections.

Aside from the Pontiac manuscript, or the Navarre journal, the source materials contain relatively little regarding Pontiac himself. The Bouquet Papers at the Canadian Archives, the Amherst correspondence at the Library of Congress, and the Gage Papers at the William L. Clements Library include much general material relative to the Indian war of 1763, but almost nothing concerning the events immediately preceding the outbreak of the war. Much must be left to a close examination of the letters of the frontiersmen and soldiers who were involved in the conflict.[7]

One thing is clear: by the spring of 1763 the tribesmen along the whole northwestern frontier were ripe for vengeance against the whites. Only a spark was needed to start the conflagration.

A plan had even been developed by the Senecas, who with some 1,050 fighting men were perhaps the strongest military power in the Iroquois confederacy. Sir William Johnson found these people, who had had close contacts with the French for so many years, the most difficult to control of all his Indian wards, but he wisely treated them with the consideration that their fighting strength justified. After the conquest of Canada in 1760, however, the Senecas, like all the other woodland Indians of the Northeast, found themselves at the mercy of the sometimes arrogant officers who commanded the British forts.

Not surprisingly the Senecas had taken steps to free themselves from the British yoke. In his diary George Croghan reports that the Senecas planned a major attack on the British in 1761.[8] The tribes living in the vicinity of Detroit were to capture the fort, murder the traders, and seize the booty. At the same time the Miamis, the Delawares, and the Shawnees and all the other tribes living between the Ohio River and Lake Erie were to attack the forts between the frontier of Pennsylvania and the stronghold at Fort Pitt. The scattered villages of the Iroquois in the Ohio region were to launch surprise attacks on Presqu'Isle, Le Boeuf, and Venango, and lines of communication between German Flats in the Mohawk Valley and Fort Niagara would be severed by fighting men from the Six Nations and Susquehanna tribes. Meanwhile, the Cherokee towns were to be visited by a delegation of some one hundred Iroquois. The Cherokees, who had already been at war with the British from 1759 to 1761, were to be told that an invading French army would join the northern Indians (a belief held by Pontiac, according to Parkman), while the western and southern Indians would clear the remaining frontiers of whites.

Although this secret plan was uncovered by British agents before it could be put into effect, the strategy of the plan is important because it shows that the Senecas were willing to fight on the side of their historic enemies, the Cherokees.* The details of the plan also help to buttress

---

* The ancient feud between the southern woodland tribes and the Iroquois was an almost insurmountable barrier to concerted action by the British. As late as October 1762 the Iroquois notified the Pennsylvania government that they desired a route through the settlements so they could continue hostilities against "their old Enemies, the Cherokees." *Minutes of the Provincial Council of Pennsylvania* (Harrisburg, 1851–53), 8, pp. 779–80. A year later "neutral" Senecas were collecting Cherokee scalps in the middle of Pontiac's uprising. Sir William Johnson hoped in the summer of 1763 to use the historic enmity of the Indians to turn the Cherokees and Catawbas

Francis Parkman's weakly-documented thesis that an extensive "conspiracy" under the leadership of Pontiac did take place. Parkman was convinced that the great Ottawa chief skillfully wrested the leadership of the Indian resistance from the Senecas, the only Six Nations tribe that later joined the uprising against the British.[9]

It is not hard to see why the remaining members of the Six Nations failed to seize the leadership of the war from the Ottawa. The Iroquois had long since given up their position as a balance of power between the French and the English, and in 1759 they publicly abandoned their traditional policy of neutrality, giving whole-hearted support to the British forces under Sir Jeffery Amherst.[10] After the conquest of Canada in 1760, most of the chiefs of the Six Nations had been won over to the British by Sir William Johnson. But the Seneca, never particularly pro-British, became more and more dissatisfied. They missed the courtship of French emissaries like the Joncaire brothers and yearned to be rid of the encroaching Anglo-Americans.

The Senecas had been voicing their discontent and informing other tribes that their main reason for wanting to attack the British was that the British refused to give them ammunition. But other tribes were also desperately short of powder and lead and made similar complaints and threats. It seems probable that in 1761–62 the Senecas may really have wished to conceal schemes that their chiefs were discussing with French colonials. One such Seneca chief was the able and violently anti-British Kaiaghshota.* It was Captain Donald Campbell, commander of Fort Detroit, and deputy Indian superintendent George Croghan who discovered the ambitious plan of the Senecas.

While the Senecas, led by Kaiaghshota had inflamed the smoldering anger of the Indians, Pontiac, a more able leader, emerged to direct what might have been no more than a savage explosion of discontent into a long and bitterly fought war. Pontiac, as well as the Senecas, is known to have sent messages to many of the western tribes, even to the Sioux, before his initial attack on Fort Detroit.[11]

Once the hostilities began, Sir William Johnson did all in his power to prevent the conflagration from spreading to the friendly tribes. The

---

against the northern Indians, but Cadwallader Colden condemned such action because "it nourishes the fierce and cruel spirit of the savage." See E. B. O'Callaghan, *et al.*, eds., *Documents Relative to the Colonial History of the State of New York* (Albany, 1853–57), 7:524–25, 609–10.

* Sometimes known as Guyasuta, Guyashusta, or Kiasola. The secret Seneca plan that Pontiac himself seems to have used in his assault upon the British forts was attributed to Kaiaghshota by the archivist-historian Lyman C. Draper, who interviewed the chief's son and nephew. Draper concluded that Kaiaghshota was "an arch-plotter with Pontiac" in the uprising "occasionally known as Guyashusta's War." State Historical Society of Wisconsin, *Collections* of the (1908) 18:240–41n.

Seneca tried to induce the other members of the Six Nations to join the uprising, but the remaining Iroquois, moved perhaps by a message from Johnson entreating them to remain loyal to the British, did not choose to ally themselves with Pontiac. To show their loyalty, the Mohawks even declared their intention of "living and dying with the English."

Sir William, however, was not able to prevent nine strongholds, among them forts Le Boeuf, Presqu'Isle, Venango, and Michilimackinac, from falling into the hands of the attacking warriors. The stubborn bulwarks of the British defense system, Fort Pitt and Fort Detroit, remained. Once the attacks were underway, they were carried on with determination and persistence strongly suggesting the Indians were under a leader of the caliber of Pontiac. *The Annual Register,* a faithful English chronicler of events in America, commented on the special qualities of the Indi n campaign:

> Upon the whole of this war, so far as it has hitherto proceeded we cannot help observing, that the Indians seem to be animated with a more dark and daring spirit than at any former time. They seem to have concerted their measures with ability, and to have chosen the times and places of their several attacks with skill; to have behaved themselves in those attacks with firmness and resolution; to have succeeded on some occasions, and to have no decisive loss in any.[12]

The fact that all the attacks did not begin on the same day does not mean that the Indians were lacking in an overall plan. Communications in a vast wilderness, interspersed with lakes and mountains, even for native Americans who lived in the forest, were sometimes slow. Moreover, each force of attacking warriors had the difficult task of securing for itself what was a scarce item indeed—ammunition. Another factor adding to the problem of launching a simultaneous assault was the sometimes inferior ability of local chiefs. The Indians at Fort Pitt, for example, had no such leader as Pontiac to help them. Nevertheless, available sources show that they tried every bluff possible to obtain a peaceful evacuation of the fort; failing that, they fought with tenacity and courage.

Pontiac, with his massive influence over the Indians of the Old Northwest, was almost certainly the leading mind behind the Indian uprising. When it came to making the peace, the British were well aware that he was the most important of all the Indian chiefs and that no lasting peace was possible without his approval.[13] His thirst for knowledge marked him as an unusual man, and his reliability in carrying out agreements— protecting messengers or restoring property—showed a degree of leadership not often found among Indians. Indeed, his authority over the Indians was declared to be absolute, an almost unheard of achievement among the tribesmen of the North American wilderness.[14] Such a man may well have put into motion a secret plan for freeing the Indians from the irritating presence of Anglo-American whites.

At any rate, nobody has succeeded in showing that Pontiac was not the mastermind behind the campaign. On the contrary, accounts of a great war belt being sent by Pontiac's messengers among the western tribes, even as far west as the Illinois country, supports the assumptions that the war was carefully planned and prepared for, and that Pontiac took the leadership away from the Seneca. Pontiac appears to have been shrewd enough to perceive that he could make use of underlying Indian grievances to weld the Indians into a force capable of carrying on a prolonged assault against the enemy.

The uprising that mushroomed among the Indians also had a mystical side, however, a result of the message from the "Master of Life." According to the Pontiac Manuscript, the Master of Life, speaking to the Indians through brother Wolf, had urged specific reforms (renunciation of liquor, the taking of more than one wife), but his central message was to take possession of the land:

> . . . This land where ye dwell I have made for you and not for others. Whence comes it that ye permit the Whites upon your lands? Can ye not live without them? . . . drive them out . . . Send them back to the lands which I have created for them and let them stay there.[15]

The widespread influence of the message from the Master of Life was such that certain tribes (Shawnees or Eries—the exact identification is difficult in the Pontiac Manuscript) declared that "we have also fallen upon the English because the Master of Life by one of our brother Delawares told us to do so. . . ."[16] This is an indication that their assault on the British may or may not have been because of messages sent by Pontiac. And it appears that Pontiac himself, later in 1766, denied sending "bad [wampum] belts" to other Indians.[17] But it was customary among Indian leaders to disclaim responsibility among whites for unsuccessful warlike acts. What would Pontiac have to gain by admitting guilt of a warlike action at the time of his defeat when surroun.'ed by his enemies? It seems probable that he minimized his position as a leading figure in an unsuccessful Indian revolt, especially in connection with incidents where white prisoners were killed.

The special role that Pontiac had in the Indian war of 1763 is perhaps most clearly described by anthropologist Anthony Wallace in his searching book on *The Death and Rebirth of the Seneca*. After examining the writings of Henry R. Schoolcraft, John Heckewelder, Howard H. Peckham, and other sources, Wallace concludes that Pontiac, as a convert to the teachings of the Delaware Prophet, accepted the teachings of the

Master of Life, and used the doctrine "as supernatural sanction for his conspiracy." [18]

The Delaware Indians were especially aroused against the whites by an Indian known as the Delaware Prophet, or Neolin, a religious messiah of 1762–63, who claimed to have had contact with the Great Spirit and who urged the Indians to return to their old way of life. Pontiac was also able to make use of the teachings of the Master of Life. In a speech before representatives of the Ottawas, the Hurons, and other tribes, he asserted that the Master of Life (who apparently put forward no military program in the teachings of the Delaware Prophet) desired that the Indians drive the whites out of their country and make war upon them.[19] Thus he aroused the Indians to a fighting frenzy; even the Illinois warriors attacked the British because of such a message from the Master of Life. The teachings of the Delaware Prophet, already well known to the warriors, were thus given special interpretation by Pontiac. Much of the tenacity and fury of the Indians in battle may be attributed to religious zeal. Perhaps some of the mutilation and torture of prisoners by Indians had its origin in religious emotionalism. Pontiac used the teachings of the Prophet to "spirit up"* his warriors and confederates.

Wallace stresses the powerful influence of the Delaware Prophet's teachings throughout the Indian world of the Northeast where the Prophet's spiritual chart was actually sold (one copy for each Indian family, the Prophet recommended) at the charge of two doeskins or one buckskin per copy. The Delaware Prophet, like his successor Handsome Lake of the Senecas, called for a God over both whites and Indians and made other references that showed his familiarity with Christianity. As Wallace notes, "his code was a syncretism of native and white elements." [20] Yet at the same time his teachings were in rebellion against traditional Christianity and the white man's culture.

In his account of Pontiac's war Wallace also stresses the fact that a second prophet, an Onondaga leader of 1762, preached that the Great Spirit would punish the whites if they persisted in seizing lands in the Indian country. In short, the Indian frontier of the North was alive with religious prophets hostile to white culture. Certainly there is no doubt that Pontiac's war had deep religious overtones; it was almost a religious crusade against the white man's culture and his religion. Pontiac very quickly saw the possibilities of sparking an Indian rebellion that had already been encouraged by religious prophets. If the Delaware Prophet was "an emotional catalyst" [21] of Indian discontent, Pontiac was the war chief who led an aroused Indian population against the British.

* General Thomas Gage's term to describe 1763 Indian unrest.

But if this is what Pontiac actually did, are we justified in using the word "conspiracy"? A conspiracy usually refers to a plot carried out by a small group for evil or unlawful ends. From the British point of view the ends were evil. The Indians, notwithstanding, saw their aspirations as legitimate.

Had the tribesmen lacked grievances, the word "conspiracy" might have been justified. As it was, however, Pontiac canalized existing grievances and provided leadership for a rebellion that could more accurately be described as a war for native independence. The American Revolution, though considered by many British leaders of the time as a criminal conspiracy, is usually thought of by Americans as a glorious moment in history.[22] In using the word "conspiracy," Parkman and other writers failed to do justice to American Indian aspirations for self-determination.[23]

Parkman's sins did not stop with the use of a single word; he conjured up a deliberate image of Indian treachery and savagery in molding the character of Pontiac. For Parkman, there are no wild Indians capable of aspirations for self-determination, for, as he says, ". . . all savages, whatever may be their country, their color, or their lineage, are prone to treachery and deceit." [24] What is more, Parkman skillfully portrays the great Ottawa chief as a typical savage, one who by his racial heritage was naturally treacherous because "treacheries . . . to his savage mind seemed fair and honorable." [25] Pontiac, in short, "was a thorough savage, and in him stand forth, in strongest light and shadow, the native faults and virtues of the Indian race." A more ominous portrayal of the American Indian is hard to imagine than Parkman's statement that Pontiac was capable of "the blackest treachery," or that he was "the Satan of this forest paradise." We are told that "his complexion was darker than is usual with his race," a hint that this remarkable chief was capable of manifest perfidy. When Pontiac's plot at Fort Detroit was exposed, Parkman's scathing pen at last found its mark in a vivid metaphor: "an entrapped wolf meets no quarter from the huntsman; and a savage, caught in his treachery, has no claim to forbearance." [26] In this instance, Parkman found his metaphor, but in the end he gave his readers a stereotype.

Even with this stereotyped, racist characterization of Pontiac, Parkman nevertheless builds at the same time a heroic image of a "prime mover of the plot," an image necessary for the dramatic fabric of his narrative. It is in this second portrait of Pontiac that the noble warrior of the wilderness steps forth to command the conspiracy against the English: "his muscular figure was cast in the mould of remarkable symmetry and vigor"; he "roused in his warlike listeners their native thirst for blood and vengeance"; he "addressed himself to their superstition . . . the Master of Life." To build an image of his finer qualities Park-

Francis Parkman, c. 1850. Courtesy, Massachusetts Historical Society.

man compared him with legendary figures of antiquity: "In generous thought and deed, he rivalled the heroes of ancient story." Besides, Parkman tells us anecdotes about Pontiac which, he argues, "will evince that noble and generous thought was no stranger to the savage hero of this dark forest tragedy." [27]

Thus, in the image of Pontiac, Parkman has given us a kind of mixed bag of coloration: a noble, generous, masculine figure who was capable of dark conspiracies and treachery against the white man. Although Parkman occasionally demonstrates that whites as well as Indians at this time were capable of cruel, barbaric conduct,[28] he still reserves his special racial blackwash for the Indians and their leaders. In this book as well as in others in his series Parkman dwells at length on Indian torture and savage violence, whereas white violence tends to be pictured as a rational response to Indian outrages. Indeed, in his own day such writers as Herman Melville as well as Theodore Parker blasted Parkman for giving his readers such a barbaric, bloodthirsty image of the Indian.[29]

By contrast to his able contemporary and friend, the eminent anthropologist Lewis H. Morgan, Parkman certainly appears to have left us with a racist view of the Indian whose demonic character drove him to savage brutality. Yet, there are parts of *The Conspiracy of Pontiac* as well as other volumes in Parkman's great *History* that give the reader an unforgettable and vividly accurate portrait of Indian culture. There is, furthermore, much truth in the portrait of Pontiac himself, for Parkman knew as much about Indians as any historian of his day. He had read everything about Indians that had been published; he had lived and camped in their country as a youth and as a man, and he had, at the risk of his life, made himself at home on the eastern slopes of the Rockies with a wandering Sioux tribe during the summer of 1846. Partly as a result of pouring over the writings of an astute Jesuit missionary of the Canadian Indians,[30] who advocated studying Indians to understand the societies of antiquity, Parkman, a pioneer in comparative ethnology, seized upon the plan of studying the nineteenth-century Sioux, virtually untouched by the white man, in order to comprehend the woodland tribes' society of the seventeenth and eighteenth centuries.

For one to understand Parkman's classic work, *The Conspiracy of Pontiac,* he must appreciate the fact that this is, in truth, a work of art, a drama of Indian-white relations woven by a master craftsman who made an exhaustive search of the sources. Even the most persistent, the most painstaking critic, who has examined all his volumes and unravelled the threads of narrative, may find it difficult to make a conclusive judgment about Parkman's shortcomings. Great writer that he was, however, we may pin him down to this criticism; his dramatic fabric at times seems to have been overcolored in such a way that he sometimes ob-

scured the truth to capture reader interest.[31] Certainly in the characterization of Pontiac as "the Satan of his forest paradise" we have what is
now a familiar but questionable stereotype of Indian treachery in early
American history. Given this kind of interpretation, whitewashing acts
of white brutality becomes easy because they can so easily be explained
as just retribution for evil plotting.[32]

On the whole, however, Parkman seems to have been correct in as-
sessing Pontiac's qualifications as an outstanding native leader—the only
chief capable of planning and 'carrying out the attack against the whites
and the guiding spirit behind the war. As a figure enshrouded in the
cloudy sources of Indian history, Pontiac nevertheless emerges in Parkman's narrative as a truly formidable leader of his people. This is why
Parkman's *Pontiac* is a great book. In fact, Parkman, in a youthful letter
before his book was written, had discovered that Pontiac seemed "to be
looked back on as a hero, by the Indians." [33] Is it possible that this singular chief might now be accepted as a national figure of heroic caliber
for all the American people? And further, why not call the struggle he
led, "Pontiac's War for Indian Independence"?*

---

*Parkman's interpretation of Pontiac as the major leader in the uprising of 1763 is confirmed
by research embodied in a detailed biographical sketch, "Pontiac," by Louis Chevrette, in
Dictionary of Canadian Biography, vol. II, 1741-1770, edited by George M. Brown et al.
(Toronto, 1974), pp. 525-31. Chevrette portrays Pontiac in much the same language as
Parkman's in evaluating his ability:

> Pontiac did not lack stature and fought with exceptional discernment and tenacity. . . .
> he perceived with great acuteness the problems that would afflict Indians for generations
> to come: the threat of assimilation and the slow taking over of their lands by a European
> population. (P. 531)

CHAPTER 9

1763—Year of Decision on the Indian Frontier

The year 1763 was one of decision on the Indian frontier. At no previous time in early American history had there been such widespread destructive violence from Indian attack. The entire wilderness frontier belting the long northern line of white occupation had been engulfed in war. During the summer warriors battered at scattered British fortifications that were isolated from the nearest colonial settlements by vast forests and mountain ridges. These frontier settlements followed an irregular line connecting German Flats on the Mohawk; Carlisle, Pennsylvania; Winchester, Virginia; Wachovia (now Winston-Salem, North Carolina); and Augusta, Georgia.[1] Closely paralleling this line of white settlement was the retreating frontier of the Indian.[2] Almost two hundred miles west of these parallel frontiers was Fort Pitt, the stronghold of the British fortification system, located at the forks of the Ohio. The other great fort, Fort Detroit, was situated in the heart of the wilderness over two hundred miles northwest of Fort Pitt.

Occupying the expanse of primeval forest was a race of hunters who, according to Indian superintendent Sir William Johnson, were "the most formidable of any uncivilized body of people in the World." [3] "Hunting and war," he observed, were the main occupations of these warriors, and one occupation increased their skill in the other. Such a people could not be held in subjection by a thin series of fortifications in the North American wilderness.[4]

In 1763 the native population of the great eastern Indian linguistic families was impressive enough to form a barrier to British westward expansion.* The Algonquian family was scattered throughout much of Canada, the Great Lakes region, and the northeastern Mississippi Valley. One reliable report listed four thousand fighting men in the powerful Ottawa confederacy alone. The most feared of all the Indian families, however, were not the Algonquian but the Iroquois. A glance at the famous John Mitchell map of North America in 1755 reveals that nation after nation of the aborigines had either been "extirpated" or "subdued" by the proud Six Nations. Only the Cherokees in the South and the bison hunters of the Great Plains were able to resist these conquerors.† Although the Mohawks, often regarded by contemporary colonial officials as leaders of the Iroquois confederacy, had dwindled to a mere 160 fighting men by 1763, there still remained almost 2,000 of the fiercest warriors in North America in the Six Nations.[5] Over half of these were Seneca tribesmen whose leaders had an abiding hatred for the British.[6]

While the Iroquois and the Algonquians formed a very real barrier to western emigration in 1763, large numbers of the so-called Indian gun men lived in close proximity to the southern colonies.[7] Superintendent John Stuart estimated that the total warrior population in the southern district was almost fourteen thousand,[8] while Sir William Johnson estimated that about twelve thousand [9] tribesmen were located in the northern department. Thus in 1763 a total of some twenty-two thousand fighting men were potentially available for the destruction of the English frontier settlements.

---

* The Indian linguistic families were not necessarily units of a political organization. The Algonquian, like all linguistic families, were divided into tribes, subtribes, bands, and clans.
† Despite their traditional hostility to the Six Nations, the Cherokee were linguistic brothers of the Iroquois and spoke substantially the same language. At Winchester, Virginia, during an Indian conference on June 20, 1757, the Mohawk sachems, speaking for the Six Nations, declared that their brethren the Cherokee should "hold fast by the chain of friendship existing between them, the English, and the Six Nations, and join their forces in order to defeat the dark schemes of their common enemy the French and Indians." The Cherokee head men, no doubt astonished by this unusual expression of good will, expressed great satisfaction in "having from the mouth of the Six Nations that they were so hardy in our Interest." See E. B. O'Callaghan et al., eds., Documents Relative to the Colonial History of the State of New York (Albany, 1853–87), 7:283 (hereafter cited as New York Col. Docs.). It seems obvious that Edmund Atkin, southern superintendent, and George Croghan, who presided at the meeting, were responsible for this declaration.

A general lack of political cohesion appears to be the main reason why all Indians, both in the North and South, did not join the uprising. The traditional hatred between the Cherokee and the Iroquois in itself presented a tremendous obstacle to the waging of an all-out war against the whites. Petty feuds prevented cooperation; only in the North was there a degree of unity among the tribes, since historically most of the Great Lakes and Ohio tribes had been either allies of the Iroquois or subject peoples.

The Indians proved strong enough to seize nine of the frontier forts north of the Ohio area, although the main bulwarks of defense held out despite the savagery of the fighting. Numerous atrocities were committed by both tribesmen and the settlers during the war, and in the end the much-tried frontiersmen of Pennsylvania at Paxton came to the conclusion that all Indians, including peaceful tribesmen who had adopted Christianity and were living under protection at Conestoga and at Lancaster, should be slaughtered.[10]

The fighting along the Indian frontier adjacent to the colonies gradually came to an end in the fall of 1764 after Pontiac himself signed a capitulation on October 31.[11] Pontiac and other Indian leaders had no choice but to give up the sieges at Fort Pitt and at Fort Detroit with the arrival of overwhelming numbers of British troops. But even after Pontiac had made a peace with his enemies, General Thomas Gage, who succeeded General Amherst in command, complained that the great chief still maintained "as much influence as ever" over interior tribes whom he could "manage as he pleases." [12] Gage urged his subordinate, Colonel Henry Bouquet, who had forced an end to hostilities at Fort Pitt and a return of prisoners from the Ohio Indians after Pontiac's capitulation, to contact Pontiac. The influential "Pondiac," as Gage called him, "should, if possible, be gained to our interest." [13]

Pontiac, meanwhile, quietly drifted into the western forests, unmolested, escaping punishment, capture, or actual military defeat. He met with the British in 1766, promised to recall war belts he had sent, and then disappeared into the Illinois country. Here he moved from village to village, sometimes with his sons, until 1769 when he was unexpectedly assassinated by another Indian, possibly as he left a trading house in the old French town of Cahokia. A few of the quaint, original French buildings of the time still stand as part of a church school. One of them, it is said, was frequented by the renowned chief who, from time to time, came to trade at the village.

Who was Pontiac's murderer? The evidence seems to point to a Peoria chief whose fellow-headmen desperately wanted to end the powerful Ottawa's maneuvering among the Illinois tribes.[14] The fact that there are at least two remembered versions of the assassination of the great chief may be due to the attempts of the murderers to cover up their deed.[15]

As peace returned to the frontier, hundreds of white captives abandoned their wilderness homes among the tribesmen to resume once again their lives with families and friends in the white settlements. Surprisingly enough, a number of the white women captives rejected their white husbands and insisted upon returning to the routine of wigwam life with their warrior mates.[16] The women had been treated with kindness, and once they had been adopted into the tribe by an Indian ceremony that "washed" the white blood from their veins, they were tribal members sharing the tribe's future of abundance, adversity, war, or peace.[17] Warrior husbands, some deeply attached to the white women who had lived with them, accompanied troops far within the settlement limits at risk of their lives and patiently watched at a distance at evening encampments, if only to catch a glimpse of a former mistress.

The women who escaped from the settlements to return to such devoted warrior husbands also had undoubtedly suffered from accusations because of real or fancied disgrace in having accepted an Indian husband. Why not flee to the wilderness and escape a lifetime of critical moralizing about one's past? Intermarriage with Indians was seldom looked upon with favor by the colonists, especially if it was not sanctioned by a proper ceremony. In fact, in all of colonial history, there are few examples of marriages between British white colonials and Indians.[18]

The British home government was not involved in the immediate problem of family mixups, although it did, through its military command, insist that prisoners held by Indians be returned. A main point of concern by British officials had been to bring about a cessation of hostilities with the Indians and to enforce the Royal Proclamation of 1763, pinpointing the Appalachian watershed as the line between savagery and civilization. The only contemporary map, showing a proclamation line following the crest of the Allegheny Mountains (the western ridge of the Appalachian chain), was published in the October 1763 issue of the *Gentleman's Magazine*.[19] Apparently no official map was published by the home government.

Confusion resulting from a stroke of pen that limited colonial westward expansion according to the *Gentleman's Magazine* map, was partly rectified by a "Plan of 1764," which directed northern and southern Indian superintendents to work out more exact boundary lines separating white settlement from Indian territory.[20] A line established at the Indian congress at Augusta was extended between 1763 and 1773 by a series of treaties and purchases so that it could be followed with reasonable accuracy from a point beginning on the Florida coast near modern Orlando. From here the line ran northwest on an irregular course through what is now Jacksonville and from there on to a point midway between mod-

Proclamation Line of 1763
Indian Cessions
and the Land Companies

— — — The Proclamation of 1763 forbade the purchase or settlement of Indian lands westerly of a line running through the heads of the rivers which fell into the Atlantic from the west or northwest.

—x—x— Tryon's Line, 1767, (by agreement with the Cherokee) directed that no white settlement should be made westerly of a line running from a point where Reedy River was intersected by the then North Carolina-South Carolina boundary, to Tryon's Mountain and thence to Fort Chiswell.

—+—+—+ The Treaty of Fort Stanwix, 1768, (with the Iroquois) extinguished Iroquois claims to the lands southeasterly of a line running from Fort Stanwix to Fort Pitt, and thence along the southern bank of the Ohio to the mouth of the Tennessee (Cherokee) River.

—o—o—
—x—x— The Treaty of Hard Labor, 1768, (with the Cherokee) confirmed Tryon's Line of 1767 and extended it from Fort Chiswell to the mouth of the Kanawha River.

—•—•— The Treaty of Lochaber, 1770, (with the Cherokee) moved the northern part of the line established at the Treaty of Hard Labor westerly to run from six miles east of Long Island of Holston directly to the mouth of the Kanawha River. Lochaber was the name of the plantation of Alexander Cameron, Assistant Commissioner of Indian Affairs for the Southern Provinces.

—••—••— Donelson's Line. When Col. Donelson acting for Virginia, and Chief Attakullakulla and Alex. Cameron, acting for the Cherokee, came to run the Lochaber Line, some agreement was entered into by which it was turned westward and made to run with the Kentucky (Louisa) River.

The Treaty of Sycamore Shoals, 1775, negotiated between the Transylvania Company and the Cherokee, consumated the sale, by the Cherokee, of TRANSYLVANIA, comprising the land lying between the Kentucky River and the south watershed of the Cumberland River plus a path from the white settlements to the newly acquired lands.

•••••••• VANDALIA originated in the grant, by the Iroquois at the Treaty of Fort Stanwix, of a tract, between Pennsylvania and the Little Kanawha, known as "Indiana."

Settlements on the Watauga and Nolachucky are indicated thus- ⚬ ⚬

Reproduced by permission of Charles Scribner's Sons from *Atlas of American History*, edited by James Truslow Adams. Copyright 1943 Charles Scribner's Sons; renewal copyright © 1971.

MILES
25   0   50   100

Drawn under the supervision of DAN E. CLARK

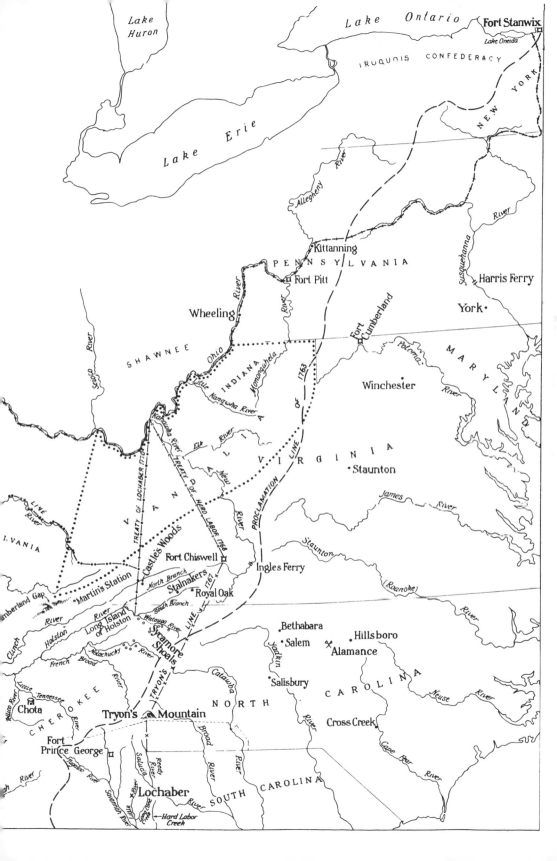

ern Atlanta and Athens, Georgia. Then it followed a northerly course
to the vicinity of the Cumberland Gap.[21] From the area of the Gap the
line ran in a northwesterly route to meet the Ohio River near modern
Louisville, Kentucky, leaving some Indians east of the boundary, including the Catawbas, who remain on small reserves of their ancestral lands
even today.

This southern Indian boundary line coincided with a northern boundary negotiated by superintendent Sir William Johnson at the treaty of
Fort Stanwix in November 1768. The northern line also had its western
tip on the Ohio River, reaching, according to a map printed in the *New
York Col. Docs.*, to the mouth of the Tennessee (then called the Cherokee
River).[22] The line then followed the Ohio eastward to the forks at Fort
Pitt up the Allegheny and overland in a northeasterly course to the
west branch of the Susquehanna River and once again overland to Owegy
(modern Owego, New York). From this point, on an irregular course
the boundary ran north to a point just west of Fort Stanwix, now Rome,
New York. Here the Fort Stanwix line seems to join what was the northern
extremity of the Proclamation of 1763. The boundary, thus negotiated
by Sir William with the Iroquois chiefs, still left a large portion of what
is now New York State to the confederacy. At the same time, however,
land speculators were pleased to have confirmation of their claims to
a bonanza of forest lands that could be sold to settlers who would clear
the woods. Although the Indians seem to have accepted the settlement
as well as the whites, the British home government withheld its approval
because Johnson exceeded his instructions in making extraordinary concessions to land speculators. Among these was the Wyoming Valley,
lying between the forks of the Susquehanna, which had been promised
to the Delaware Indians as a settlement at the Easton conferences in the
late 1750s.[23]

By the year 1768, two connecting boundary lines separated whites
from Indians. The lines, which met on the Ohio River, silhouetted a
huge geographical arrowhead directed to the heartland of America, a
garden of seemingly boundless forests, meadows, and teeming wildlife.
This rich prize, of course, was only temporarily held by the populous
woodland tribes. Pointing toward the rich Midwest as it did, the por-
tentous boundary line, fronting the great edge of settlement of the British
North American colonies, forecast the oncoming waves of white population that would sweep across the entire continent to the Pacific in little
more than a half century.

Though the negotiations concerning land speculation schemes were
haphazard and most details of bargaining will probably never be known,
the Indian boundary lines were nevertheless a fact of life for both tribesmen and colonists. In this sense, the boundary was a recognizable barrier

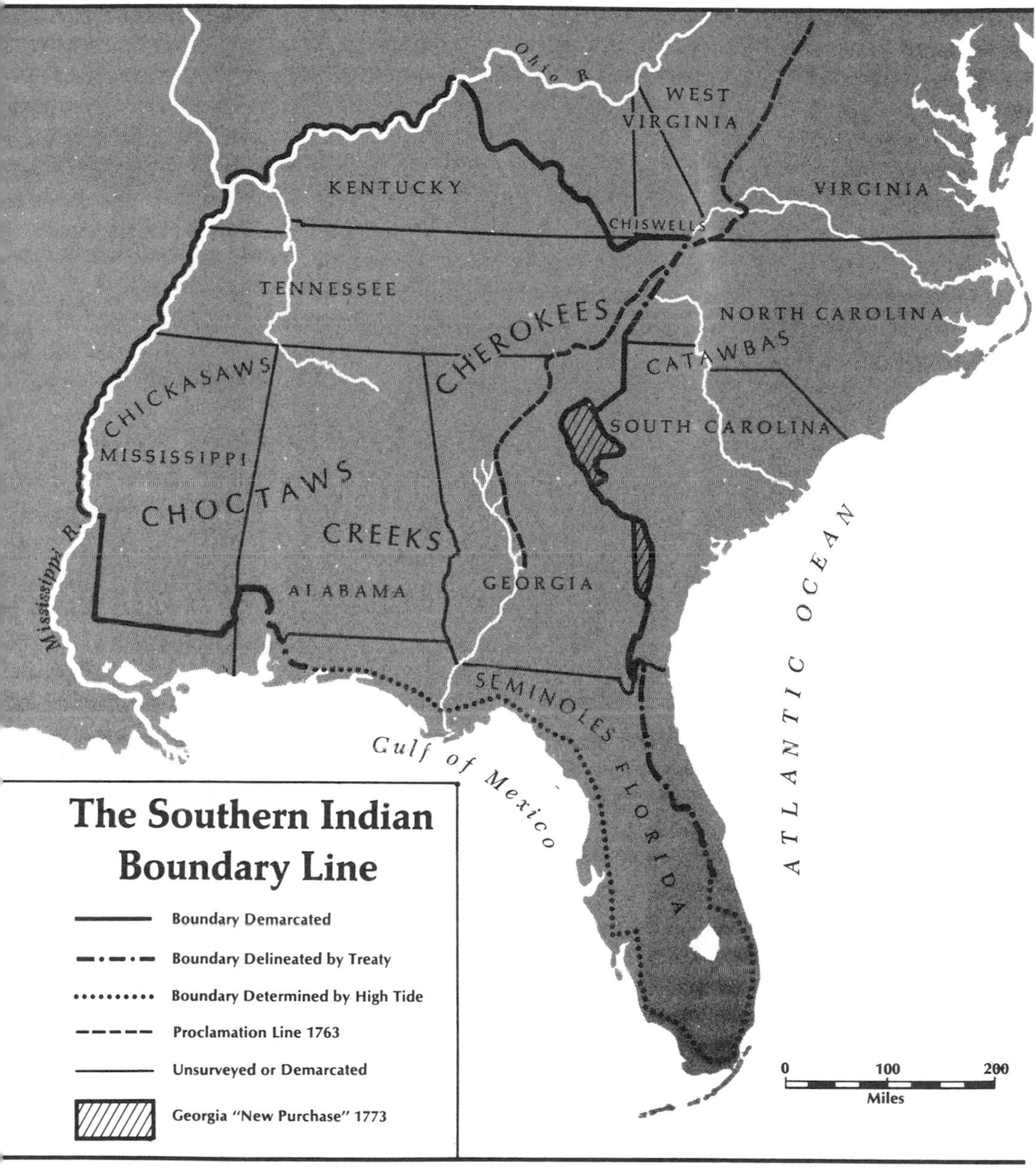

The Southern Indian Boundary Line
Boundary Demarcated
Boundary Delineated by Treaty
Boundary Determined by High Tide
Proclamation Line 1763
Unsurveyed or Demarcated
Georgia "New Purchase" 1773
Ohio R.
WEST VIRGINIA
KENTUCKY
VIRGINIA
CHISWELLS
TENNESSEE
CHEROKEES
NORTH CAROLINA
CATAWBAS
CHICKASAWS
SOUTH CAROLINA
MISSISSIPPI
CHOCTAWS
CREEKS
Mississippi R.
ALABAMA
GEORGIA
SEMINOLES
FLORIDA
Gulf of Mexico
ATLANTIC OCEAN
0
100
200
Miles

in moderating the pace and direction of white occupation of Indian lands.[24] Had the American Revolution not occurred so soon after the establishment of the connecting boundary lines, it is possible that they could have had a greater influence upon the development of a policy to insure a more orderly occupation of the West, possibly avoiding the tragic Indian wars that punctuate nineteenth-century American history.

One might expect that the boundary line concept would die with the Revolution. But this was not so. Even after England was no longer a power in negotiating with Indians on behalf of the Americans, new state governments and later the new national government set up a series of frontier boundaries separating whites from Indians. Washington's views, as set forth in a letter of September 7, 1783 to a congressional committee attempting to formulate policies toward the defeated Indians, advocated placing the Indians west of a boundary line, "beyond which we will endeavor to restrain our People from Hunting and Settling." [25] Washington cautioned that the new government should not attempt "to grasp too much." As Reginald Horsman has pointed out, Washington never regarded such a boundary line as permanent: "policy and economy point very strongly to the expediency of being upon good terms with the Indians," Washington argued. To attempt to drive them out of their lands, he maintained,

> is like driving the Wild Beasts of the Forest which will return . . . the gradual extension of our Settlements will as certainly cause the Savage as the Wolf to retire; both being beasts of prey tho' they differ in shape. In a word there is nothing to be obtained by an Indian War but the Soil they live on and this can be had by purchase at less expense, and without that bloodshed, and those distresses which helpless Women and Children are made partakers of in all kinds of disputes with them.[26]

Washington's voice advocating the isolation of the Indian barbarian was echoed by many other Americans, including some of his chief advisors such as Generals Henry Knox and Philip Schuyler. Underlying their arguments for the boundary line was also the concept that the Indian himself would be better off separated from whites. Indeed, white officials from Cadwallader Colden to Andrew Jackson maintained that the government could not protect Indians from exploitation unless they were removed to an Indian territory.[27] What other solution was there? What other solution was there that would be feasible for a white political leader to advocate?

The inevitable decision was to remove the woodland tribes westward to one "final" boundary, the Mississippi River, and not unexpectedly many of the arguments justifying the historic removal were reminiscent of the discussions that Anglo-Americans had about the need of a Proclamation Line in 1763.[28]

It was a long step from the Royal Proclamation of 1763 to the establishment of an "Indian Territory" by federal government legislation of May 28, 1830. Then, of course, followed the sad, bitter Plains Indian wars culminating in complete victory for the whites and the creation of reservations where tribesmen could be herded in and completely surrounded by another kind of boundary line separating them from white society.[29] The sequence of events dating back to the 1760s shows that turmoil on the Indian frontier helped to set forces in motion that eventually decided the fate of the Indian in the next century. Certainly the boundary line concept, which made physical separation of whites and Indians a fact of life, is not unrelated to the growth of white prejudice against Indians, a factor that must now be recognized as a powerful force in the history of the American people.[30] Further detective work in tracing the emergence of boundary lines and the identification of pressure groups behind them may throw new light on the evolution of the reservation system[31] and the special kinds of prejudice that underlie Indian-white relations in the last hundred years of our history.[*]

[*] Arrell M. Gibson, *The American Indian, Prehistory to the Present* (Lexington, Mass., 1980), pp. 217-484, has a readable, authoritative account of the origins of the reservations that followed a long era of violence. The best description of the tragic federal policy that brought on the reservation system is Robert A. Trennert, *Alternative to Extinction: Federal Policy and the Beginnings of the Reservation System, 1846-51* (Philadelphia, 1975). A history of *The Indian in America*, by Wilcomb E. Washburn (New York, 1975), pp. 168-69, appraises U.S. Indian policy as both "malevolent" and "benevolent" and supports the argument that Indian removal was inevitable "given the nature of the system" (p. 169).

PART III

INDIAN-WHITE CONTACT: FINAL PERSPECTIVES

Cultivate the earth, ye gods! The Indians did that as much as they needed. And they left off there. Who built Chicago? Who cultivated the earth until it spawned Pittsburgh, Pa.?

. . .

Man is a moral animal. All right. I am a moral animal. And I'm going to be turned into a virtuous little automaton as Benjamin would have me. "This is good, this bad. Turn the little handle and let the good tap flow," saith Benjamin and all America with him. "But first of all extirpate those savages who are always turning on the bad tap."

D. H. Lawrence
Studies in Classic American Literature

CHAPTER **10**

The Noble Savage Theme: Attitudes and Policies toward the Indian in the British Colonies

Was there a noble savage type among the woodland Indians? The question is as controversial today as it was in the colonial era because so much depends upon the viewpoint of the one who writes about Indian-white relations. Those who see a semblance of true nobility in the Mohawk warrior are probably not those who have been impressed with his savagery in warfare and torture of captives. White attitudes toward Indians, as we have seen in the introduction to this volume, can be very complex in their origin. Certainly such attitudes are different from those that the Indians have about themselves or about their heroes in American history who led them in the long, futile wars against their white adversaries.

The truth is not easy to uncover, as a glance at the wide range of opinion and interpretation in this field of early American history makes clear. The article on Indians in the *Large Soviet Encyclopedia*, for instance, paints a particularly black picture of this segment of our history, emphasizing the brutality of the English settlers in Indian-white affairs. The first colonists are portrayed as rapacious invaders:

> The original development of America's native population was disrupted by
> the intrusion of European colonizers. The entire history of embattled
> America is one of unheard-of violence and treachery, of mass destruction
> of native peoples and their enslavement. The Indians resisted in despair
> but were defeated.[1]

The theme of Anglo-American maltreatment of the Indians persists in
almost all Soviet accounts of United States history and is a dominant
thread in Soviet histories dealing with the early American frontier. My
initial reaction to this point of view, which I first encountered some years
ago while completing an article on the Soviet image of American history,[2]
was one of rejection. I resented what seemed to be an inaccurate and
unfair account of early American history in which the colonists were depicted as greedy, selfish invaders who exterminated Indians in order to
take possession of the land. Yet further study of Indian history (and of
the writings of others who have studied the subject) has convinced me
that there is, unfortunately, much truth in the Soviet encyclopedia account.

If we cannot be proud of the history of Indian-white relations in colonial America, we must also recognize that this is not a simple story to
tell. There were those colonials who admired the Indians, especially native leaders such as Pontiac of the Ottawas or Joseph Brant
of the Iroquois, and saw in them an image of a noble savage. There
were others who viewed the Indian as something less than a human being,
certainly not a hero, and perhaps closer to the devil. As has been noted in
the Prologue of this volume colonial racist attitudes toward the Indian
had a psychological basis. When the early Virginians conjured up an
image of a belligerent Indian they tended to overlook the generous,
friendly Indian who had done so much to help the first colonists. To
stereotype the Virginia Indians as treacherous savages allowed the
colonists to justify their actions in taking native lands. In a sense, the
colonists overcame a feeling of guilt by anticipating hostile, violent,
brutish savages who would resent white encroachment on their lands.
After the Indian war of 1622 Virginians found less and less to admire
among the Indians. Although John Smith had written at length and sometimes favorably on Indian politics and customs, writers after the Virginia
Indian war of 1622 tended to portray the natives as brutish, wild, lazy,
and "bloudy." [3]

One can thus trace changing attitudes toward the Indians that ma-
terialized within a short space of time, sometimes within a decade. The
friendliness of the Pilgrims toward the Wampanoag and Massachusetts
tribes, which had suffered population losses in an epidemic about 1616–
19, differed from the attitudes of later Bay Colony settlers toward the
Indians after the Pequot War of 1637 and King Philip's War of 1676.

John Smith's attitude toward Powhatan, leader of a confederacy of some thirty tribes surrounding Jamestown was respectful and friendly since Smith was concerned with bargaining for Indian food and protecting his infant colony against what might be a formidable attack. Smith's initial friendliness with the Indians would no doubt have been altered had he remained in Virginia long enough to survive the Indian wars of 1622 and 1644.

From the evidence in early Virginia and New England history we may conclude that colonial Indian-white relations differed from time to time, and colony by colony. Even in the proprietary colonies, where one might expect to find a more clearly recognizable pattern of Indian-white relationships, there is also considerable variation. Quaker-Indian relations, for example, are unique in terms of the orderly manner in which land was occupied and the extreme care that was taken to maintain cordial relations with adjacent tribes.[4] When the Quakers lost control of policy making, however, the Pennsylvania frontier in 1756 became the scene of a savage Indian war led by the outraged Delawares. Yet Pennsylvania's response in fighting off attacking warriors did not result in putting captured Indians into a work force of slave laborers. In provincial South Carolina, on the other hand, the planters did just that by enslaving hundreds of Indian captives who fell into their hands.[5]

The Indian superintendency system, formed by the imperial government along the format of the Edmond Atkin plan of 1755, represented a high point in British efforts to gain more control over all Indian-white relations throughout the colonies. Opposition, however, poured forth from headstrong governors. They in turn were often frustrated by powerful provincial assembly committees who attempted to control Indian land purchases, fur and skin trade regulations, and military defense. As a result, the effectiveness of the Indian superintendents was much reduced by interference from the various colonies. Another complicating factor was the role of British generals such as the Earl of Loudoun and Sir Jeffery Amherst who attempted to direct all Indian policy that related to military matters.

At the end of the French and Indian War Britain attempted to halt western expansion by issuing the Proclamation of 1763 and, in a series of treaties concluded with western tribes (in 1764, 1768, and 1775), attempted to set boundary lines that would satisfy land speculators and bring about an orderly occupation of the frontier.[6] Regulations concerning land purchases and trade with the Indians also showed Britain's increasing concern for the Indian. These measures, however, proved ineffectual. The frontiersmen and the land speculators had, in the years from 1763 to 1775, become far more independent. Eager for frontier lands, they were not at all ready to accept regulations imposed by the British.

Not unexpectedly they joined the revolutionaries in the War of Independence and exposed themselves to Indian hostility.[17]

Throughout the colonial period the mother country had had no real choice but to permit a large degree of colonial control over Indian affairs. Confronted with the increasing demands of semi-independent commonwealths in North America, the British frequently did not possess the power to enforce their authority over far-reaching wilderness frontiers. Nor is there much evidence to show that the English, before the 1750s, were particularly interested in Indians other than as providers of lands and furs or as auxiliaries in fighting the French and Spaniards.

A wide assortment of contemporary records reveals that the seventeenth-century colonials, who helped mold early Indian policy, generally considered themselves superior to the aborigines. The first settlers' writings often record that they were repelled by Indian religion, Indian sexual mores, Indian illiteracy, and Indian ideas of dress, personal modesty, and adornment.[8] There are frequent portrayals of Indians as depraved, savage brutes, as impious rascals who lived in filth and ate nasty food.[9] Even Francis Parkman, one of the first serious students of the Indian, portrayed him in colonial history as a Stone Age savage whose homicidal fury in war gave him a demoniac character.[10]

There is evidence that seventeenth- and eighteenth-century colonials tended not only to despise the Indian but also to distrust him. By tradition, Europeans associated the "heathen" or "infidel" with warfare and conflict, and the primitive Indian was expected to be hostile. Sometimes Indian friendliness was actually viewed with suspicion; such friendliness might well mask deceit and treachery. As Wilcomb Washburn points out, the almost atavistic fear of Indian treachery can be traced back to Jamestown in 1607, when Christopher Newport recognized the friendliness of the native, but commented that they were "naturally given to treachery." [11] This point of view later became a basic ingredient in the histories of Virginia. In 1898, for example, the historian Alexander Brown wrote that friendly Indians "probably boded the little colony a future harm." [12] There was in fact a widespread belief that Indians were enemies of the Commonwealth. The saying, "The only good Indian is a dead Indian," owes its existence to this shrunken, distorted view of the natives.

The Puritan settlers were equally suspicious of the Indian. Their prejudice was rooted in the morality of the Old Testament and refined and strengthened by such historical phenomena as the Pequot War. The assumption that the Indian was an obstacle to the progress of civilization made it difficult for the Puritans to recognize Indian virtue. Indian generosity was explained as an act of God, for His intervention had caused the Indians to behave temporarily in a benevolent fashion. In Puritan annals we therefore find such statements as, "God caused the Indians to help us with fish at very cheap rates. . . ." [13] Such bias against the Indians was of course partly due to the fact that early Puritan fathers saw their life in the New World as part of a preordained plan, the unfolding of God's will. The natives were merely God's agents on earth. Thus the religious beliefs of the Puritans and many other colonials encouraged them to look on the tribesmen as part of the hostile environment of the New World. The Bible (particularly the Old Testament) continued to be used as a guide in Indian affairs. In the late eighteenth century, for instance, James Adair, a South Carolina Indian trader, concluded that the culture of the southern Indians was a survival of customs from the ten lost tribes of Israel. [14]

The erroneous belief that the Indians were treacherous and unreliable persisted among British and provincials throughout the colonial period. English generals such as Edward Braddock and Sir Jeffery Amherst exhibited this attitude, and, in 1763, influenced by this concept, the Paxton Boys of a frontier hamlet of Pennsylvania butchered harmless Conestoga Indians. The fact that a number of the Christian "Moravian Indians" were housed in barracks in Philadelphia caused a spokesman for the Paxton rioters to write an angry "Remonstrance" to the governor of Pennsylvania and the Assembly:

> The Indians now at Philadelphia are His Majesty's Perfidious Enemies, & therefore to protect and maintain them at Public Expense, while our suffering Brethren on the Frontiers are almost destitute of the necessaries of Life, and are neglected by the Public, is sufficient to make us mad with rage, and tempt us to do what nothing but the most violent necessity can vindicate. [15]

The colonials liked to regard the Indians as members of a nomadic hunting race with no fixed habitation, roaming over thousands of acres of virgin wilderness. [16] This wish-fulfilling dream of the nomadic Indian (which Presidents John Adams and Theodore Roosevelt, among others, later used as an excuse for taking Indian land) ignored the fact that many of the tribes of eastern North America lived in populous towns and villages. Such towns contained houses, streets, fortifications, centers for civic and religious events, as well as corn fields, orchards, and garden plots. [17] North American Indians were generally good fishermen, hunters, and farmers. Many Indian societies were in certain ways highly developed —in terms of occupational specialization, social controls, and class structure, for instance—but complicated political and social customs were not easily understood by the European, and the colonials were generally content to remain ignorant of Indian society, with little reason to doubt their own superiority.

Fortunately, some early explorers, as well as British officers and colonials, were free of the prejudice that tainted the judgment of the majority and saw more admirable qualities in the Indians. Among those who recognized Indian virtues were many of the Spanish explorers such as Christopher Columbus, Alvar Nuñez Cabeza de Vaca, and Francisco de Coronado; such well-known figures as Jacques Cartier, Samuel de Champlain, John Smith, William Bradford, and Roger Williams also left favorable accounts of the Indians. The seventeenth-century Virginia Indians are described by contemporaries as "the most gentle loving faithful people . . . such as live after the manner of the golden age"; the Wampanoags, Bradford wrote, were "a spetiall instrument of God." [18] Early missionaries praised the freedom-loving Indian who lived in a world untainted by the corruption of European society.

Robert Rogers, famed ranger, fighter, and Indian agent, and probably one of the best eighteenth-century judges of the Indian character, was full of praise for the Indians south of the Great Lakes: "These people of any upon earth seem blessed in this world: here is health and joy, peace and plenty; care and anxiety, ambition and the love of gold, and every uneasy passion, seem banished from this happy region." [19] Sir William Johnson, the Irish-born New York Indian diplomat for the British, who had married the Mohawk woman Molly (Joseph Brant's sister), was no romantic idealist where Indians were concerned. His experience in frontier diplomacy, trade, and land speculation exceeded that of any other British colonial official in the eighteenth century. Writing to a British scientist in 1771 about the Six Nations Iroquois, Johnson praised the sachems of the grand council at Onondaga for conducting their deliberations with "regularity and decorum." The speaker was never interrupted; harsh language was never used, no matter what the speaker may have been thinking at the time.[20] Moreover, Johnson judged many Englishmen to be ignorant of the customs of the Indians, which, if better known, would be admired and respected.[21]

Examples of colonial expressions of respect and admiration for the Indian can be multiplied. Various delegations of Indian chiefs who visited London in the eighteenth century were cordially received and much admired everywhere. Some of them were painted by Sir Joshua Reynolds. Copies of the paintings circulated throughout Britain, and a few of these survive as rare prints in the Huntington Library vaults and in other libraries. British officers who had been among the Indians in America reinforced the favorable impression made by the chiefs. In June 1756, for example, a young British military officer, Charles Lee, recorded his impressions of the Indians for his sister in England. He had seen the Indians at their worst and had been with Braddock on the Monongahela, but he insisted that the sympathetic account of the Indians that Cadwallader Colden

had given in his *History of the Five Indian Nations* was "literally true." Of
the Mohawks, the tribe of the Iroquois that he had come to know from
personal experience, Lee wrote:

> I can assure you that they are a much better sort of people than com-
> monly represented; they are hospitable, friendly and civil to an immense
> degree; in good breeding I think they infinitely surpass the French or any
> other people that I ever saw, if you will allow good breeding to consist
> in the constant desire to do ev'rything that will please you, and in strict
> carefulness not to do anything that may offend you. . . . [These warriors]
> acquire something of an ease and gracefulness in their walk and air which
> is not to be met with elsewhere, their Dress I like most wonderfully. . . .
> Their Complexion is deep olive, their eyes and teeth very fine, but their
> skins are most inexpressibly soft and silky. Their men are in general hand-
> somer than their women, but I have seen some of them very pretty.[22]

Other comments on scalping and warfare may strike us as less flattering
to the Indians, but it is clear that Lee is quite sincere in his praise of the
Mohawks; indeed, he finally decided to marry a daughter of one of the
Seneca chiefs, "a very great beauty." "You may think," he wrote his sister, "that I am endeavoring to make my letter Romantic but I give you
my word and honour that it is every syllable facts."[23] Later Lee turned
against the Indians and, as a Revolutionary general, was accused of be-
traying the patriot cause. But for many years he kept in touch with his
Indian wife who had borne him twins.

Edmond Atkin, the southern Indian superintendent who had long experience in the Indian trade, gives us another favorable view of the Indians. In a long report addressed to the Board of Trade, Atkin had this
to say about the Chickasaws:

> The Chic[k]asaws are of all Indians the most Manly in their persons,
> Sentiments, and Actions; being of large graceful figure, open Countenance
> and Manners, and generous Principles; Vigorous, Active, Intrepid, and
> in appearance even to Fierceness; expert horsemen (having perhaps the
> finest breed of Horses in N. America); by much the best Hunters; and
> without Exception (by acknowledgement of all Europeans as well as
> Indians that know them as such) the best Warriors. Even their Women
> handle Arms, and face the Enemy like Men.[24]

In this same report, Atkin praised the Indians as being more faithful
to the terms of treaties than any other people on earth. In the making of
treaties, he said, "no people are more open, explicit, and Direct."[25]

Thus the refutation of the various charges made against the Indians—
that they were treacherous, barbaric, and inferior to the white man—came
from those who knew the Indian very well indeed: from early explorers
and missionaries, and later from soldiers and Indian agents. Moreover,

a few colonials and British officers clearly recognized something akin
to the noble savage in the Indian, though many years were to pass before
that concept was to gain fame in French and American literature. The
fictionalized Indians may in fact be less unrealistic, less romanticized,
than we have assumed, their virtues based on those actually possessed
by native Americans.[26]

If there is any doubt of the American Indian's superb natural qualities
one need only turn to Robert Beverley's *The History and Present State of
Virginia* of 1705, in which the author, a distinguished Virginian and a
careful observer, argued that his "true account of the *Indians*," as well as
the rest of his book was based only on data that "I can justifie, either by
my own Knowledge, or by credible Information." Beverley treats the
religion, laws, customs, sports, crafts, entertainment, government, and
hospitality of the native people in rich detail. This follows an account
of seventeenth-century Indian-white relations that stresses the English
as well as the Indian responsibility for atrocities. Beverley's *History* is all
the more valuable because it was partly written to revise incorrect statements appearing in an English historical work* that he had examined
in manuscript before it was printed.[27]

What does Beverley have to say about the woodland tribes of Virginia's
frontiers? His description of "the Persons of the Indians" gives us a remarkable portrait indeed:

> The *Indians* are of the middling and largest stature of the *English;* They
> are straight and well proportioned, having the cleanest and most exact
> Limbs in the World: They are so perfect in their outward frame, that I
> never heard of one single *Indian*, that was either dwarfish, crooked, bandy-
> legg'd or otherwise mis-shapen.† . . . Their Colour . . . is a Chestnut
> brown and tawny. . . . Their Women are generally Beautiful, possessing
> an uncommon delicacy of Shape and Features, and wanting no Charm,
> but that of a fair Complexion.[28]

Beverley seems to have gone out of his way to shock his contemporaries who tended to look down upon the Indians. In passages describing
the beauty and chastity of Indian women, he stressed their natural
beauty and charming personalities. Refuting a report that Indian girls
sold their bodies for wampum, Beverley retorted that the story was
"an aspersion cast on those innocent Creatures by reason of the freedom

* John Oldmixon's *The British Empire in America* (London, 1708).
† Beverley argued that such physical perfection did not result from killing deformed
infants: "But if they have any such practice among them, as the *Romans* had, of
exposing such Children till they dyed, as were weak and mis-shapen at their Birth,
they are very shy of confessing it, and I could never yet learn that they had." Robert
Beverley, *The History and Present State of Virginia*, ed. Louis B. Wright (Chapel
Hill, N.C., 1947), p. 159.

Left: Bush ranger of the French and Indian War. *Right:* French *coureur de bois,* woodsman-trader. These two sketches by Frederic Remington, whose work was based upon painstaking research, combine many traits of both Indians and whites. Courtesy, Remington Art Memorial.

they take in Conversation, which uncharitable Christians interpret as
Criminal upon no other ground than the guilt of their own Consciences."
In warming up to the topic of the virtues of Indian women Beverley went
so far as to say:

> The *Indian* Damsels are full of spirit, and from thence are always inspir'd
> with Mirth and good Humour. They are extremely given to laugh . . .
> the excess of Life and Fire which they never fail to have, makes them
> frolicksom, but without any real imputation to their Innocence. [29]

Such favorable views of Indians expressed during colonial times were
unfortunately muted and finally all but smothered by prevailing attitudes
of white superiority. Most colonials seemed to have rejected the idea
that the Indians could have a certain nobility and that their fine
natural qualities could be absorbed into white society through marriage
or assimilation.[30] Yet at a later date Thomas Jefferson thought that probably a portion of the Indians, after the passing of the frontier, might well
become acculturated and adopt the white man's way of life, or at least
his methods of agriculture.[31] In fact, however, tribes like the Conestoga
in Pennsylvania—who survived in a sea of white settlements—were not
assimilated into Pennsylvania rural society. There are scattered examples
of Indians who attended the various colonial colleges,[32] including Harvard and William and Mary (which set up a special program for the
education of promising Indians), but not a single one seems to have
risen to prominence in colonial, white society. One exception was Joseph
Brant of the Iroquois, who had been a student at a missionary school.
Nevertheless, Brant's offspring did not achieve distinction. One of these,
young Issac Brant, a drunken ne'er-do-well, assaulted his father with a
knife and in return received a scalp cut from which he later died.[33]

The gap between the races was occasionally bridged by intermarriages,
for example, among the Indian traders who occasionally had native wives.
But theirs were usually marriages for convenience and not based upon
concepts of racial equality. Sir William Johnson is said to have had two
Indian wives after the death of his first wife. But Johnson was alone
among those who intermarried with Indians and spoke glowingly of their
finer qualities and what might be called their nobility of character. There
were surprisingly few known cases of mixed marriages between Indians
and British colonials, although many Virginians have attempted to trace
their ancestry back to John Rolfe and Pocahontas. Certainly there were
many Indians who lived as Indians but were undoubtedly the offspring
of white men and Indian women, for it was customary among many
tribes to offer attractive young women as hostesses, who spent the night
with visiting strangers. Robert Beverley, writing of this custom, saw

parallels in classical times: "After this manner perhaps many of the Heroes were begotten in old time, who boasted themselves to be the Sons of some Way-faring God." [34]

Andrew Montour, a self-educated Indian interpreter from the middle colonies, is a rare example of a half-caste who attained some prominence in the eighteenth century. But his case is a special one, for his father was probably Iroquois, and his mother Canadian (she too may have been the offspring of a mixed marriage). Although Montour seems to have been illiterate, he was nevertheless a master of Indian dialects and was fluent in both English and French. The Moravian missionary, Count Zinzendorf, wrote the following description of the interpreter in 1742:

> Andrew's cast of countenance is decidedly European, and had not his face been encircled with a broad band of paint, applied with bear's fat, I would certainly have taken him for one. He wore a brown broadcloth coat, a scarlet damaskan lappel-waistcoat, breeches, over which his shirt hung, a black Cordovan neckerchief, decked with silver bubles, shoes stockings, and a hat. His ears were hung with pendants of brass and other wires plated together like the handle of a basket. [35]

Andrew owned property and demanded and received compensation for his services. He was a kind of "cultural broker" between two races. One point seems to have distinguished him clearly from his Indian contemporaries: he wore European breeches. Though many items of clothing were given as presents to the Indians, breeches were not among them.

In the few recorded cases where children were born of unions between Indians and women settlers, the white mother was usually a prisoner who had been captured by the Indians in war. At the end of Pontiac's uprising, however, when female captives were given the chance to return home to their families and white husbands, many of the women preferred to remain with the Indians. [36]

There were practical obstacles to intermarriage as well:

> An Indian wife was an asset to the trader among the Indians. But the agricultural settlers, both French and British, did not want Indian women as wives. Farmers needed wives who knew the ways of European housekeeping and husbandry, who knew how to milk cows, fry eggs, and so on. The farmer, even in Virginia, so late as 1682, often preferred to pay the expense of importing women of questionable repute from European cities, at considerable cost, than to take Indian women who would be helpless on a farmer's homestead. [37]

The reluctance of the average British colonist to accept intermarriage was, in the opinion of Robert Beverley, as well as other Virginia writers, a basic cause for Indian-white jealousies and misunderstandings. "Intermarriage," Beverley pointed out, had been "proposed very often by the Indians . . . urging it frequently as a certain Rule, that the *English* were not their friends if they refused it." Beverley then goes on to argue that white intermarriage with Indians might well have prevented "the Abundance of Blood that was shed on both sides" and the accompanying "Errors and Convulsions in the first Management" of the colony of Virginia. It is likely, he concludes, that intermarriage with Indians would have resulted in their being "converted to Christianity" and that "the Country would have been full of People, by the Preservation of the many *Christians* and *Indians* that fell in the Wars between them." One of the most telling arguments that Beverley made for intermarriage was the example of the union of Pocahontas and John Rolfe in 1613.[38] The result was "a firm Peace with her Father, tho' he would not trust himself at her Wedding. Both the *English* and the *Indians* thought themselves intirely secure and quiet." The marriage, Beverley added, also helped to bring about better relations with an adjacent tribe, the Chickahominy Indians.[39]

That racial prejudice had prevented intermarriage, and therefore the peaceful interrelations of Indians and whites, was a theme found in the writings of another eminent colonial Virginian. In his *History of the Dividing Line* of 1728 William Byrd of Westover suggested that colonists intermarry with Indians, a people who, he wrote, "are healthy & Strong, with Constitutions untainted by Lewdness and not enfeebled by Luxury." Echoing Beverley's persuasive arguments, Byrd wrote that ". . . the Indians, "coud, by no means perswade themselves that the English were heartily their Friends, so long as they disdained to intermarry with them." If the colonists were serious about converting and civilizing the native people, Byrd said, "they would have brought their Stomachs to embrace this prudent Alliance. . . . For, after all that can be said, a sprightly Lover is the most prevailing Missionary that can be sent amongst these, or any other Infidels." [40] Byrd suggested, with just a touch of irony, that the Indians might be prepared to give up their lands peacefully as a form of dowry if they were convinced that their daughters would be accepted as equals in white society.[41]

Governor Alexander Spotswood, writing to the Lord Commissioners of Trade and Plantations in 1717, also commented on the absence of intermarriage:

> And as to beginning a nearer friendship by intermarriage (as the Custom of the French is), the inclinations of our people are not the same with those of that Nation, for notwithstanding the long intercourse between ye inhabitants of this Country and ye Indians and their living amongst one another for so many Years, I cannot find one Englishman that has an Indian Wife, or an Indian marreyed to a white woman.[42]

The Board of Trade in England was displeased with this state of affairs and recommended to the crown in 1721 that intermarriage be encouraged:

> It was for this reason, that, in the draught of Instructions for the Governor of Nova Scotia, we took the liberty of proposing to your Majesty that proper encouragement should be given to such of your Majesty's subjects as should intermarry with the native Indians; and we conceive it might be for your Majesty's service that the said instructions should be extended to all other British colonies.[43]

Even the Quakers and pacifist German sects in Pennsylvania seem to have rejected intermarriage, although they were interested in establishing friendly relations with the Indians. Penn's message to the Indians, sent before his arrival in Pennsylvania, was full of good will and friendship: "I have great Love and Regard toward you," he told the Indians, "and I desire to win and gain your Love and Friendship by a Kind, Just and Peaceful Life." The Indians seem to have accepted this message; they loved and respected Penn and trusted the Quakers, who were generous with gifts and treated them with fairness. It was not until the middle of the eighteenth century that Pennsylvania suffered the terror of Indian attack.[44] Penn's descendants had abandoned his faith and had adopted a far less humane policy toward the Indians than that of the first settlers; the Indians were cheated in land transactions and in trade, and exposed to the ravages of rum. In a complete reversal of the earlier policy, attempts were made to dominate the Indians by constructing forts rather than by giving presents. The original Quaker policy was defended by Superintendent Edmond Atkin who wrote that it was necessary "to begin building Forts in their hearts . . . after which we may build Forts wherever we please." [45]

Before extensive fortifications could be built along the wide Pennsylvania frontier, war broke out. In 1756 Lieutenant Governor Robert H. Morris and the Pennsylvania Council drew up a declaration of war providing for bounties for native scalps ($130 for a male over twelve years, $50 for a female). Although attempts were made to thwart this plan, it was pushed through the Council with the support of nonQuakers; the Assembly was consulted only after hostilities had commenced. Yet the Pennsylvania Assembly cannot be completely exonerated on the matter of scalp bounties. On July 4, 1764, following a proclamation of war against the Delaware and Shawnee Indians, the Assembly approved an elaborate scheme for scalp bounties for all "Enemy" Indians over the age of ten! This act marked the end of the era of friendly relations between Indians and whites in Pennsylvania.[46]

The imperial Indian superintendent, Edmond Atkin, spoke out forcibly against the barbaric practice of offering scalp bounties. He declared that the Earl of Loudoun, British commander-in-chief in the colonies in the late 1750s, "detests the practice." Such bounties, Atkin argued, encouraged what he called *"private scalping,* whereby the most innocent & helpless persons, even Women & Children, are properly murdered." Such a policy, Atkin asserted, was "only becoming the greatest Savages, & unworthy of any Christian people." Atkin also said that he had reason to believe that the royal governors had "been cautioned" to discourage the practice of giving "Rewards" for scalps. Atkin, who was, of course, interested in establishing the authority of the Indian superintendent, pointed out that Sir William Johnson never rewarded warriors specifically for bringing back scalps.[47]

Atkin's protests were futile. Like a number of other imperial officers, he found himself at odds with colonial assemblies and colonial governors over the questions of policy and its implementation. The authority that he claimed as an officer of the crown was frequently defied; he found, like other imperial officers, and indeed the British Parliament, that the wishes of the crown often had little influence on the decisions of the colonials.

To make matters worse the imperial officers themselves often disagreed over Indian affairs. Governor William Shirley of Massachusetts had a long and bitter feud with William Johnson over questions of authority in dealing with the northern Indians, and Governor James Glen of South Carolina was responsible for calling a large conference of Cherokees at the very time when Governor Dinwiddie of Virginia had contracted with these same Indians (some five hundred warriors) to lead Braddock's army through the woods toward Fort Duquesne.[48] Dinwiddie concluded that Governor Glen was "wrongheaded," but he himself quarreled with Atkin about a "monsterous account" for Indian gifts, and he harassed his deputy, young George Washington, with detailed instructions for dealing with Indians. Washington found Atkin almost impossible to work with and finally decided to ignore the superintendent's instructions.[49] Muddle and strife were two of the main characteristics of British-Indian policy throughout most of the colonial period.

The lack of clarity in British policy may help to explain why the various colonies insisted on making their own decisions on questions related to their own Indians. Moreover, the authority of the British was challenged by the Indians as well as by the colonials. The Iroquois and other Indians declined to be referred to in treaties as "subjects" of the crown. They treated British officials and governors as equals and often gave them Indian names. Virginia's governor was called Brother Assaraquoa; Brother Onas was the name for the governor of Pennsylvania; and Maryland's governor had a special name, Brother Tocarry-Hogan, to denote his geographical position between the neighboring colonies. Significantly, the Indians did not use the term "Father" in addressing the English as they sometimes did in treaty talks with Count Frontenac, who insisted on this title (although the Iroquois perhaps humored him by using it).

To understand exactly what the colonists and the British government wanted from the Indians, we cannot do better than to take a careful look at the terms of one or two fairly representative British-Indian treaties. The Pettaquamscut Treaty of July 15, 1675 was concluded between Major Thomas Savage (not an inappropriate name) and his fellow officers representing Massachusetts and Connecticut, and the various sachems of the friendly Narragansett Indians. According to the treaty the sachems were to deliver King Philip's subjects "dead or alive"; all "stolen property" was to be returned to the whites; disputes over property where the case was not clear were to be judged by "impartial men"; pilfering and "acts of hostility" toward the English "shall for the future forever cease"; certain chiefs were to be held as hostages to insure the peace; the award for the capture of Philip alive was two coats and for his head, one coat; all land grants, sales, bargains, conveyances of lands, meadow, timber, grass, stones "bought or quietly possessed" by the English were renewed, confirmed "forever"; "God" was called "to witness that they [the Indians] were and would in the future remain true friends of the English."[50]

The hard terms of this treaty would scarcely lead one to suspect that the Indian partners to the treaty were friendly toward the whites. What the Puritan fathers wanted was the death or capture of their enemy; the protection and restoration of the Puritan settlers' property; and finally, approval for their occupation and possession of land—to all of which God was to act as witness. When the Narragansett tribesmen did not live up to the letter of this demanding treaty, the Puritans (aware of the value of the Narragansett land) launched a vicious attack against them.[51]

Another representative Indian treaty was written almost a century later. The Treaty of Logstown of 1752 was agreed to by the British government, the Ohio Company of Virginia, and several individual colonies on the one hand, and by the Ohio Iroquois and other tribes, on the other. The demands made were somewhat similar to those of the Pettaquamscut Treaty, but this agreement covered a far greater territory; the British laid claim to almost the whole Ohio Valley. After elaborate preparations, including the transportation of what was said to be the largest gift of goods ever presented to the Indians, the sachems were persuaded to ratify older treaties giving the British ownership of a large part of the upper Middle West. The whites piously defended the "pen and ink work" of the almost certainly fraudulent treaties, but Half King, an Iroquois sachem, protested: "We never understood, until you told us Yesterday, that the Lands then sold were to extend further to the sun setting, than the Hill on the other side of the Alleghany Hill." [52] The conference was a friendly one with the whites listening to Indian complaints, yet on questions of land ownership the whites won on every point.

Land was not the only concern at this meeting. The commissioners tried to calm Indian anger over fur trade abuses, to warn the Indians about French duplicity, and to cultivate Iroquois friendship with presents and fine speeches. Inquiries about an Indian murderer were made, and the question of religious instruction for the Indians was raised. The conference was, from the white point of view, successful, for within a few years the Iroquois tribesmen were allying themselves with the British against the French.

At a great Indian conference held at the headquarters of William Johnson in June 1755, Iroquois warriors were recruited for a campaign against the French at Lake George. The Treaty of Logstown had helped to smooth the way for this later conclave. Extant minutes of the conference detail the arrival of group after group of warriors until finally the Mohawks and their missionary came on the evening of June 21, 1755. "At Dinner time," according to the minutes, "the Sachems & warriors of the hither Mohawk Castle March'd to Col. Johnson's with the Revd. Mr. [John] Ogilvie their Missionary & their chief Sachem at their Head & made a fine appearance." [53]

These three conferences cover a time of near a hundred years. [54] They document the colonists' very low opinion of the Indians and their overwhelming greed for land; both colonists and crown officials were prepared to fight for it, pay something for it, or cheat for it. Next in importance, the whites wanted the Indians' services. If they could not win them as allies, they wanted them as mercenary soldiers, and in the later colonial period they paid certain tribesmen in money to fight for them. The colonials were also prepared to make use of forced labor. King Philip's wife and child, for instance, were sold into slavery, and hundreds of Indian women and children were sold into slavery in South Carolina. [55] Even the Puritans used Indian slaves. [56] Boston newspapers carried advertisements for the capture of runaway Carolina Indian slaves. Local New England Indians as well were enslaved or hired from jails to act as servants. Sometimes they were assigned to reservations called "villages" where, if they did not revolt, they were forced to live under a stern code of law that discriminated against minorities—black, mulatto, and Indian. The "wild" Indians of the frontier were left to their own devices until disease, war, or other factors left them weak enough to be brought under the legal jurisdiction of the whites. [57] In South Carolina soldiers and allied Indians on slave-catching raids plundered the Spanish mission towns of tribesmen who were unarmed and easy victims for the Carolina slavers.[58] A census of 1708 recorded 1,400 Indian slaves in South Carolina, about half the number of black slaves.

By the later part of the eighteenth century Indian slavery in South Carolina seems to have diminished, for little mention of Indian slaves is found in documentary material of the period. A Carolina physician, Dr. George Milligen-Johnston, writing in 1763, took the view that free Indians had become important to the white planters because they helped to maintain an equilibrium of strength preventing black slave revolts. Because the Indians performed this function they should not be exterminated. Dr. Milligen-Johnston set forth his racist rationale in this fashion:

> [The blacks] are in this Climate necessary, but very dangerous Domestics, their Number so much exceeding the Whites; a natural Dislike and Antipathy, that subsists between them and our *Indian* neighbors, is a very lucky Circumstance, and for this Reason: In our Quarrels with the *Indians* . . . it can never be our interest to extirpate them, or to force them from their Lands; their Ground would be soon taken up by runaway *Negroes* from our Settlements, whose Numbers would daily increase, and quickly become more formidable Enemies than *Indians* can ever be, as they speak our Language, and would never be at a Loss for Intelligence.[59]

The strong antipathy between blacks and Indians described by the Carolina physician is not borne out by examination of sources on Indian history in colonial South Carolina, but the argument made by Milligen-Johnston is extremely significant because it reveals the attitudes of callous indifference toward the welfare of non-whites that certain colonials had.

It is difficult to know who or what was responsible for the disastrous treatment accorded the Indians during the American colonial period. Certainly the ignorance of the colonists concerning the culture of the native tribes made it possible for them to regard the Indians as inferior to themselves. And their prejudice, in turn, made it easier for them to acquiesce to, or actually take part in, the maltreatment of the Indians. The situation is not without modern parallels to other cases of widespread racial or religious prejudice—in Nazi Germany, in South Africa, or even in America today.

But the whole weight of blame cannot be placed on the settlers. If British policy makers had been firm in their resolve to protect the Indian, the situation might have been different. In fact, however, British policy was frequently weak and ineffectual. Corrupt governors like Lord Cornbury gave away whole sections of western New York in order to pocket patent fees and were rarely disciplined or removed from office.[60] In short, there was no important body of imperial aw for the protection of the Indians and their lands.

The Noble Savage in Bronze. Massasoit, Chief of the Wampanoags, extended hospitality to the Pilgrims and honored his vows of peace. Photographed by the author at Plymouth, Massachusetts.

The immediate causes of violence, however, lay not so much in the underlying societal factors already discussed—an ignorant and prejudiced white population, a negligent and ineffectual imperial authority—but in the tinderbox atmosphere at the points of contact: in the wilderness and, especially, at the cutting edge of the provincial agricultural frontier. The whites were greedy for furs and land, and far from established authority they were often not inhibited by a fear of the law. The Indians, cheated by the whites in trade and treaties, saw their hunting grounds encroached upon and their very lives endangered. Indians and whites alike were inflamed and one atrocity provoked another. Liquor, disease, and firearms helped to turn an ugly situation into a tragic and disastrous one. Explosions of violence, when they came, were not confined to small areas; self-ignited and self-propelled they swept like wildfire through whole sections of the colonial frontier.[61] Neither the British home government nor a combination of the colonies could prevent the holocaust from devouring whole Indian societies. This explosive force, along with the violent forces within the Indian world and the malevolence of the supposedly civilized whites (who nevertheless murdered for scalp bounties), brought about convulsions that continued well into the national period. Uncontrolled passions—greed, hate, fear, and anger—erupting into a whole series of Indian wars must be assigned some responsibility for what the Cherokees have called the long trail of tears.[62] The British, unlike their rivals, the French and Spaniards, never developed an overall eighteenth-century colonial policy that gave the Indian a place and a future in the imperial structure of empire. The colonials, certain of the superiority of the white race and supported by the knowledge of their own power, pushed the Indians aside, took possession of the coastal lands, and then occupied the hinterlands of the new continent.

Over the years we have created and accepted as true our own version of early American Indian history. We have been all too inclined to glorify our ancestors, to portray them as heroic frontiersmen who conquered the wilderness and subdued the wild natives, meanwhile ignoring the persistent struggle of the Indian to preserve his lands and his way of life. Of all the early writers who encountered the Indians and attempted to understand the issues and problems of Indian-white relations, it was probably Robert Beverley, the early eighteenth-century historian, who put his finger on the nub of the matter. In concluding his chapters on Indians, Beverley almost wistfully commented on the nobility of "this harmless people," whose simplicity of life, closeness to nature, and freedom "without the Curse of Labour" made them a symbol of God's creation. With the subtle perception of Henry David Thoreau, he praised the natural beauty of the land and the bloom of the native people that had been despoiled by the colonists:

> Thus I have given a succinct account of the *Indians;* happily I think, in their simple State of Nature, and in their enjoyment of Plenty, without the Curse of Labour. They have on several accounts reason to Lament the arrival of *Europeans,* by whose means they seem to have lost their Felicity, as well as their Innocence. The *English* have taken away great part of their Country, and consequently made every thing less plenty amongst them. They have introduc'd Drunkenness and Luxury amongst them, which have multiply'd their wants, and put them upon desiring a thousand things, they never dreamt of before.[63]

Among those woodland Indians who had been so profoundly changed by the whites were those of the hinterlands who survived and retreated before the whites. Some of them attempted to stem the white invasion. If we find no nobility in such figures, fighting for native self-determination, in what kind of figures in history will we ever recognize superiority of mind and character? Pontiac, as we have seen in previous chapters, was a native American who possessed (at least from the Indian point of view), heroic qualities of leadership. If such a man was also a savage, let us concede that in him we have a grand image of the noble savage of the North American woodland wilderness.

CHAPTER 11

The Price of Progress: Native People on the European Frontiers of Australia, New Guinea, and North America*

Those who have scrutinized the fragmentary record of man in prehistory tell us that Stone Age peoples in many parts of the world evolved a culture that gave them a reasonably satisfying life largely governed by the ecology of their habitat. In the Pacific islands, in Australia, and in North America, although patterns of life varied, native cultures seem to have put little strain on the land and biota. The beliefs and institutions of native people encouraged them to live in balance with the natural resources. For example, in hunting, there are only rare examples of native peoples' killing off animals that were a part of their food supply.† The Pacific

* Completion of this essay was made possible by research grants from the Huntington Library, the American Philosophical Society, the Committee on the International Exchange of Persons, and the Committee on Research, University of California, Santa Barbara, California.
† Paleo Indians and other Paleo peoples have sometimes been portrayed as destructive. For instance, the controversial hypothesis of the Pleistocene "overkill" of huge Ice Age mammals by certain Paleo Indians some twelve thousand years ago is examined from several sides by paleontologists, archaeologists, and ecologists in Paul Martin, ed., *Pleistocent Extinction, the Search for a Cause*

islanders who lived in delicate balance with plant and animal life evolved a culture that was governed by specialized tropical oceanic environments. The same generalization can be applied to Aborigines of Australia and many of the North American Indians to a degree. In fact, all three peoples, including the ancestors of the native people of Papua-New Guinea (the southeastern part of the island), possessed a remarkable knowledge of plants and animals in their habitat and in general lived a life that today's conservationists would praise very highly indeed.[1]

When the virgin areas were "discovered" by Occidentals, however, there were fundamental transformations in the ecological balance of the land. Superior technology brought about fundamental changes. The native people, in most instances, were pushed aside and the wild lands were utilized for missions, Sunday schools, mines, plantations, farms, and grazing land. Even well-meaning missionaries seeking to convert the natives into a labor force often destroyed the lands and culture of the people they sought to protect.

Of the native people who survived the onslaught of the aliens, few retained their lands or even a portion of them. Many natives were simply killed off by bullets and disease, some survived to become black- or brown-skinned Europeans. Fewer still maintained their ancient ways and somehow clung to their land. Next to outright extermination, the best technique for destroying natives was dispossessing them from the land. Land for the aborigines was all important because it was a spiritual ingredient of their culture; it determined their social groupings and status; and, finally, it was the source of their livelihood. If there is a test for the survival of a native peoples it must be: how much of their land have they retained in resisting the alien invasion? [2]

The three widely separated native people that are being compared here—the American Indians, the Australian Aborigines, and the natives

---

(New Haven, Conn., 1967), pp. 75 ff. The question of "Overkill or Overchill" is still unresolved. The controversy concerning the Indians and other native people as practitioners of burning (and thereby the destruction of flora and fauna) is discussed in Carl Sauer, *Land and Life* (Berkeley, Calif., 1965), pp. 189–91. Dr. Sauer, discussing the matter in a letter to me of January 28, 1971, writes:

> I think the case is pretty well made for man, and especially the Indians as practicers of burning. So the longer the aborigines and successors were around the bigger the grasslands and the more open the woodlands, the greater the number and diversity of . . . flowering, palatable plants. On balance this meant that there was more food than in fire free tracts. A forest has little food except at the tree tops and along the openings. Indian burning did change faunal composition but increased productivity of food of plant and animal.

The generally beneficial results of Indian burning are also described in Victor E. Shelford, *The Ecology of North America* (Urbana, Ill., 1963), pp. 56, 396, 424. Shelford states that the Indians were conservationists, but whites have in some cases obliterated original biotic communities from 98 percent of the land (p. 91).

of New Guinea—exhibit striking similarities. All of them had lived for
centuries isolated from either western or Oriental civilizations. Although
North American Indians had copper ornaments, all groups lived in
what is called the Stone Age, in a social world of clans, tribes, and
tribelets, many of them part of larger cultural groups loosely related by
ancestral and linguistic ties. All used wooden and stone tools and
weapons, and all constructed artifacts for a variety of religious, civic,
and utilitarian purposes. All lived in a world of sorcery and medicine
men. In their societies, the men mainly occupied themselves with hunting, and in making weapons, tools, and shelters, and in some cases
gardening, while women were generally concerned with child care,
gathering and preparing food, and often in making mats and baskets.

    The history of these people is primarily known to us through the
records of explorers, missionaries, government agents, and settlers, all
expressing the white man's point of view.[3] Historical materials are, of
course, supplemented by modern anthropological studies.[4] All these
people had early relations with Europeans, especially English-speaking
Europeans. The Indians of North America, it will be recalled, had their
frontiers invaded by waves of Spaniards, Dutch, French, Swedes, and
English in the seventeenth and eighteenth centuries, and by Russians,
Canadians, and Americans in the nineteenth century. Australia was
visited by Captain James Cook* and by many European explorers,[6] but
the real invasion came when an English penal colony was planted there
in 1788. The large island of New Guinea was reached by Portuguese,
Spanish, and Dutch explorers in the early 1700s and by Captain Cook
in 1770. Europeans established small settlements on the coasts of New
Guinea in the early 1800s.

    The native populations of the three areas resisted European occu-
pation of their land, and all of them had strong religious, social, and
economic ties with the lands that were eventually taken over by the
whites. In general natives respected territorial rights of other native
groups in spite of tribal rivalries and conflicts. Identification with specific
areas of land was almost always characterized by sacred landmarks and
place-names.[7] These native people lived according to what the conservationist Aldo Leopold has called a *land ethic*. Indeed, their respect for
the land emerges from their close spiritual ties with nature. Their sacred
rituals, mythology, and religious songs were generally tied to the rhythm

---

* A passage from a letter written by Cook in 1771 gives a kind of noble savage
image of mainland Australian Aborigines: "These people may truly be said to be in
the pure state of Nature, and may appear to some to be the most wretched upon the
Earth: but in reality they are far more happier than . . . we Europeans, [since,]
being wholly unacquinted [sic] . . . with the superfluous . . . necessary Conven-
iencies so much sought after in Europe[,] they are happy in not knowing the use of
them. . . ." [5]

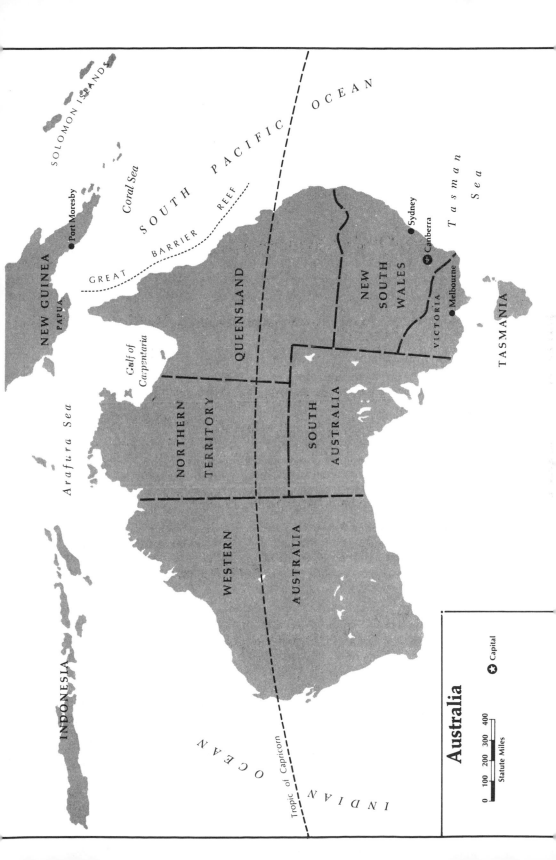

Australia

Capital ⊛

0   100   200   300   400
Statute Miles

of the seasons, the growth of plants and animals, and the ancestral deities who created the world. Groups of natives usually claimed descent from a particular totem, perhaps part animal and part human. Totemism, a concept of life unifying all living things in nature with man as a central figure, had no counterpart in European thought and was seldom understood by whites who first came in contact with native people.[8] Despite the many variations of Indian, Australian Aboriginal, and native New Guinea religious myths and totemism, all appear to have much in common. The lives these native people led, judged by our standards, were brutal and hard. Yet they succeeded in adapting themselves to their environment and lived in relative harmony with their natural surroundings. They even had certain types of population control.[*] Generations lived and died, seemingly without population explosions or widespread starvation.

Much of New Guinea, especially the western part called West Irian (now part of Indonesia), is practically as it was thousands of years ago. Village life has remained almost unchanged. Before the arrival of Europeans these dark-skinned, woolly-haired people (many of the Melanesian natives differ in stature, hair-texture, and features from each other) had established a subsistence village life based upon gardening, hunting, and fishing. Their domestic animals were the dog, the pig, and the chicken, while staple foods were yams, bananas, and the sago palm. Villages were isolated from each other by precipitous mountains, swamplands, or jungles. Feuding tribes, without a common bond of language, fought for grisly trophies of human heads and flesh. Sorcery, exchange of food and gifts, reciprocal "pay-back" justice, feasts, dances, and condolence ceremonies for the dead are all familiar to the student of the American Indian as well as the Australian Aborigines.[10]

The New Guinea natives, like all other indigenous people of tropical countries, suffer from a variety of diseases that limit population growth. Half of the infants born in the Sepik River interior villages where I visited die before their first birthday. Malaria, a repulsive skin infection called "grilli" that flakes the skin, and hookworm are age-old enemies, but the special gifts of transient Europeans and Orientals, leprosy, tuberculosis, and venereal disease have also taken their toll.[11] Voracious clouds of night-flying mosquitoes force individual natives to crawl into huge woven straw stockings to escape being almost eaten alive.

---

[*] Benjamin Franklin described Iroquois population control in this way: "The number of savages generally does not increase in North America. Those living near the Europeans steadily diminish in numbers and strength. The two sexes are of a cold nature, for the men find that the women refuse to sleep with them as soon as they become pregnant. For they believe that makes childbirth difficult. Further, they suckle their children for two and a half or three full years and for the whole time they refrain from sleeping with men." [9] See also Epilogue, p. 163.

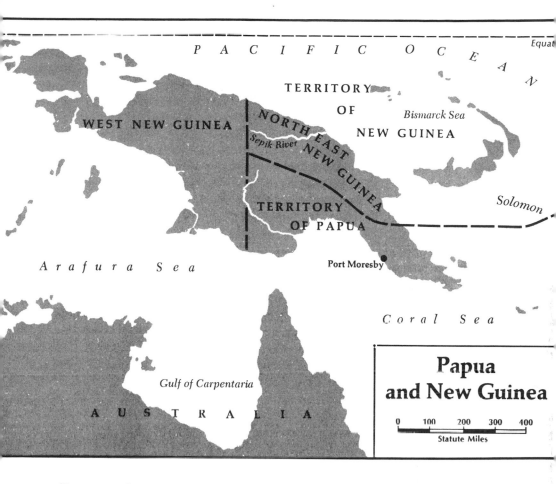

P A C I F I C   O C E A N

TERRITORY

OF

NEW GUINEA

Bismarck Sea

WEST NEW GUINEA

NORTH EAST NEW GUINEA

Sepik River

TERRITORY
OF PAPUA

Solomon

A r a f u r a   S e a

Port Moresby

C o r a l   S e a

Gulf of Carpentaria

A U S T R A L I A

Papua
and New Guinea

0   100   200   300   400
Statute Miles

Yet everywhere in Papua-New Guinea the natives appear to live today
in reasonable prosperity on their own lands. Mountain villagers own
coffee plantations that encircle their gardens and straw-roofed matted
buildings. The river and jungle villages of rows of homes, many with
second-story apartments, are owned by the tribes who have lived there
for centuries. The garden-sorcerer, who produces yams as huge as a
man, gardens in a plot used by his ancestors for generations [12]

Why, we may ask, have the natives of New Guinea been allowed to
keep their land when the Australian Aborigines and the American Indians were dispossessed? Why is the native population of Papua-New
Guinea nearly two million while the non-indigenous people (Europeans,
Chinese, and others) numbers only twenty-five thousand? A seasoned
British explorer of 1890 put the question this way: "Will he [the New
Guinea native] too disappear before the impact of the white race, like
the Tasmanian and the Australian aboriginals have done? I think not,"
the explorer argued, ". . . the house-building, horticultural Papuan
differs as much from the Australian nomad as the Malay or the Samoan

differ from the feebler races they dispossessed." [13] Almost immediately
the Europeans realized that they could not evict the New Guinea natives, who were firmly entrenched in their villages, and fought with
terrible ferocity when attacked or threatened. Because of the complexity and variety of New Guinea language patterns and the diversity
of local cultures, no one friendly tribe or village could easily be used
to conquer others or to aid whites in seizing control of the interior. The
harsh climate, the virulent jungle diseases, the forbidding swamps, im-
penetrable jungles, and steep mountain cliffs gave villagers additional
protection. Certainly there was no question of native claims to ownership of the land. Villagers clearly defined their systems of land tenure
and garden plots (somewhat similar to those of the Iroquois) through
a complex mixture of village, family (descent groups), and individual
rights allowing householders exclusive privileges of cultivating certain
allotments.[14]

Although the Dutch, Germans, British, and later the Australians
acquired limited areas of land for trade and plantations near white settlements, there was never a concerted attempt to take over native land
rights. The history of Papua-New Guinea reveals that soon after their
1886–87 occupation of Papua the British decided to prevent dispossession
of the natives. The Special Commissioner's report on New Guinea of
1886–87 states, for example, that "the land question is no doubt the
cardinal one upon which almost everything connected with British
policy will turn." [15] Within two years the "protectorate" administration,
as it called itself, published regulations clearly outlining basic rules
governing native-white relations. Whites were not permitted to purchase land or to have any interest in land obtained from native people,
who, in turn, were forbidden to sell to whites. Only the imperial government could negotiate purchases. This discreet policy, along with
regulations prohibiting the sale of arms and intoxicants to natives or
the exploitation of natives as laborers, helped to prevent native explosions
of outrage against occasional white abuses. An ordinance of 1888, for
example, prohibited "removal" of natives from their own district except
"for purposes of education or the advancement of religious teaching." [16]

When the British imperial government formally annexed Papua by a
proclamation read at Port Moresby in 1888, some decades after the
beginning of British penetration of the area, the Germans had already
established themselves in the area immediately to the north, and the
western part of the island had been annexed by the Dutch as Netherlands New Guinea. The native people on the coast and on neighboring
islands had been exposed earlier to Moslem and European slave recruiters
and to a variety of Christian missionaries, Catholic, Anglican, Lutheran,
and Methodist. A large number of the islanders had served as laborers

on Queensland or on German Samoa plantations and had brought back
bitter reports of exploitation. In 1883 more than thirty ships recruited
native labor on the shores of New Guinea.*

However, when whites angered headmen by cutting through into the
interior, the islanders fought back. Papuan ferocity in combat was not
easily forgotten. Native people of New Guinea had fought each other
for centuries, and whites seemed (at first) like strangers from another
remote village. Why not kill them? Missionaries suffered incredible hard-
ships. A British commentator in 1886 complained that the native response to "the message of Christ" was that of "a savage race of inhuman
murderers." [18] In German New Guinea, white control went no further
than the fringes of settlement. Newspaper files at the Library of the University of Papua-New Guinea show the remarkable slowness of the penetration of European government into the wilderness even after British-
Australian authority was extended over the eastern part of the island in
1914. As late as 1931 a Port Moresby newspaper writer complained
that "the remote tribes . . . have hardly been under [European]
influence at all." [19] Handicapped by the tropical climate, rugged terrain,
and the bewildering complexity of native languages, patrol officers
found they had another foe in sorcery, which was, as one visitor puts it,
"the very air of Papua." [20] When native officers took the field, they
sometimes brought sorcerers before white magistrates for such bizarre
offenses as "causing rain to fall at an inopportune time." In a land where
there are sometimes two hundred inches of rain a year, the rainmaker
could be a formidable villain. [21]

The remarkable perseverance of sorcery and customs such as "pay-
back" justice until today indicates how slow the white man's civilization
has been in penetrating New Guinea. The natives have never really been
conquered by Europeans. They have never been deprived of their lands
by an encompassing frontier of white settlement. There has been native
acculturation, but without dominance or assimilation. Like many of
the American Indians and Australian Aborigines, some New Guineans
have accepted the white man's money, his religion, his items of dress,
and other tangibles of civilization, but they have kept their old customs
and rituals. Like some of the Indians and Australian Aborigines, they
have resisted spiritual domination by the white man. The native people
in New Guinea, however, seem to have been moderately successful in
maintaining their old ways and a larger degree of self-determination
because they still control the ownership of the great mass of land. The
original British penetration of the area around the large native village
at Port Moresby in 1883 did not go far beyond the double rows of

---

* This labor trade, sometimes called "blackbirding," often differed little in practice
from slaving. [17]

native houses and rows of swaying coconut palms where an extensive trade in pottery, garden products, and sago palm flour flourished.[22]

Today, Port Moresby is much changed, but the center of the city today has a large native market. It is in this city that the native people have a strong voice in self-government through an elected legislative House of Assembly.[23]

The history of early native-white contacts on the frontiers of Papua-New Guinea, then, is different from that of North America or Australia largely because the American Indians and the Australian Aborigines were driven from their lands, especially in areas of rich soil where climate sustained lush vegetation. When the native peoples were over-run by advancing white frontiers, as in Australia and North America or on Pacific islands such as New Zealand, investigators have discerned three distinct periods in the acculturation of certain tribes or groups of Aborigines. In the first stage of white contact friendly relations often developed because of native hospitality and presents offered by the whites. As whites encroached upon native lands, early friendship soured and within decades native resentment grew. Finally, warfare resulted in defeat of the natives, their bewilderment, and a loss of respect for their own culture.[*]

In the second period (which may cover several decades or even a half century), the native people often developed a scorn for many of their own customs in an era of depopulation and despondence. This was usually a time when they suffered from the onslaught of smallpox, tuberculosis, venereal disease, and alcoholism. After portions of their lands and sacred places had been occupied by whites, they were often without leadership.

The final stage has been called an era of contra-acculturation by noted Australian anthropologist A. P. Elkin.[25] In this period the natives tended to revive their culture in modified form with renewed appreciation of their own arts, crafts, and rituals. If native societies reach this third stage, as the Seneca Indians did with the rise of the prophet Handsome Lake, they usually survive as a people with their own cultural heritage. Otherwise they perish or are assimilated by the whites.

The Senecas took nearly two hundred years to complete this cycle of acculturation. Like the Maoris of New Zealand, who experienced a similar cycle in their confrontations with whites, the Senecas were fierce warriors who had at first held Europeans at bay. The Senecas, in fact,

---

[*] A. P. Elkin has criticized Australian missionaries who had good intentions but nevertheless were destructive pioneers of white civilization in breaking down native cultures without making a replacement. Missions appear to have created a cycle of destruction that is typically uniform among both the Australian Aborigines and the California Indians causing the virtual disappearance of full-blood native people within fifty years.[24]

prospered after their initial contacts with the Dutch, French, and British in the seventeenth century. Despite the disappearance of fur-bearing animals from their country in western New York, they profited from their role as middlemen in the fur trade between the Anglo-Dutch traders at Albany and the Indians of the Great Lakes. They sustained themselves with a diet partly based upon maize, squash, beans, and nuts, and protected themselves by "the Great Binding Law" or Iroquois "Constitution" that bound the Senecas to the Five Nations confederacy.[26]

In their prime the Senecas, with their fellow-Iroquois, almost maintained a balance of power between France and England in the 1750s.[27] But when the eighteenth-century wars of the forest ended, they lost much of their land. After the American Revolution they were forced into a reservation life that has been called "slums in the wilderness." The 1799 vision of Handsome Lake, a reformed drunkard and Seneca chief, marked the beginning of a new era for his people, a renaissance in Iroquois technology, a rehabilitation of the Iroquois cultural health, and the beginning of the Longhouse or Handsome Lake Church.[28]

Not all Indian prophets had the success of Handsome Lake. A Delaware prophet of the 1750s had his message taken over by the Ottawa chief Pontiac, who unsuccessfully led northeastern tribes in one of the last great wars of the forest. These religious movements, when they appeared among the Plains tribes in the nineteenth century, have sometimes been called "cults of despair." Across the Pacific, full-blood and half caste Australian Aborigines attempted to revive the rites and beliefs of their ancestors.[29]

Most of the aboriginal peoples of North America and Australia have worked out a semiassimilation on their own as a result of living within a conquered territory, but a few have offered steadfast resistance. Such are the Navajos, who stem from the Athapascan Apaches and who borrowed weaving and planting of corn from the Pueblo tribes, and later silversmithing and sheepherding from the Spaniards. By skillfully adapting these to the arid land left them by the whites, they have increased in population and today are a proud, largely self-sustaining people who have strongly resisted assimilation into white society.[30]

The histories of the Senecas and the Navajos are exceptional in the overall story of Indian-white confrontations on America's frontiers. Many tribes were simply unable to withstand the powerful impact of white frontiers of exploration and settlement. In both Australia and America there was a disintegration of native societies directly adjacent to white settlements, especially in areas where there had been a native population density.

Rainfall variations and climatic conditions had a significant influence on the growth of native cultures and population densities. The highest concentration of native population in both North America and Australia was in areas of moderate rainfall and lush vegetation along the coasts and islands of the continents. The harvesting of maize by the eastern Indians and the gathering of acorns by the California Indians contributed to the density of Indian population.[31]

Among the coastal Indians and Aborigines of Australia, hunting and living areas were well defined by a few hundred miles. These were the areas quickly penetrated by land-hungry whites because of the fertility of the soil and the agreeable climatic conditions similar to those in Europe.

The advance of the white frontiers of settlement was generally conditioned by the same factors that originally determined native population patterns and the character of native hunting, harvesting, and food gathering areas. In great arid regions such as the Aranda Plain of central Australia, a tribal hunting and food gathering territory might extend to twenty-five thousand square miles.[32] Whites, concentrating on exploiting the most valuable, fertile lands, generally avoided arid "wastelands" except during periodic mining booms. Native people of the interior, scattered thinly throughout a wide desert zone were not quickly conquered or assimilated. In fact, a few remain as wild and free today as they were at the time of the discovery of Australia, when there were an estimated three hundred thousand Aborigines, about one individual for every ten square miles.[33]

North American Indian population densities are not so easy to set forth because of the controversies about prehistory populations. I am inclined to accept the most recent, detailed estimates by the anthropologist Henry F. Dobyns, who argues that the aboriginal Indian population in North America at the time of discovery was 9,800,000. What happened to all those Indians? In personal conversations with me and in his publications Dobyns convincingly argues that millions of Indians were killed off by waves of a virulent sixteenth- and seventeenth-century disease frontier resulting from first contacts with European explorers, fishermen, and settlers. Smallpox, typhus, the bubonic plague, influenza, measles, malaria, and yellow fever were among the most deadly diseases for the Indian. Smallpox was perhaps his worst killer because it sometimes returned a second and third time in new epidemics that all but exterminated whole Indian tribes. *

___

* By 1900 the Indian population in the U.S. had dwindled to some 250,000, but according to Dobyns' projections from 1970 census data, the American Indian population may be near 700,000 today. Dobyns' statistical study that has generated debate is "Estimating Aboriginal Indian Population, An Appraisal of Techniques with a New Hemisphere Estimate," *Current Anthropology*, 7 (1966):395–449. Dobyns' final conclusion is that "the New World was inhabited by approximately ninety million persons immediately prior to discovery." If Dobyns' estimates are reasonably

Despite the superior fighting qualities of the Indians (as compared to most other native peoples), and the large number of warriors who survived the onslaught of disease, the Indians were unable to hold off the advancing Anglo-American colonial frontier, and without the alliance of French fur-trading interests, it is doubtful that the British colonials could have been held at the Appalachians after 1750. In Australia a small white population of settlers and convict laborers in a few decades easily overran the best areas occupied by the Aborigines on the southeastern shore of Australia and the large island of Tasmania. Fragmentary evidence suggests that epidemic diseases decimated thousands of the Aborigines as they came into contact with Europeans.

New Guinea, by contrast, a land of rugged terrain and lush tropical vegetation supported a native population said to be as high as five hundred per square mile in some areas, a strong barrier to whites who at first barely held their own on the island's edges.[35] In the tropical New Guinea climate whites seemed at first to suffer more from epidemic diseases than the native people.

In many respects the Australian Aborigines who were so easily dispossessed and conquered resembled the California Indians. The latter tribesmen were easily forced into the Spanish mission system and later had to fend for themselves after the secularization of mission lands and the occupation of California by the advancing American frontier.[36] These Indians were particularly vulnerable to exploitation. Living by hunting, fishing, acorn and root gathering, they had no art except basketry, no elaborate dances, no cultivated gardens or fields of maize. They lived in rude huts in small communities, and, though often naked, had rush aprons or skin robes. To the Europeans, their open brush lands might appear useless, but they yielded rabbits, birds, and other animals for food.[37] Forest stands sheltered browsing deer. Each tract, well defined in area, was a source of food to be harvested. Many tribelets moved from area to area each season, fishing in winter and spring, hunting during summer and fall. Like the Aborigines of Australia they did not tame and breed animals except the dog. Acorns were a primary food, and there was a variety of other wild foods: fruits, berries, seeds, and fleshy root stalks.[38]

These tribelets resembled the subtribes of the Aborigines, small food gathering groups called *hordes*. Unlike the Indians, the Aborigines had no villages; they were seminomadic hunters, fishermen, and collectors. The men stalked the kangaroo or emu or speared fish. The women

accurate (and they are carefully evaluated by qualified experts who offer critiques in accompanying pages in the article), Europeans may well now be considered invaders of the New World lands since Europe, in the age of discovery, had about the same population as the Western Hemisphere.[34]

collected wild fruits, yams, nuts, seeds, grubs, stems, and roots.[39] Each Aboriginal horde's hunting and living territory was clearly defined and respected by other groups. Yet, as one Australian pioneer opined, such people are "strolling savages" without a particular home or habitation.[40]

Other Australian pioneers questioned this approach, which tended to justify the dispossession of nomadic people. In 1839 a sympathetic Australian defended the natives and their right to the land:

> In short every tribe has its own district & boundaries [and these] are well known to the natives generally; and within that district all of the wild animals are considered as the property of the tribe ranging on its whole extent [,] as the flocks of sheep and herds of cattle that have been introduced by adventurous Europeans, are held by European law & usage the property of the respective owners. In fact as the country is occupied chiefly for pastoral purposes the difference between the aboriginal and European ideas of property and the soil is more imaginary than real.[41]

The author of this interesting comparison between Aborigines and Australian settlers, probably a Presbyterian clergyman and pioneer anthropologist,[42] went on to compare the kangaroos and the wild cattle. "The only difference being," he argued, "that the former are not branded with a particular mark like the latter, & are somewhat wilder and more difficult to catch." Furthermore, his argument runs, "particular districts are not merely the property of particular tribes, particular sections of these districts are universally recognized by the natives as the property of individual members of the tribes." Finally his argument is expanded to point out a factor of great importance: "The infinity of the natives' names of places, all of which are descriptive & appropriate is of itself prima facie evidence of their having strong ideas of property and the soil." [43]

There were few other whites who wanted to consider property rights of the Aborigines in pioneer Australia. Most clergymen, and even the various "Protectors"* of the Aborigines, had a condescending, fatalistic attitude toward the natives.[44] To justify the occupation of Tasmanian lands, a prelude to complete extermination of the natives (after Lt. Governor George Arthur organized a man-hunt across the island in 1830), one clergyman wrote, "it cannot be supposed that providence would desire any country to the occupancy of a few savages who make no further use of it than wandering from place to place when at the same time millions of human beings in other places are crowded upon one another without means of subsisting." [45]

---

* Usually former clergymen appointed by the government to round up native tribes and move them to a new area.

The nomadic Aborigines of Australia were also held in low esteem by almost all whites from the time of early exploration and settlement. Most Europeans shared the opinion of the seventeenth-century explorer William Dampier who described their "great bottle noses, pretty full lips, and wide mouths." "Their Eye-Lids," he said, "are always half closed, to keep the Flies out of their Eyes." These people, he continued, "differ but little from Brutes" having no houses, domestic animals, fruits, or "skin garments." [46] Anthony Trollope's harsh judgment two centuries later is representative of the prevalent white attitude toward the natives: "Of the Australian black man we may certainly say that he has to go. That he should perish without unnecessary suffering should be the aim of all who are concerned in the matter." Trollope went so far as to write that should the "race" increase, it "would be a curse rather than a blessing." [47] He reached this decision despite the remarkable "proficiency" of the children in school. The blacks, he tells us confidently, "are being exterminated by the footsteps of the advancing race." [48]

In the early 1800s the eminent Anglican clergyman of Australia, the Rev. Samuel Marsden, held the blacks in such contempt that he felt they were not worth missionary effort for conversion. Indeed, their misery, he held, resulted from a special punishment inflicted upon them because of the sins of their ancestors in the Garden of Eden.[49] Marsden, though enthusiastic about missionary work among the Maoris in New Zealand, concluded that the Australian blacks ". . . have no Reflections —they have no attachments, and they have no wants." [50]

The comments of Marsden, Trollope, and Dampier on Aborigines span two centuries but illustrate the unchanging contempt for these native people. In the 1780s and early 1800s the Aborigines were quickly killed off in Tasmania and pushed inland from the southeastern shores of Australia. Although log forts were built at first, the farming and pastoral frontiers soon occupied fertile areas of the interior. Great pastoral estates, the squatters' "stations," as they were called, spread into the hinterlands, widely separated from each other because there was no real military threat from the natives.[51]

Governor Sir George Gipps divided Port Philip of southern Victoria into four districts in 1838. He provided a "Protector" for the Aborigines after a House of Commons committee reported on the pitiful condition of these vanishing people, degraded by liquor, disease, and poverty.

There is evidence that squatters put arsenic into flour for "black savages," as they were called, to retaliate after natives lighted dry grass with fire sticks, ate sheep or cattle, or occasionally attacked and killed isolated whites.[52] The attempt of the British government to halt violent, mass extermination of natives by hanging seven whites who had murdered blacks at a settlement near Myall Creek only made whites more

secretive about their punitive raids on the natives.[53] The last Tasmanian
woman died in 1888, completing the extinction of her race. As late as
the 1890s native police in Queensland were raiding other Aborigines in
punitive expeditions.[54] Reservations and missions eventually evolved
in the late nineteenth century but failed to stop the decline of Aboriginal
population. As one concerned modern Australian described the story:

> When our British forefathers took this land they termed it "waste and
> unoccupied": in reality they conquered the Aboriginal people by force
> of arms, disease, starvation and the destruction of Aboriginal social sys-
> tems. We are heirs to a colonial empire which was built largely on force
> and a deep abiding belief in the superiority of British people and their
> institutions.[55]

The author of this encapsulated history of native-white relations is a
scientist who has studied the same problem in several areas of the
world. He concludes that the Australian policy that first permitted
occasional extermination, and then, in the twentieth century, encouraged
assimilation is based on " 'racism' . . . the conscious or unconscious
belief in the basic superiority of individuals of European ancestry,
which entitles white peoples to a position of dominance and privilege."
He reasons that this attitude not only permitted, but encouraged exploitation of primitive peoples.* The policy of assimilation, he argues further,
has been based upon ignorance and disdain for the life-style of the
Aborigines with the objective of turning them into "dark-skinned Europeans." [56]

In America the wars of the forest culminated in Pontiac's War of Indian
Independence in 1763, and after the Indian conflicts of the American Revolution, there was never any real threat to white expansion into the interior.
The idea of a boundary line separating whites from Indians was rapidly accepted and finally became national policy after Calhoun proposed moving
the Indians west of the Mississippi into a permanent reserve.[57] That land
was penetrated by the massive westward trek of Americans in the
1840s. After fur traders, miners, military leaders, farmers, and rail-
roaders persuaded the government that Indians belonged on reservations,
the land was finally subdivided.

As in Australian history, the Indian was often portrayed as a nomadic
heathen with nasty habits whose beliefs and customs left him almost a
beast.[58] When Theodore Roosevelt wrote that "justice" was on the side

---

* Similar indictments of Europeans in their relations with Indians are in William
Christy MacLeod's fine volume, *The American Indian Frontier* (New York, 1928)
and William Brandon's eloquent *American Heritage Book of Indians* (New York,
1964), a paperback edition. See also Chapter 10 for a discussion of the views of these
and other writers.

of the pioneers because "this great continent could not have been kept as nothing but a game reserve for squalid savages," [59] he echoed the opinions of such eminent figures in American history as John Winthrop, John Adams, Lewis Cass, John C. Calhoun, and Thomas Hart Benton, who argued that a nomadic, primitive race must give way to a Christian agricultural civilized society. [60] Much of their justification rested upon biblical quotations to show that white people had prior rights to the land because they "used it according to the intentions of the creator." [61] The argument that nomadic hunters could be forced to alter their economy by an agricultural or pastoral people had first, though not systematically, been advanced by John Locke who saw a relationship between cultivation of the soil and ownership of property. [62]

Anthropologists such as the Australian A. P. Elkin and the American Nancy Lurie, have pointed out that the Europeans who dispossessed the natives had no appreciation or understanding of native culture, native occupational specialization, social control, or economic concepts. White ideas about native literacy, sexual mores, modesty, and Christian beliefs, and white pride in technological superiority (especially the use of guns) buttressed arrogant European assumptions of superiority. [63] There was no real understanding of the natives' preference for their own culture and way of life over the European system.

For example, the Reverend John Clayton of Virginia in 1687 described the occupation of the male Indians as "Exercise," when he meant hunting. Woman's work, the Reverend Clayton briefly noted, was gardening, mat weaving, pottery making, and cooking. [64] Clayton's comment here is typical of hundreds of untrained observers of native peoples who have given posterity an Indian stereotype: hardworking, industrious women and lazy, pleasure-loving men. This image also emerges from much of Australian and New Guinea literature on native-white contacts. Indeed, it is the impression this writer had when first visiting Australian Aboriginal reserves in central Australia, in Queensland, and in the Darwin area and primitive villages off the tributaries of the Sepik River in northern New Guinea. My initial observations led me to think that men in such villages in New Guinea spent almost all their time talking and smoking in their sacred club houses, tall, well-proportioned buildings constructed without nails, called the *haus tamberam*. Meanwhile the women, it appeared, worked almost as slaves, caring for children, grinding the pulp of sago palm, and straining it to obtain the white cheeselike starchy food that comprises their main diet. But I was mistaken and found that the main occupations of the men in the villages were varied, physically exhausting, and complex, resembling those of the male in an American Indian village. The man in the New Guinea village busied himself with hunting, house and canoe building, the making of artifacts, and participation in a variety of colorful civic and religious ceremonies, many of which concerned the governance and cultural life of the village at large.*

Similar cultural patterns are found among the Indians of colonial Virginia. According to Lurie, there were marked similarities between the Indians and the early colonists in male and female division of labor for building houses, hunting, housekeeping, child care, garment making, and cooking.[65] The similarities of both cultures in practice did not lead the white to adopt conciliatory attitudes in the inevitable disputes that arose over occupation of the land. Actually the stereotype of the Indian in early Virginia history was expanded. Not only was the Indian warrior a lazy, pleasure-loving rascal, he was also treacherous, unclean, a pagan savage who ate nasty food, and might turn upon one at any time despite his sly professions of friendship.[66] In American history there are occasional portrayals of Indian nobility and the natural advantages of native life in the forest by such writers as Roger Williams, and such soldiers and Indian superintendents as Robert Rogers and Sir William Johnson.[67] And in Australian history one finds that early European artists visiting Australian shores drew pictures of manly, athletic, handsome natives, akin to the noble warrior of early Iroquois and Cherokee portraits. However, later pictures of Australian Aborigines are almost caricatures of human beings, little black people with huge heads, ugly faces, and stick-like legs.[68] Both in Australia and in America the contemptuous stereotype seems to have submerged the favorable portrait in order to justify unjust policies.

Misconceptions about both American Indians and Australian Aborigines were based upon ignorance of native culture and its development after it confronted white society. There was little in the Europeans' technology that the early Indians in Viriginia could not evaluate in terms of their own experience. They had made copper ornaments. As soon as they became accustomed to the noisy blast of firing, they familiarized themselves with guns as well as other metal tools. Similarly, fabrics were a part of native technology, and Indians had already made their own nets, weirs, and garden tools. English ships, to Indians, were almost like big canoes. Indian religion was polytheistic, based upon a pantheon, thus a Christian deity could be added, just as the Indians could adopt the use of guns, needles, and scissors. What whites had difficulty in comprehending was that many of the seventeenth- and eighteenth-century Indians viewed

* During the summer of 1969, with a native missionary of the Seventh-Day Adventist Church who spoke fluent Pidgin English, I traveled by outboard motorboat some sixty miles beyond the Sepik River town of Ambunti to "Swago" village, an interior jungle settlement located on a small tributary of the Sepik. Here, with two other visiting whites, I lived for several days in one of the most primitive, isolated native villages in Papua-New Guinea.

Photographs on the following pages were taken by the author.

An Australian government sign restricting entrance to the Amoonguna Territorial Aboriginal Reserve near Alice Springs.

A typical "Swago" village house with elevated family living quarters connected by a retractable log staircase and a lower area for storage and shelter from the heat.

View of a native house in Lai, Papua-New Guinea.

Australian Aboriginal children at school on the The Amoonguna Territorial Reservation.

School children at a Lutheran mission near Mt. Hagen, Papua-New Guinea.

A highland man making matting on a native-owned coffee plantation near Mt. Hagen, Papua-New Guinea.

Native man making a dugout canoe in a "Swago" village on the Sepik River.

Native people at an outdoor market, Port Moresby, Papua-New Guinea.

A highland headman posing at Mt. Hagen, Papua New Guinea.

A Sepik River headman from the jungle interior.

Native artisan presenting an unusual artifact, one of the chief sources of trade for interior Sepik villages.

themselves as equal to the Europeans. Although they would borrow a
deity or a technological innovation, they were for the most part un-
impressed with the trappings of European civilization.[69] Even those
colonial sachems and chiefs who had been to England failed to urge
the white man's ways on their fellow tribesmen.[70]

Indians of the colonial period did not consider assimilation a solution
to the problem of dealing with the whites. This path would have meant
servitude, perhaps slavery, educational programs, adoption of their
children, and possibly intermarriage (which the Indians approved, but
the whites themselves generally rejected), all proposed by Europeans
at one time or another during the colonial era. The Indian solution was
to attempt to remove the source of anxiety by direct attack on the whites.
Pontiac's aim, in the great Indian war of 1763, was to drive the British
frontier back into the sea. Indians who fought the English during the
1760s were fighting for self-determination in a war for their independence. For generations they had governed themselves under a complex
pattern of self-government in their towns and villages. Their fortifications
and buildings for families, and civic and religious affairs were impressive
even to the colonists. Gardens, orchards, and grain fields attested to their
agricultural skill. Indians had no desire to abandon their own culture.
The Cherokee who made a last stand against the English in 1760 were
such expert farmers that William Wirt, their legal defender in the controversy over their later removal to the Far West in 1830, found whites
fearful that Indian skills would prevent Georgia's occupation of Cherokee
land. The Georgians insisted upon regarding the Cherokee as hunters
and argued that these Indians "had no right to alter their condition to
become husbandmen." [71] This remarkable argument denies, of course,
the right of the Cherokee to become farmers within the area of Georgian
territory. Georgia's argument was carried forward until "it was made
clear that, though the Georgian soil was destined to be tilled, it was
destined to be tilled by the white man and not the Indian." [72] Thus
white racist rationale was twisted to justify taking lands occupied by
the Cherokee, one of the great Indian people who had tilled the land
for centuries. Dispossession of nomadic Plains Indians or seizure of
lands occupied by the more primitive California Indians required no
such Byzantine reasoning. Whites could call upon John Locke and the
"Creator" to justify their land grabs.

At least the early record of Canada in dealing with the Indians is
notably better than that of the United States. The fur-trading tradition
of the Hudson's Bay Company and Montreal required that understanding
friendship with the Indians be maintained to exploit the resources of
the land. Thus in Canadian relations with the Indians, private or exclusive occupation of the land was not necessary or even desirable in most

areas.[73] In both the United States and Australia, however, the persistent clamor of the pioneers for land was the basic factor in the desire of frontier settlers to rid themselves of aboriginal people.[74]

In New Guinea, as we have seen, the indigenous people were never conquered and treated as captives. They were saved from the worst evils of white racism, dispossession, and possible decimation. Geography, climate, and the physical and cultural vitality of these and other native people all played a part in determining the fate of individual tribes in their confrontation with whites. Europeans, sometimes brutalized by their own cruelty toward aborigines, have yet to seek accommodation by understanding the land ethic of the native people.

Yet even today nations that are led by a powerful white citizenry are often unsympathetic to the aspirations of native peoples. For instance, the popularity of the Turner frontier theory in North America and in Australia is evidence of the historian's concern for the development of white civilization and the exploitation of the land. In this important interpretation of history, native peoples play only a minor role. Turner, in his influential essay of 1893, dismissed the Indian as "a consolidating agent" who helped to encourage intercolonial cooperation for border defense.[75] Turner also mentioned Indians in his lectures as if they were some kind of geographical obstacle to the westward movement of whites.[76] Australian and British writers who have applied the Turner theory to Australian history sometimes equate the Blue Mountains with the Blue Ridge range and the bushranger with the mountain man, but they are hard pressed to explain the Australian character as an outgrowth of occasional conflicts with the Aborigines, because the fighting was so completely one-sided.[77] A leading Australian historian tells us, without tongue in cheek, that the timid, peaceful Aborigines may have helped to bring a friendly, law-abiding society to Australia where whites usually settle their quarrels without violence.[78] Be that as it may, Indians and Australian Aborigines have surely influenced the course of history in America and Australia more than is often recognized, if only to give a special tincture to the society of the whites who occupied their lands.*

There are no writers at the University of Papua-New Guinea who see Turner's frontier theory applicable to that country, for New Guinea largely belongs to the indigenous people. The frontier theory, an interpretation of the development of white characteristics in a new setting,

---

* There is disagreement among Australian historians about the amount of violence in Aboriginal-white contact and the length of time during which it occurred. Usually the period of violence was short, a decade or two, because the Aborigines could not hold a sizable band of fighting men together for a long time. But in some parts of Queensland, fighting in a type of guerilla warfare, tribes fought off white invasion for a generation. I am indebted to Professor B. J. Dalton, James Cook University of North Queensland, for this information.

cannot be applied to a country where the natives still control the mass of their own land and outnumber the Europeans. It represents not only an interpretation of history but essentially an attitude that historians have taken toward the land, the native people, and the expansion of white civilization.

In New Guinea today, the Australian government has made a persistent effort to give the native people a share in social services and in self-government. This accords with the attitudes of fair-minded Australians whose influence has been so powerful that Australian public opinion now supports a policy of enlightened treatment for the Aborigines at home.* The fact that the New Guinea native people still retain most of their land and cultural heritage is probably due to luck, a fortunate combination of circumstances that enabled them to withstand the powerful forces behind the white frontiers of exploration, missionary activity, and trade. A different set of circumstances allowed European greed to prevail over a retreating native people on the frontiers of Australia and North America. If we condemn the white man in his relations with the Indians and Australian Aborigines, let us be aware that the example of history shows that the same kind of abominations can occur again if the stakes are high enough. A case in point is the policy of the United States in protecting oil, mineral, and land rights of the Alaskan Indians and Eskimos.

The history of native-white relations shows that the price of progress is sometimes bitter disillusionment on the part of the native people who become enmeshed in nativist movements because older values have been lost and newer ambitions are difficult to realize. In Australia, in New Guinea, and among the American Indians† such activist movements have a fundamental disagreement with a white man's culture that has taken so much and given so little.[80]

* All Aborigines of Australia are now citizens, and in theory possess the voting franchise and are eligible for a whole range of social service benefits. Dept. of Territories, *The Australian Aborigines* (Sydney, 1967), pp. 66–110. Yet I observed that Aboriginal people are still deprived of their civil rights as is the case of the reserve off the coast of Queensland at Townsville. Here the administration seems to be entirely under the Queensland police and an executive officer who was formerly a plantation manager. The Queensland state government still does not recognize Aboriginal land rights in the territory under its control, and recently a Northern Territory judge held that Aboriginal land rights were obliterated when Governor Arthur Philip announced British sovereignty at Sydney Cove in 1788. This interpretation supports the British decision that nullified John Batman's land purchase treaty with the Aborigines in 1835, apparently the only treaty of its kind ever made in Australia. C. M. H. Clark, ed., *Select Documents in Australian History, 1788–1850* (Sydney, 1969), pp. 90–93. In recent years the Australian Commonwealth government has passed over Aboriginal protests in opening their reserves to bauxite mining and has permitted copper mining in Bougainville, despite objections of native people.[79]

† See essays by D'Arcy McNickle and William C. Sturtevant and others in Eleanor B. Leacock and Nancy Lurie, eds., *North American Indians in Historical Perspective* (N.Y., 1971), pp. 29, 92ff.

Epilogue:
What We Owe
the Woodland Indians

The fatal confrontation between whites and Indians was not seen in colonial times as the clear-cut moral issue that it sometimes appears to us today. Along the white frontier, adjacent to the Indian country, there was an almost quiet desperation in the eager plowing up of virgin farmland. In the eighteenth century a great wave of settlement swept through the colonies, particularly in Pennsylvania where there was a peaceful invasion of the "Pennsylvania Dutch," or Germans. Close after these farmers came a flood of poverty-stricken Scotch-Irish who with axes and plows forced back the wall of forests. These restless, enterprising immigrants, led by a bevy of flinty Presbyterian ministers, inevitably collided with woodland Indians who fought to keep their ancestral lands in the interior valleys of the Susquehanna River and its tributaries.[1]

Indian savagery in counterattacking caused unspeakable suffering for the Scotch-Irish during the last phases of the French and Indian War. One estimate is that by the time of Pontiac's War of Indian Independence about two thousand whites had been killed or had vanished as prisoners of raiding parties. Further south, settlements of Virginia pioneers penetrated the beautiful green valleys beyond the Blue Ridge. At intervals these farmers hurriedly enclosed cabins with crude stockades for refuge in time of attack. The frontier Virginia farmers were, in many respects, the historical ancestors of *Leatherstocking*, woodsmen and marksmen schooled in Indian warfare. They fought skillfully with the aid of a Virginia militia while their families had temporary protection in scattered fortifications.

The numerous war parties that ravaged the borders carved a path

of total destruction. Whole districts were depopulated after having
suffered the ordeal of the tomahawk and the firebrand. The thinly
settled valleys of Appalachia were practically devoid of whites after
widespread Indian attacks left slaughtered cattle, blazing dwellings,
and the remains of clay-built chimneys. There were instances of torture,
and the bodies of men and women remained lashed to trees, where they
had died a fiery death.[2]

Certainly the moral question is not a simple one. It deserves our attention because throughout history men have had to decide between
what they believe is necessary or moral.[3] If we make conclusive moral
judgments on the confrontation between settlers and Indians, we may
find ourselves eclipsed by righteous indignation. Most of us share, I
think, a feeling of sympathy for the Indian because of the injustices he
has suffered at the hands of the white man. There is, however, a danger
of being locked into a sympathetic position so that one's indignation
spills over against all those who had anything to do with Indians. One
can rant equally against colonists, governments, missionaries, individual
officials, military men, pioneers, and even against the Indians themselves
who were corrupted by the whites who lavished gifts on them as a
bribe for lands.

Nowhere is found the irreducible truth. But we can make an assessment of the human wreckage left in the debris of violence if we
stand back from the details of the conflict. It is possible, even in analyz-
ing the dispossession of the Australian Aborigines, or the valiant stand
made by the native people of New Guinea against the Europeans, to
view it all as part of a complex historical process in the growth of nations. In the case of the long conflict between the whites and woodland
Indians, one may view the whole story as part of a process that trans-
formed provincial America into the modern American nation of today. If
we step away from the series of events to look at the trends behind them
we can more clearly see the historical processes at work.

For instance, it is not difficult to see that harsh living conditions, contact with Indians both in peace and war, and remoteness from central
authority, all influenced the emergence of a tough new American breed
among the white settlers. The early frontier (as well as later frontiers)
was a powerful force from the beginning in molding the national character and in promoting rugged democratic ideals. Frederick Jackson
Turner talked little about the Indians or blacks because his was primarily an interpretation of history that concerned itself with white
people.[4] If we look at the same historical process to understand what
happened to the Indian, we come to the inevitable conclusion that in
early American history we are watching the expansion of one people
into the territory occupied by another.

As the chapters in this book show us, native peoples have shared a somewhat common experience in their struggle to survive in a world once dominated by Euro-American civilization. The Indians who occupied the territories claimed by France in North America seem to have fared better than almost any other native people. Certainly the French were ingenious managers of Indians and adept at dominating their chiefs with special types of gifts. Essentially the history of New France tells us that Indian policy was channeled toward peaceful exploitation of the fur trade because the economy of Canada was never based primarily upon agriculture, but on fishing and trapping. Yet, despite their plan of coexistence with the Indians, the French could not prevent the involvement of Indians in a whole series of border wars with the English. It must nevertheless be said that the French, more than any other great European power seizing possession of a large area of North America, and despite the diffusion of trading goods,[5] minimized the displacement of Indians and left native society relatively undisturbed.

Spain, though not dealt with in the foregoing chapters, deserves mention here because her actions differed from those of the French and other European powers. Spanish policy seems to have been very much to the point: develop and exploit the surface of the land and send riches back home. Indians were to be conquered, converted, and used. As in the case of French policy, the Indian had a place in the overall imperial scheme of empire.[6]

British policy, however, as we have seen illustrated in various chapters of this book, allowed no particular place for the Indian. In a sense, he was a nonperson. British and colonials tended to use the Indians and then eliminate them or shove them aside. In the end, there was no real home left for the American Indian. Here again is a historical process that one can observe by scanning hundreds of treaties with exchanges of gifts, promises, and wampum belts.

It was the woodland Indians who had the longest series of contacts with Americans during the formative period of the American nation. They were the tribesmen who generously gave corn to the fledgling settlements at Jamestown and Plymouth. Indeed, they may have saved these small outposts of Europe from disappearing in the shadows of early American history that close off details of first attempts at colonization. Once the colonies were going concerns, the colonists saturated their public records with matters concerning the Indians. Their archives as we know them today are punctuated with accounts of treaties, wars, messages from headmen, chiefs and sachems, and news about enemy Indians who allowed themselves to become allies of the Spaniards or French. As the roots of settlement reached into the coastal river valleys, the fur traders, squatters, and land speculators fill records with controversies about their activities. Indians, Indians, Indians! The niagara of paperwork regarding them in the colonial archives leaves no doubt that there was continual border contact between whites and natives as the frontier moved westward. Although the daily contact was there, a kind of no-man's zone, or neutral belt of land, seems to have always separated Indian territory from the zigzagging white cutting edge of settlement. It was in this tinder box zone where, more often than not, friction so easily sparked a conflagration of violence.

One singular aspect of the tragic historical process that finally eliminated the woodland Indian's way of life was that he fought back. He had a stubborn resiliency. Furthermore, native Americans produced brilliant leadership that on occasion brought the whole westward movement to a halt. The Delaware Prophet and Pontiac are examples of Indian leaders who distinctly perceived the irreversible harm that Euro-American influences had had upon Indian societies. Pontiac became such an outstanding leader because he clearly diagnosed the permanent damage his people had suffered as they bore the brunt of fierce white competition for rich midwestern lands.[7]

Fortunately for the Indians who fought under Pontiac and collaborated with him, the colonials were handicapped in carrying out their traditional scorched-earth campaigns in which stored surpluses of food as well as orchards and grain fields were put to the torch.[8] Pontiac and his tribesmen on the woodland fringe were partly free from such danger because they were mobile and flexible in their attacks and because their old hunting ethos allowed them to live off the animal life of the forest. The great wilderness gave them shelter and provided a sanctuary when retreat became necessary. But even with this significant advantage, the Indians could not win. Pontiac and his confederates were doomed because in the long run all the advantages were on the side of the Anglo-Americans. What left its mark on the Indian as well as the white man was the very bitterness of the struggle. If, in the ordeal of Indian war, the whites developed stereotypes of a lowly savage, they also retained the image of a gallant warrior who fought for freedom to live his own life on his own land.

The retreat of the woodland tribes before the relentless advance of the Anglo-American agricultural frontier is dramatically illustrated in the fate of the Delawares. After the peace settlements of the Delaware War of 1756–57, these once loyal, peaceful allies of William Penn were promised lands of the Wyoming Valley in the upper Susquehanna. But friction developed during the latter part of the eighteenth century after squatters moved into the area.* In a bloody confrontation the Indians

* According to a treaty of 1778, the Continental government actually proposed statehood for the Delawares, but there was no attempt to gain approval of the thirteen

counterattacked, but were finally beaten off. The Delawares were later scattered in the removal, some as far west as Texas. Francis Parkman in 1846 saw remnants of a once proud people near Fort Leavenworth on the edge of the Great Plains where he described them as a dying tribe, "worn and dingy" but nevertheless dangerous scavengers who lived by preying on other tribes.[9]

What happened to the Iroquois league, composed of the most powerful of the woodland tribes? A large proportion of the league members finally decided to maintain their alliances and fight on the side of England during the Revolution. Their severe attacks on border outposts resulted in the Continental Congress sending a punitive military force under General John Sullivan that in 1779 left the main Iroquois towns, fields, and orchards in flames. Sullivan's thoroughness in making a wasteland of the Iroquois strongholds at last and forever broke their power.[*]

Joseph Brant, the daring Mohawk chief who led his people against the Americans, had been a student at Eleazar Wheelock's academy at Lebanon, Connecticut (where Indian and white youths were given Christian missionary training).[10] Combining the role of a British gentleman-officer and an Iroquois warrior-diplomat, Brant led his "civilized Indians" in hard-fought campaigns that won the respect of his enemies. Brant's forces, well aware of European ideas of superiority, waged a war that seldom violated European standards of conduct. Butcheries committed by some of his Indian allies, reminiscent of the seventeenth-century cruelties of the Iroquois, were the work of roving bands eager for plunder and revenge against the Americans.[11]

After the war Brant led a group of his people to Canada where they were given a reserve on the Grand River adjacent to the modern city of Brantford, Ontario. Since the 1783 treaty of peace after the Revolution made no provision for the Iroquois, those that remained in the new United States were at the mercy of a government that classified them as "dependent nations." Soon they were engulfed in a sea of white population that flooded all around them. The Cayugas were quickly swept before the tide, and the once proud Senecas, desperately clinging to a small portion of their lands, were victimized by a hungry specu-

states to admit an Indian state into the union. See William T. Hagan, *American Indians* (Chicago, 1961), 35.

[*] General George Washington's orders to Sullivan were specific: "the immediate objectives are the total destruction and devastation of their settlements. It will be essential to ruin their crops in the ground and prevent their planting more." Indeed, Sullivan's army in destroying beans and corn almost destroyed an aboriginal civilization. Washington's orders are quoted in Thomas R. Wessel, "Agriculture and Iroquois Hegemony in New York, 1610–1779," *The Maryland Historian*, 1 (1970):100. See also Barbara Graymont, *The Iroquois and the Revolution* (Syracuse, N.Y., 1972), pp. 192–222.

lative group known as the Ogden Land Company that used rum and promises to win its concessions. As Lewis H. Morgan wrote disgustedly, protesting the exploitation of the Iroquois, "It is no small crime against humanity to seize the fireside and property of a whole community, without an equivalent against their will; and then to drive them, beggared and outraged into a wild and inhospitable wilderness." [12]

Fortunately the Iroquois, after their revitalization movement under Handsome Lake, with some white help, were able to ward off those who would take all their land. The Iroquois emerged from a horticultural and hunting culture to an agricultural way of life by adding domestic animals and the plow about 1800. Individual Iroquois later took up skills as blacksmiths and as other types of artisans so that in the next generation they worked for wages at a number of trades. Then came schools and literacy. Though the Iroquois are "civilized" and some live in American cities, they still cannot be regarded as an urban people. Troubled by factionalism, a gradual erosion of their rich ceremonialism, and the loss of their lands, they survive in the midst of their conquerors. Modern Iroquois have at last capitulated to white civilization by joining it but mostly on their own terms. In the words of the prophesy of Deganawidah:

> Hail, my grandsires!
> . . . the Great League which you established has grown old . . .
> You have said that
> Sad will be the fate of those who come in later times.[13]

Today, still battling utility companies, they control minuscule reservations in New York.* Those Iroquois at the Brantford, Ontario reserve, which I visited not too long ago, eke out a living as workers in nearby white industries and carry on limited farming on their own land. Their Longhouse religion still prospers. Its main rivals are the Mormon and various Protestant religions. Some of the Iroquois, it will be recalled, were converted by Jesuit missionaries and later by Protestants, but Mormon proselytizing is recent. Despite the sullen tone of resentment among a few of the Indians (some of the Longhouse people I met objected to sending their children to the white man's schools), they still have a lively sense of humor, they still love their dances, their championship lacrosse teams, and their games. Those Wyandot-Hurons who have

---

* Lewis H. Morgan in his writings on the Iroquois, set forth the thesis that they would in time, through a natural law of progress, emerge in proper stages to attain the threshold of civilization. Modern Iroquois appear to fit "Morgan's scheme imperfectly." William N. Fenton, "The Iroquois Confederacy in the Twentieth Century: A Case Study of the Theory of Lewis H. Morgan in 'Ancient Society,'" *Ethnology*, 4 (July 1965):263.

Top: Iroquois Longhouse Church. *Bottom:* Six Nations' Council House. Photographed by the author at the Iroquois Reservation, Brantford, Ontario.

long intermarried with whites and now live in a reserve fronting the modern city of Quebec are by contrast almost indistinguishable from their fellow-French Canadians, although they treasure their Indian heritage and certain financial benefits accruing from it.

The removal of the Cherokees and other tribes of the Old South is surely one of the darkest chapters in American history. Today most of their descendants live in Arkansas and Oklahoma, sometimes as prosperous farmers and businessmen, although poverty haunts most of them as they, like the Iroquois, are slowly blended into the mainstream of American society. Still, the shock of being completely uprooted from their homes and removed during the age of Andrew Jackson will always be recalled by modern Cherokees, the Creeks, the Choctaws, and other descendants of Indian tribes. Jackson's implementation of the removal, with all the callousness of his military tactics in herding Cherokees and other Indians into compounds where they suffered from hunger and disease, will forever be associated with his name.[14] Actually and surprisingly, the demand for removal of the Indians was President Thomas Jefferson's most significant and all-important innovation in the development of federal policy toward the Indians. Jefferson's ideas implied a kind of "human cattle drive" in which the whites pushed the woodland Indians ahead of them as range after range of new states were created up to and beyond the Mississippi. The whites would advance "compactly," Jefferson wrote, "as we multiply." [15]

As Jefferson predicted, the Indians on the woodland fringe, belting the shores of the Mississippi, were also pushed westward during the 1830s. The swift retaliation against Blackhawk, who led Sauks and Foxes back across the Mississippi to their ancient homelands, brought about the so-called Blackhawk War. In his autobiography Blackhawk eloquently described his feeling for the land that had been lost by his people:

> My reason teaches me that that land cannot be sold. The Great Spirit gave it to his children to live upon, and cultivate, as far as is necessary for their subsistence, they have the right to the soil. . . . Nothing can be sold, but such things as can be carried away.[16]

       .   .   .   .

A distinguished British writer who has written several impressionistic books about America one told me at a London conference on Anglo-American history that "it was the red Indians who had such an influence on the American character." What he meant by this sweeping generalization, he later told me, was that Americans are somehow vastly different than Englishmen, other Europeans, and Australians. The extent of that difference, he maintained with eyes twinkling, was probably the result of historic relationships between Americans and those fierce red Indians!

Could it be that many of us are really part Indian and we don't know it? Maybe the woodland tribes didn't intermarry much with the colonists, but thousands of them and their western brethren have since intermarried with whites and thus contributed to what Margaret Mead calls the "mongrelization" of the American people. Such classifications of race under white, black, or anything else are really meaningless, she argues, because even white American European types, if they did not just get off an immigrant boat from a small village in Sweden, may have a grand mixture of bloodstreams including Indian.[17] If the genes of an Indian warrior are not actually transmitted, is it possible that his way of life provided a kind of root system for American culture that has nourished us so long that we could never completely disown it?

We may think that such an argument exaggerates the Indianism of Americans, but the influential psychoanalyst Carl Jung in 1928 believed he could detect an Indian side to the personality of his American patients.[18] To what extent this unique side of the American character is derived from our frontier heritage or from the Indian is a matter of speculation. Some influence, notwithstanding, should be attributed to the Indians.

Do we really owe the Indians anything? Have they made any singular contribution to our culture other than the mystical notion about husbanding the land and the natural environment? Is it possible that their special attitudes toward wildlife will ever help to cure our myopia about the natural balance that allows the wholesale poisoning and killing of eagles, bears, mountain lions (as well as a host of small animals) disrupting the food chain and affecting the populations of dependent species? Will we ever get away from the idea that the animals in their natural state are not there for "harvesting" by men?

Perhaps the study of Indians, particularly the woodland Indians, will show us the advantages of hunting with restraint and the importance of cultivating an attitude of respect toward animals and the ecological balance wheel. What seems likely, however, is that the white man will never understand Indian attitudes of reverence toward wildlife (just as he has not understood Indian attitudes toward the land). The bear could not be killed without an apology and ceremony of atonement by woodland Indians. How different the white man is. We permit extractive or exploitative industries to wipe out whole populations of animals without a whisper of protest. Lumber companies, for example, have concocted an ingenious kind of cyanide bomb, attractively baited but triggered to explode in any inquisitive bear's mouth if he is so foolish as to enter the domain of privately owned forests.[19] Even our own government foresters have developed a competitive system announcing proudly the number of porcupine killed in their "green" sheet newsletters.[20] Indeed, it almost seems as though our national policy is to exterminate any animal that is not deemed useful to business or bureaucrats. But, fortunately, there are voices of protest, and among those are representatives of the increasing population of the Indians themselves. As Vine Deloria, a Standing Rock Sioux, has phrased it:

> . . . American society could save itself by listening to tribal people. While this would take a radical reorientation of concepts and values, it would be well worth the effort. The land-use philosophy of Indians is so utterly simple that it seems stupid to repeat it: man must live with other forms of life and not destroy it. . . . Reorientation would mean that public interest, indeed the interest in the survival of humanity as a species, must take precedent over special economic interests. . . . All of this must change drastically so that the life cycle will be restored.[21]

Vine Deloria speaks for all Indians here in demanding that we listen to what he has to say. "Every time we have objected to the use of the land as a commodity, we have been told that progress is necessary to American life," he argues. "Now," he says, "the laugh is ours." The white man's "dollar-chasing civilization" is based on a conception of nature that Deloria classifies as "obscene . . . it is totally artificial and the very existence of the Astrodome with its artificial grass symbolizes better than words the world visualized by the non-Indian." For Deloria an even greater symbol of the white man's obscenity is the artificial world of the foul-smelling city.[22]

We may come to appreciate the importance of the Indian's message to us if we pay more attention to the outright gifts the Indian made that have contributed to the prosperous, unique side of our life. The woodland Indians, for example, gave us their accumulated wisdom stored in experience gained by generations of native people. The settlers in all the early colonies learned quickly about the value of Indian maize (corn), squash, and pumpkins and soon adopted native planting and cooking techniques. Tobacco, regarded by the Indians as sacred with particular medicinal properties, was of course also readily planted by the first pioneers, although we may now question how beneficial a gift it was.

Of all the bounties the Indian turned over to the first European settlers, corn was perhaps the most significant contribution to the colonial boom in prosperity.* Of those plants domesticated by the Indians corn is only less important than the potato (domesticated by Meso-American and South American Indians and brought to Europe by the Spaniards in the

---

* Edmund S. Morgan has documented the fact that as late as 1620–21, after fourteen years, the Jamestown settlers were still dependent upon the Indians for corn because of their need of "plentie of victuall everie daie." E. S. Morgan, "The First American Boom: Virginia 1618 to 1630," *William and Mary Quarterly*, 18 (April 1971):172–73.

1570s, eventually reaching Ireland about 1606) in feeding the modern world. Records for production of world staple crops in 1966 show that two from the Indians of the western hemisphere, maize and potatoes (531,641,000 metric tons), are second only to two crops from the Old World, wheat and rice (562,185,000 metric tons).[23] There is more maize raised in North America than on any other continent, though most of it is used for cattle and hog feed. In the American South, corn bread, Johnny cake, and hominy are longtime favorites, as is "corn on the cob" in the American Midwest.

Besides items of food, the settlers borrowed Indian buckskin clothing and Indian canoes (the Chippewa birch-bark style is still reflected in modern canoes), snowshoes, and toboggans. Iroquois-style moccasins survive today. Woodland Indians, as one would expect, were expert craftsmen who had long experience in developing techniques of bending wood without splitting it for basket handles, frames for snowshoes, canoe ribs, and lacrosse rackets. They surely and swiftly tempered the wood with hot water or, in the case of dugout canoes, with burning. The Iroquois were among the best Indian carpenters, easily felling huge trees and fashioning beams and boards from a wide variety of woods. White pioneers and explorers survived in the wilderness because they mastered Indian techniques of building shelters in the woods or making utensils, weapons, or tools fashioned from wood. For example, those whites who knew how to make a strong rope from the inner bark of the willow, or how to build a good canoe in the woods, had prepared themselves for living alone beyond the limits of civilization.[24]

Indian medical cures and skills, many of them lost with the passage of time, have also been of considerable value to those colonials who knew how to use them effectively. Indians had an almost astonishing number of remedies for toothaches, gangrene, ulcers, backaches, headaches, rheumatism, weak or sore eyes, and other complaints. They were also able to perform primitive surgery when required, and their medicine men, sometimes called conjurers, were not far behind modern physicians as successful practitioners in certain areas of psychiatry. The Iroquois, for example, were masters at interpreting the unconscious as it expressed itself in dreams.[25]

To be sure, some of the Indian drugs were given in huge doses (enough for a horse), and some are known to be overrated or valueless. For instance, Seneca snakeroot (*Polygala senega L.*) was valued as a cure for coughs and other ailments as well as for snakebites. Though not recommended for snakebites, the *Pharmacopeia of the United States of America* reports its use today as an expectorant, cough remedy, emetic, and a stimulant. A particular favorite among the woodland Indians was the hemlock tree (*Tusuga canadenssis Carr.*, and other species), which

Iroquois recapture the past. *Top:* Elm-bark longhouse. *Bottom:* Birch-bark tepee and canoe similar to those once made by Chippewas and other Great Lakes woodland tribes. Photographed by the author at the Tuscarora Reserve, Niagara, New York.

is thought to have been used by Indians to cure scurvy among Cartier's men in 1535. A seventeenth-century New England writer, John Josselyn, reported that the natives healed sores and swellings from the inner bark of a young hemlock. The Ojibwas are said to have pulverized the bark and swallowed it to treat diarrhea. The Pottawatomis combined it with other materials for "flux," or diarrhea, and made tea from its leaves to bring on perspiration as a cure for colds. Other woodland tribes used the bark to stop bleeding and to heal cuts; they made hot tea with the leaves for sweat baths. Even the twigs were boiled by the Penobscots to make a tea for curing colds.[26] About 170 drugs still listed in the *Pharmacopeia of the United States of America* and the *National Formulary* were known to the Indians north of Mexico.[27]

Robert Beverley, an able writer on the early Virginia aborigines, had a high opinion of the curative powers of Indian medicine. Their medicine men, he wrote, were "very knowing in the hidden qualities of Plants and other Natural things." In an age when whites were more apt to dodge a bath than take one, Beverley noted the Indians "take great delight in Sweating, and therefore in every Town they have a Sweating House."[28] Moreover, most Indians culminated the sweat bath with a dive into a nearby stream, a most exhilarating physical shock that some modern anthropologists believe is beneficial for nervous anxiety and illnesses that are today classified as psychosomatic.[29]

Very significant for modern Americans are Indian contributions to what we now call obstetrics, gynecology, and pediatrics. The Indians were more rational than their white neighbors about relieving pain, especially in connection with labor, which some whites felt was a form of punishment justified by the original sin. Europeans, not always aware that the Indians aided childbirth by herbal medicines, often expressed amazement at the ease with which Indian babies were born. Ezra Stiles, a president of Yale College, was almost typical in his comment on the subject when he wrote: "I have often been told that a pregnant Squaw will turn aside & deliver herself, & take up the Infant and wash it in a Brook and walk off."[30]

Since woodland Indian women suckled their babies for as long as three years, few Indian children, reared on mother's milk, were deformed because of malnutrition. Furthermore, the arrival of babies was spaced. John Lawson, writing in the eighteen century about Sioux woodland tribes on the Virginia frontier, argued that Indian women controlled family population because they had "an art to destroy Conception," an art that modern writers feel was based upon the use of certain herbs.[31]

What is especially fascinating about Indian medicine is that some techniques that were employed are difficult if not impossible for the modern physician to duplicate. For instance, the enthusiastic participation of a whole aboriginal tribe in a healing rite with religious overtones combines to bring about hidden psychotherapeutic results. How could we ever hope to do as well as the Indian community cheering a sick person on to recovery? Medical science may yet still benefit by study of medicine men's techniques.[32]

Indian medicine shows that the historical arrogance white Americans have had toward the Indian is misplaced. It is misplaced because clearly the Indians, in this case the woodland people, were, in certain areas of medical science, far in advance of their European contemporaries. Some of the colonial doctors, often part-time barbers or apothecaries, with standard remedies of calomel, bleeding, or opium, were superstitious rustics compared to the woodland Indian medicine man with his vast store of herbal medicines and his understanding of the psychological needs of his patients. Even Benjamin Rush, no doubt the leading physician of the Revolutionary generation, showed that he misunderstood Indian medicine when he said in 1774 that native remedies "were few in number," though he did acknowledge them to be "simple . . . full of strength." [33] Whatever merit the Indian health remedies had, Rush correctly concluded, they were no match for the white man's plagues of smallpox and venereal disease.[34]

If it has taken Americans centuries to come to appreciate the genius of Indian health remedies, a more self-evident contribution from the tribesmen is the thousands of Indian names and words that have enriched our vocabulary and made our language more euphonious. A number of our states have Indian names, and most place-names of those in the Midwest and East are taken from the woodland tribes: Milwaukee, Massachusetts, Illinois, Wisconsin, Michigan, Ontario, Mississippi, Alabama, Arkansas, Minnesota, and Pontiac are examples. One investigator identified some five thousand Indian place-names for New England alone! Many specific names and phrases reveal the historic influence of the woodland tribes and their brethren upon our society: "wampum," "wigwam," "mugwump," "caucus," "powwow," "papoose," "sachem," "tepee," "succotash," together with such phrases as "bury the hatchet," "take up the hatchet," "smoke the peacepipe," or "run the gauntlet." Scholars have found that Indians all over North America have modified our language, and that the number of Indian place-names in the one state of California numbers in the thousands.[35]

Woodland Indians (as well as all other Indians) have over the centuries left a clear imprint on American culture, not only in language but in literature and in art. Take, for example, the colorful cycles of pioneer history and Indian-white relations that form the backdrop of James Fenimore Cooper's *Leatherstocking Tales.* The hero, a scout as we see him in the *Deerslayer,* has the spunk to resist worldly temptations. In the *Path-*

finder he marries himself to the wilderness after giving up his girl to another. Natty Bumppo's portrait, as it unfolds in later novels, *The Last of the Mohicans, The Pathfinder, The Pioneers,* and *The Prairie* reveals a character whose virtues are those of the woodland Indians and pioneers. He is courageous, reverent of nature, and just. Above all, he is a woodsman-hunter par excellence. By contrast, the pride and disillusionment of the Delaware Chingachgook shows another dimension of Indian character. Similarly, Henry Wadsworth Longfellow, poetically inaccurate in historical details, nevertheless immortalizes a symbolic but heroic figure of woodland Indian traits in *Hiawatha*. Out of this kind of tradition the Indian guide, or scout, the frontier ranger, the plainsman, the mountain man, and finally the cowboy emerge as character types combining traits of both white and Indian to become heroes of American history, literature, and drama.

Seldom is the image more clearly drawn than in the true life depiction of Henry Chatillon, the modest, soft-spoken, tall plainsman, "a man of extraordinary strength and hardihood," [36] who appears as a leading figure in Francis Parkman's *Oregon Trail,* a personal narrative of 1846 that has had millions of readers. Parkman was expert in conjuring up heroic frontiersmen figures. In his famous *History,* the frontier ranger Robert Rogers is colored in such a way as to point up his virtues as a bold frontier ranger and to ignore charges of counterfeiting that have been leveled against him. Rogers and his rangers are also heroes of Kenneth Roberts' stirring historical novel, *Northwest Passage*. So popular was Rogers that his story appeared on the silver screen with actor Spencer Tracy in the lead. Why the intense interest in such a figure? Rogers, like Leatherstocking, is a figure who combined the best traits of Indians and whites, a daring woodsman who was a past master at Indian methods of survival in the wilderness. Rogers' Rangers, clad in green-colored buckskin, were so much a part of the forest in following Indian tactics of camouflage, ambush, and surprise, that they almost outdid the Indians themselves.

What Rogers did for America (at one time his journals were so widely printed in the colonial newspapers that he was better known than George Washington) was to publicize Indian methods of fighting in which, as Edmond Atkin once claimed, "Glory cannot be acquired without cunning & Stratagem." [37] Rogers taught British commanders, as he was taught by the Indians, how to fight in the woods. He respected the woodland warriors as British generals finally learned to respect them after Braddock's defeat in 1755—a British military disaster that showed the extreme importance of Indian tactics.

With spears, arrows, hatchets, bullets, and war paint, the woodland Indians held their own against the finest troops that Europe had. They went down in defeat not because they were beaten by better warriors or strategists, but because they could not fight off the overwhelming number of the enemy and his two-horned devil: disease and liquor. Even today we imitate him. There is no higher calling in the military service than that of the commando-ranger who gallantly fights our battles the world over. And no modern military ranger commander has better solved the problem of food logistics than the Iroquois raiding war chief whose men carried, in skin bags, parched maize flour, pulverized and mixed with dried berries and maple sugar. When water was added to this curious mixture, a handful could sustain a warrior for a day.[38] In fact, he could sustain himself for months at a time while laying siege to the mission settlements of Canada and almost bringing the entire colony to its knees.

Yet even the formidable Iroquois were known as peacemakers and peacekeepers. It is probable that the Five Nations, having established "the Great Peace" between themselves with their historic constitution before the time of the first invasion by the white man, might never have embarked upon the long Huron war had their country not been depleted of furs by the Dutch fur trade. The sachems, drawing on their long cane pipes over the Onondaga council fires, could easily argue that despite the border wars over beaver, they wished to extend the Great Peace to Canada. As their representatives told the Jesuits, "If you love, as you say you do, our souls, love our bodies also, and let us henceforth be but one nation." [39] They proposed peace with the French under the "Great Tree" many times. Fierce Iroquois warriors hidden behind a screen of forest looked on to see if their negotiators could ever persuade the French to share the Canadian beaver pelts so they could leave their deadly work undone. Finally the Iroquois war parties had to carve out their own destiny by physically opening up the Great Lakes beaver country. And in doing so, they all but killed off the Hurons. Later, during the Anglo-French wars of the eighteenth century, they preserved a policy of neutrality that was constantly attacked by the machinations of Sir William Johnson who plied their sachems and war chiefs with gaudy clothes, rum, and other gifts.

A recent book of documents dealing with the Indians of the southern colonial frontier, shows that the Cherokees and their allies were likewise eager to stop the bloody conflict in which they found themselves engulfed. We have in these documents, or "Indian Books," an expression of the Indian point of view as found in long communications from chiefs and headmen (and occasionally headwomen) among the Creeks, the Choctaws, the Catawbas, the Chickasaws, and the Cherokees. These lengthy "talks," as they were called, set forth a clear argument that the Indians, above all, wanted a fair deal in trade and honest clarity in treaty terms and negotiations. Time and again we find the Indians pleading that their "hearts is [sic] streight" and that they wanted "to live in Peace and Friendship." When the Cherokees in 1759 declared to the English, "we desire to keep free from any Disturbance or Blood," they spoke for most of the woodland tribes of the Old South.⁴⁰ Is it possible that the American penchant for peace has an anchor chain deep in the historical past that ties us to the Indian?

It has often been said that the woodland people were so generous with their food and other possessions that when one starved, they all starved. Much of the present-giving took place because the Indians shared whatever they had with each other, with white colonists, and even with prisoners taken in war. Is it possible that the American proclivity for sharing, for philanthropy, for generous gifts, is related to the magnificent tradition of generosity among the woodland tribes? There was even a joyful element of play and ceremony around native giving.⁴¹ If Americans have similar feelings about sharing today, who is to say that the Indian was not at least partly responsible in making that subtle contribution to the American character? Indeed, gift-giving seems to have had profound implications for the American way of life.⁴²

The fact that the colonial Indians refused to be drafted into slavery by their white conquerors, is the subject of much comment among the colonists. Except for some individual cases, Indians, praised for their fine physiques and intelligence by leading colonials, nevertheless resisted all colonial efforts to convert them into a labor force of field hands. True, there were sporadic efforts among the Carolinians to force native tribesmen removed from Apalachee Spanish missions into slavery, but even this effort was doomed to failure.

Why would the average woodland tribesman choose death as an alternate to being the white man's slave? Freedom was the Indian's element: freedom of movement, freedom of speech, freedom of action, freedom to do what he pleased to do whenever he chose to do it. Travelers among the Indians often spoke about mild parental discipline used to control Indian children who seemingly were only swayed by affectionate counseling. In the tribal relationships existing between adults, few leaders had any real semblance of authority. Sachems, subchiefs (or sagamores) medicine men, and conjurers had little personal dominance over their fellow-tribesmen except as they exerted it by sheer force of leadership and personality. White colonials, eager to identify Indian leaders who would authorize bargaining over lands and trade looked in vain for actual Indian "kings." Whites, however, did contribute to the prestige of particular chiefs by rewarding favored "treaty chiefs" with special medals, gorgets, and elaborate gifts, and this practice may well have had an influence in strengthening the posture of Indian leaders such as Teedyuscung of the Delawares and Pontiac in the late colonial period. Yet neither of these chiefs were despotic leaders who commanded underling tribesmen. In fact it is difficult, if not impossible, to find in the woodland Indian languages words that convey the full meaning of despotism, authoritarianism, or dictatorship, so far removed are such concepts from Indian thinking.

The religion of the woodland Indians, varying in rites and details from tribe to tribe in various linguistic families, was not forced upon those Indians who were adopted, nor did particular medicine men, conjurers, or prophets, attempt to stamp out religious beliefs of neighboring tribes. Of course the Indians did not attempt to force their beliefs on the white man. Despite the white man's arrogant assumption that his was the only religion, the Indian from the beginning believed in freedom of choice, a concept that eventually became one of the highly treasured "freedoms" of Americans today. Freedom of choice, of course, also meant freedom of religion. American ideals, in a host of different kinds of freedom, may not be entirely of European origin. Is it possible that we owe the Indian more of our heritage of freedom than we have heretofore acknowledged? Nowhere do we see Indian ideals more admired than among America's young people today. Indian lifestyles involving movement from place to place, communal democracy, reverence for nature, and dialogues on peace, are imitated everywhere by a new generation of Americans. Modern, youthful, concerned citizens have gone a long way in attempting to teach their elders about values of the old Indian way of life. Such instruction, as one would expect, has not always been received with gratitude. Nor have the Indians always admired their long-haired imitators, even when they talk about ecology. But at least there is talk and debate.

Academics still argue about whether the Indian confederations of colonial times had a tangible influence upon the fathers of the Constitution. The case for the Indians is not so far-fetched as one might think. Franklin, an admirer of the Iroquois league, had good reason to know its virtues for he had been an Indian commissioner at treaties, and at the Albany Conference of 1754 he and his fellow delegates had a whole series of scoldings from Old Hendrick of the Mohawks who praised the league and told them their disorganized, womanlike method of defense against the French was to be deplored.[43] It is known that other framers of the Constitution had knowledge of Indian confederation systems and the ideals of Indian democracy. Moreover, these statesmen were avid readers of the French *philosophes* whose writings were partly influenced by descriptions of North American Indians set forth in the writings of French Jesuit missionaries. The noble savage idea, hammered into the writings of Michel de Montaigne and later French writers, including Rousseau, was embellished with the ideas of natural rights, of the equal-

Lapowinsa, a Delaware chief, participated in negotiations resulting in the notorious "Walking Purchase" of 1737 in which . . . "for large Quantities of Goods . . ." the chiefs bargained away a large parcel of Delaware River land. Generations of Indians later charged whites with duplicity and questioned Pennsylvania's title. "Indian Deed for lands on the Delaware, 1737," Samuel Hazard, ed., *Pennsylvania Archives*, First Series (Philadelphia: 1852–56), 1:541–43. This painting by Gustavius Hesselius (1734) was given to the Historical Society of Pennsylvania in 1834 by Granville Penn, grandson of William Penn; it is published here, courtesy of the society.

ity of man, and with democratic tribal traditions of North American Indians.[44] Because the great Inca and Aztec regimes were swept so quickly out of existence by invading Spaniards and their societies were shrouded in mystery, the politics of the Iroquois league and other confederations among the woodland tribes became so significant to European observers.

As the French writers were fascinated by the Six Nations Iroquois, so Lewis H. Morgan, the father of American anthropology, a century later was also attracted to them. Their grand council, he said, was "the germ of modern parliament, congress, and legislature."[45] William Fenton, the modern Iroquois scholar, went so far as to argue that the confederacy was a germ of the modern state that united tribes with adjacent territories and a common language for defense under a single political system.[46]

With all their contributions and achievements in government, politics, language, medicine, agriculture, and ecology, it is nevertheless true that the woodland tribes, as well as most other Indians of North America, were concerned with the daily business of *living*,[47] whereas the whites, especially those settlers of the British North American colonies, were largely concerned with *getting*. The Puritan ethic, so clearly spelled out in the writings of Benjamin Franklin and Thomas Jefferson as well as the Puritans themselves, stressed thrift and industry. By contrast, there was something almost sacrilegious about the lifestyle of the woodland Indians. From John Smith to Thomas Jefferson we find a whole series of Anglo-American writers who want to put these "indolent" natives to work tilling fields. The Indian, exposed to the marketplace economy and technology of the white man, could no longer continue his way of simply living. He had to be more concerned with getting in order to survive. The resulting degradation of the woodland tribes and finally the preaching of Handsome Lake's *gaiwiyoh*, "the good news," helped some of them to rise out of their demoralized state, as did the Iroquois. Other tribes had their leaders, too, such as the great Sequoia among the Cherokees, and John Ross, the Cherokee leader who helped his people to live after removal to a harsh new land.

Unfortunately whites still tend to associate "Indian" with dances, feathers, "arts and crafts," and bad whiskey. Such associations, part of the historic stereotype of the Indian, have prevented us from appreciating the tremendous potentialities of Indian wisdom. It is even feasible that Indian tribalism could have a successful impact upon the modern world in the sense that it gives self-respect to the individual as well as the group. Furthermore, it is closely identified with the land because tribal groups have been rooted in specific land areas for thousands of years. It may be that the way of life of the Indian (as well as other "savage" tribes, in the language of older evolutionism), with its web of significance in which man obtains an acceptable relationship with the world at large, the universe, and the ecology surrounding him, may have true meaning for America today.

In the tribe, competition and individual initiative are subordinated to the idea of the harmonious whole. Thus people are able to adjust more easily to each other.[48] The tribal way of judging a man by what he accomplishes is also significant because of its simplicity. If a man's I.Q. is not computed, his potential becomes an object of possible praise, and if his wealth is not hoarded to be compared with that of others, he may be judged simply by what he does. Even more important, the tribal man never is, or was, historically so conservative and unchangeable that he did not adapt to new situations. Certainly the story of humanity would have been vastly different if mankind had not adjusted to necessary changes.[49] Can modern America actually benefit from Indian tribalism as part of the American heritage? Is it possible that our huge bureaucracies and polluted, overgrown cities—unmanageable and seemingly uncontrollable—are our only alternatives?

From the historical perspective, we can see flaws in the tribal way of life that made it difficult, at times almost impossible, for the Indians to seek the best accommodation with whites. Perhaps the greatest weakness of Indian society was its own hubris. The singleminded pride of the woodland tribes may have proved to be their undoing because it tended to make them more susceptible to easy conquest by the white man's entrepreneurial economy, which, in turn, greatly weakened Indian self-sufficiency. It is undoubtedly true that the woodland tribes at first had no real concept of what an "Indian" actually was. For instance, to a Choctaw, whites, Chickasaws, or Catawbas, though human beings, were regarded as three types of outsiders. It was not until the eighteenth century that the woodland tribes of the interior began to realize that they had something in common with each other as opposed to the Europeans. We see this in speeches at Indian treaties when chiefs comment on Indian lifestyles and loss of hunting territories.[50] By the time Pontiac appeared upon the scene many woodland tribes were willing to cooperate to ally themselves and pit their strength against this white outsider whose presence blighted their manner of living.

Through study and renewed appreciation of Indian history we may, perhaps, recapture and preserve much of that rich Indian inheritance for all Americans. Is it not possible that the Indian wisdom of our heritage may help us to turn more and more toward nature, to succor the richness of the earth and the spirit of mankind?

We know that the Judeo-Christian traditions of man's dominion over nature have been at least partly responsible for the spread of the white American style of technology. Somehow we seem to have built a value structure out of this heritage which supports technological advance in the belief that this kind of progress coincides with God's will.[51] The monotheism of early Christianity "liberated" mankind from the religions of antiquity which tended to view a universe with all things having a certain spiritual essence. Although Christianity had its spirits, none were contained in animals, plants, or sacred rocks or waterfalls. As a distinguished historian of science has argued, "To a Christian a tree can be no more than a physical fact. The whole concept of the sacred grove is alien to Christianity and to the ethos of the West." [52] Despite such an interpretation, it is hard to prove by close examination of Genesis, for example, that there is biblical justification for the ravaging of the earth, that we have divine license to dig, chop, crush, and kill as we wish. And the teachings of St. Francis set forth the idea that it is the duty of all men to show respect for animal life, domestic animals and birds, as well as wildlife. Americans seem, however, to have persuaded themselves that in exploitation for immediate wealth they can do as they please without accounting for their actions. Now, perhaps, we may reconsider difficult questions that the American Indian heritage poses for us: should we have a concern, even a moral obligation, for a bear, a grove of redwoods, a sacred lake, or even a wolf, a coyote, or an alligator? From a practical standpoint, should we not regard the land as a depreciable resource in only finite supply? [53] If we are able to reassess our values, surely the American Indian concept of Mother Earth* will help us on the way to comprehending ecological righteousness in the modern world.[54]

---

*One of the leading practitioners of "upstreaming," the reevaluation of traditional historical sources on Indians with modern ethnological data, was the late Robert F. Heizer, who did extensive work in what he called "ecological types of Indian cultures." In his *Natural World of the California Indians*, written with Albert B. Elsasser (Berkeley, Calif., 1980), pp. 57–81, Heizer spells out his conclusions, based upon detailed analysis of California Indians, religion, subsistence patterns, and general life-styles. On p. 220 he makes this assessment:

> In the native peoples of California, who lived here for so very long before the whites appeared, we can see the true ecological man—people who were truly part of the land and the water and the mountains and valleys in which they lived. The environmentalists and conservationists of today feel a kinship with the Indians in their respect for nature, a feeling which at times rises to that of the sanctity of the natural world.

APPENDIX 1

Chronological Highlights of Early
Indian-White Relations

c. 1497–1600	Explorers and fishermen contact North America; probable spread of epidemic diseases among woodland tribes
c. 1559–70	Beginnings of the league of the Iroquois
c. 1584	John White at Roanoke Island; water color paintings of southern woodland tribes; possible spread of epidemic diseases among coastal tribes from contact with Roanoke colony
1603–35	Champlain's voyages; early contacts with Canadian tribes
1607	Founding of Jamestown; early contacts with Powhatan confederacy
1609	Henry Hudson contacts Mahicans (river Indians)
	John Smith's capture by Powhatan giving rise to the story of Pocahontas intercession
1613	Marriage of Pocahontas and John Rolfe
1620	Massasoit, friendly Wampanoag chief, assists Pilgrim settlers
1022	Opechancanough's first uprising in Virginia
1631	Roger Williams contends that royal charter for Massachusetts illegally expropriated land rights of Indians
1636	Roger Williams founds colony at Providence and adopts humane policy toward Indians
1637	Pequot War in New England; Roger Williams prevents alliance of New England tribes against New England colonies
c. 1640	Beaver and otter nearly exterminated in Iroquois country
1642–53	Iroquois "beaver war" eliminates Hurons as rivals
1643	Roger Williams publishes A Key to the Language of America . . . of . . . the Natives
1644	Opechancanough's second uprising in Virginia

175

1644–52	John Eliot's conversion of New England Indians at Newton and Natick
1662	Philip, son of Massasoit, becomes Wampanoag chief
1671	Plymouth colony asks Philip to give up arms; he makes token delivery
1675	Philip accused of conspiracy against colonists; after he attacks Swansea (June), he is joined by other tribes
1675	(July) Pettaquamscut Treaty negotiated with Narragansetts
1676	End of King Philip's War; Philip betrayed and killed, his wife and nine-year-old son sold into West Indian slavery
	Bacon's Rebellion, partly the result of failure of Indian fur trade policies, results in defeat of Susquehannas and other tribes, a defeat for Virginia coastal tribes
1682	William Penn's treaty with the Delewares, Susquehannas, and other tribes, the beginning of a long period of friendly relations with Indians under Quaker leadership; the presentation of "Penn" wampum belts by the Indians
1689–97	King William's War
1701	John Lawson visits Indians on the Carolina frontier
1702–13	Queen Anne's War
1705	Robert Beverley's *The History and Present State of Virginia* published
1711–12	Tuscarora War on southern frontier; about 1722 remnants of Tuscarora move north to join Iroquois as sixth nation
1715–28	Yamasee War in South Carolina destroys power of Carolina coastal Indians
1717	Governor Alexander Spotswood of Virginia writes to Board of Trade on absence of intermarriage between colonists and Indians
1721	Board of Trade recommends to crown that intermarriage between colonists and Indians be encouraged
1727	Cadwallader Colden's *History of the Five Indian Nations* published
1728	William Byrd surveys boundary line between Virginia and North Carolina; writes *History of the Dividing Line* in late 1730s
1737	Walking Purchase of 1737 negotiated, in which Pennsylvania Indians are cheated by the Proprietary government
1744–48	King George's War
1748	Treaty of Aix-la-Chapelle
1749	Céleron de Blainville asserts French claim to Ohio country
1752	French massacre of Miami Indians at Pickawillany; British treaty with Indians at Logstown
1754	Albany Conference
1754–63	French and Indian War
1755	Edmond Atkin writes Indian report for Board of Trade; superintendency system created; William Johnson appointed north-

ern superintendent (June) William Johnson persuades Iroquois to break neutrality and join him in campaign against the French (July 4) Defeat of General Edward Braddock by French and Indians

1756   Edmond Atkin appointed southern Indian superintendent; Quakers lose political control of Pennsylvania Indian policy in provincial assembly; gift-giving policy curtailed

1756–57   Delaware War envelopes Pennsylvania frontier

1757   Surrender of Fort William Henry and massacre of prisoners by Indian allies of Montcalm

1759–60   Cherokee War on the Carolina frontier

1760   British conquest of Canada by Sir Jeffery Amherst and allied forces

1761   Proclamation prohibiting settlement on Appalachian frontier by Colonel Henry Bouquet

1761–62   Senecas plan major attack on British along whole western frontier, probably under the leadership of Kaiaghshota

1762   Onondaga Prophet preaches on message of the Great Spirit

1762–63   Delaware Prophet, sometimes called Neolin, preaches message of the Master of Life

1763   (February 10) Treaty of Paris ends colonial phase of Seven Years' War

(May) Colonel Henry Bouquet urges convening of large congress with northern tribes to discuss Indian grievances; Sir Jeffery Amherst declines to hold conference

(May–June) Sir Jeffery Amherst begins policy of "oeconomy" by curtailing Indian presents and setting up new trade regulations at frontier posts

(c. May–June) Pontiac sends war belts to urge attack on frontier posts; (May) Pontiac's surprise attack on Detroit betrayed

(June) Pontiac's War of Indian Independence begins; capture of frontier forts and siege at Fort Detroit and Fort Pitt take place

(June) Amherst asks that blankets be used to spread smallpox among Indians surrounding Fort Pitt; (July) Amherst urges use of "English dogs" to hunt Indians

(June) John Stuart, southern Indian superintendent, issues invitations for Congress of Augusta on Georgia frontier

(October 7) Royal Proclamation of 1763 establishes Indian sanctuary and restricts westward movement of colonists

(November) Distribution of gifts to southern Indians at congress of Augusta by John Stuart

(December) Paxton Riots on Pennsylvania frontier, massacre of Conestoga mission Indians

1764   British reorganize Indian administration and plan for extension

	of frontier Indian boundary lines according to the "Plan of 1764"
	(October 31) Pontiac signs capitulation with British
1766	Pontiac meets with British and promises to recall war belts
1768	Fort Stanwix Treaty results in extension of a northern Indian boundary line to meet southern Indian boundary line
1769	Assassination of Pontiac
1773	Completion of extension of the southern Indian boundary line
1775–83	The American Revolution
1779	General John Sullivan's expedition against the Iroquois
1783	The Treaty of Paris
1799	Vision of Handsome Lake, Seneca chief, and beginnings of Longhouse or Handsome Lake Church
1830	(May 28, 1830) Federal government legislation establishing western "Indian territory" for removal of eastern woodland tribes

Chronological Highlights of Early Native-White
Contacts in Australia and
Papua-New Guinea
(CHAPTER 11)

c. 1500–1600	Portuguese and Spanish explorers touch shores of New Guinea and Australia
c. 1600–50	Dutch visit shores of New Guinea and Australia
1688	William Dampier, English adventurer, records observations of Australian Aborigines; visits northern coast of New Guinea now known as Dampier Strait
1770	(April) Captain James Cook visits Botany Bay, near Sydney and sails in New Guinea waters
1778	(January) Britain begins convict settlement in Australia at Sydney Cove
1830	Lt. Governor George Arthur organizes manhunt to capture or eliminate Tasmanian Aborigines in sweep across the island
1835–36	John Batman's land purchase treaty with Aborigines of 1835, nullified by the British government (1836)
1838	"Protectorate" system established on Australian mainland to control Aboriginal population
	Myall Creek Massacre of Aborigines takes place in Australia; accusations of use of poisoned flour to kill off Aborigines
c. 1840–95	European Protestant and Roman Catholic missions in New Guinea; Protestant missionaries in Australia among Aborigines
1884	British claim Papua with headquarters near native village at Port Moresby (southeastern New Guinea)
	Germany claims northeastern New Guinea
1886–87	British establish "protectorate" over Papua
1888	British ordinance prohibits "removal" of native people for forced labor in Papua
	Death of last surviving Tasmanian Aboriginal woman

c. 1890–1930   Continuing punitive raids on Aborigines of Queensland by white and native police
1901–   Australian legislation discriminates against Aborigines and other non-white people
1914   Australia occupies German New Guinea
1919   Australia given mandate to administer German New Guinea
1948   Australian Aborigines are declared citizens by the Nationality and Citizenship Act
1949   New Guinea Act provides for union of Papua and New Guinea to be administered under Australian government
1964   Elections for House of Assembly for Papua-New Guinea native people
1967   Removal of Australian discrimination legislation against Aborigines
1975   Papua New Guinea achieves political independence and joins the British Commonwealth
1976   Papua New Guinea joins the United Nations

PROLOGUE

1. Bernard A. DeVoto, *The Course of Empire* (Boston, 1952), p. xxxiii. For the viewpoint of a modern Indian writer on the sins of anthropologists, see Vine Deloria, *Custer Died for Your Sins, An Indian Manifesto* (New York, 1969), pp. 78–124.

2. DeVoto, p. xxxiii.

3. Frederick B. Tolles, "Nonviolent Contact: The Quakers and the Indians," *Proceedings of the American Philosophical Society,* vol. 107, no. 2 (Philadelphia, April 15, 1963).

4. Roy Harvey Pearce, *The Savages of America, A Study of the Indian and the Idea of Civilization,* rev. ed. (Baltimore, 1965), pp. 4–6, 48–49. In spite of such attitudes toward savagery, the first seventeenth-century settlers generally agreed that the Indians were exceptionally hospitable and helpful to those in distress. See Chapter 9. Alden Vaughan in *The New England Frontier, Puritans and Indians, 1620–1675* (Boston, 1965), pp. 42–43, argues that the early Puritans considered Indians "as pleasant as any people they encountered."

5. Winthrop Jordan, *White Over Black, American Attitudes Toward the Negro, 1550–1812* (Chapel Hill, N.C., 1968), pp. viii–xi, 3–43.

6. *Ibid.,* pp. 89–90, 276–77. Carl Degler sets forth the convincing argument that racial prejudice is rooted in visible physical differences that "easily translate themselves into intellectual and moral distinctions." Carl Degler, *Neither Black Nor White, Slavery and Race Relations in Brazil and the United States* (New York, 1971), pp. 288–89.

7. Peter Loewenberg, "The Psychology of Racism," in Gary B. Nash and Richard Weiss, eds., *The Great Fear, Race in the Mind of America* (New York, 1970), pp. 186–201.

8. See the discussion of stereotypes in Chapter 10.

9. Loewenberg, p. 191.

10. See N. Scott Momaday's penetrating essay expressing a modern Indian

point of view, "The Morality of Indian Hating," *Ramparts* 3 (Summer 1964): 29–40.

11. Wendell H. Oswalt, *This Land Was Theirs, A Study of the North American Indian* (New York, 1966), pp. 187–95; Robert E. and Pat Ritzenthaler, *The Woodland Indians of the Western Great Lakes* (Garden City, N.Y., 1970), pp. 1–32, 55–85; Harold E. Driver, *Indians of North America*, 2d ed., rev. (Chicago, 1969), pp. 66–104.

12. Oswalt, pp. 414–15.

13. Ritzenthaler, p. 67.

14. James A. Tuck, "The Iroquois Confederacy," *Scientific American* (February 1971): 32–42.

15. Conrad E. Heidenreich, "The Geography of Huronia in the First Half of the Seventeenth Century" (Ph.D. diss. McMaster University, 1970), pp. 267–73.

16. For an account of the eighteenth-century European traveler's reaction to the Indian and his conflict with white society, see Curtis B. Solberg, "As Others Saw Us: Travelers in America During the Age of the American Revolution" (Ph.D. diss. University of California, Santa Barbara, 1968), pp. 88–111.

17. W. R. Jacobs, ed., *The Appalachian Indian Frontier* (Lincoln, Neb., 1967), pp. 3–74.

18. Allan W. Trelease, "The Iroquois and the Western Fur Trade: A Problem of Interpretation," *The Mississippi Valley Historical Review* 49 (June 1962):32–51, revises interpretations set forth in George T. Hunt, *The Wars of the Iroquois, A Study in Intertribal Relations* (Madison, Wis., 1967), pp. 34–35n. Hunt's views are echoed in Robert Goldstein, *French-Iroquois Diplomatic and Military Relations, 1609–1701* (The Hague, 1969), pp. 198–204, and in W. J. Eccles, *The Canadian Frontier 1534–1760* (New York, 1969), pp. 32, 53.

19. Trelease, p. 43; Hunt, p. 33.

20. See Trelease, pp. 45, 48, for citations on the above quotations.

21. Kiliaen van Rensselaer to Willhelm Kieft, director of New Netherland, May 29, 1640. Quoted in Hunt, p. 34.

22. *Ibid.*, p. 33.

23. The late Frank Speck's investigations showed this was "the universal pattern among the agricultural Indians" of the Midwest and Northwest. Speck is quoted in George S. Snyderman, "Concepts of Land Ownership Among the Iroquois and Their Neighbors," in William N. Fenton, ed., Smithsonian Institution, Bureau of American Ethnology Bulletin, no. 149 (Washington, D.C., 1951), pp. 16–17.

24. Quotations from speeches by Tecumseh in Snyderman, p. 30.

25. The peculiar relationships between family structure and landholding among generations of settlers is described in Philip J. Greven, *Four Generations: Population, Land, and Family in Colonial Andover, Massachusetts* (Ithaca, N.Y., 1970), pp. 125–258.

26. William A. Ritchie, "The Indian and His Environment," *The Conservationist* (December–January 1955–56):23–27.

27. Calvin Martin, "The Algonquian Family Hunting Territory Revisited" (Graduate paper being revised for publication, University of California, Santa Barbara).

28. Ritchie, p. 27.

29. Wilcomb Washburn, "The Writing of American Indian History: A Status Report," *Pacific Historical Review* 40 (1971):265; Anne K. Nelson,

"King Philip's War and the Hubbard-Mather Rivalry," *William and Mary Quarterly* 27 (1970):615–29.

30. Quoted in Cyclone Covey, *The Gentle Radical, A Biography of Roger Williams* (New York, 1966), p. 162.

31. Washburn, 40: 265, and Washburn's review of Douglas Leach's *Flintlock and Tomahawk: New England in King Philip's War* in *Pennsylvania Magazine of History and Biography* 82 (1958):473–74.

32. Reflecting the attitudes found in contemporary sources, Philip L. Barbour in his *Pocahontas and Her World* (Boston, 1970) portrays Virginia Indians as "crafty" (p. 53), as "spies" (pp. 57, 61, 77, 85, 99), as "redmen" who "cheated" (p. 77), as inclined to "treachery" and "unreliability" (p. 79) and as downright "treacherous" (p. 103). See also my review of this book in *The New York Historical Society Quarterly* 55 (1971):188–89, for further discussion of evaluating contemporary sources. Indian stereotypes in early American history are discussed in chapter 10.

33. William Byrd, *The Secret Diary of William Byrd of Westover, 1709–1712*, ed., Louis B. Wright and Marion Tinling (Richmond, Va., 1941), p. 455. Even the early Spanish Jesuits in sixteenth-century Virginia complained about the "secret" machinations of the Indians. See Clifford M. Lewis and Albert J. Loomie, *The Spanish Jesuit Mission in Virginia 1570–1571* (Chapel Hill, N.C., 1953), p. 183.

34. F. W. Hodge, ed., *Handbook of the American Indians North of Mexico*, Smithsonian Institution, Bureau of American Ethnology Bulletin, no. 30, pt. 2 (Washington, D.C., 1910), pp. 986–87; Verner W. Crane, *The Southern Frontier, 1670–1732* (Ann Arbor, Mich., 1964), p. 203.

35. Hodge, 2:986–87.

36. Alden T. Vaughan, *The New England Frontier, Puritans and Indians, 1620–1675* (Boston, 1965), pp. 286, 303–04.

37. Roger Williams, *The Complete Writings of Roger Williams*, ed. Perry Miller, (New York, 1963) 7:27. In his essay, *Christenings Make Not Christians*, Williams clarified his position on not pressing Indians into being professed Christians.

CHAPTER 1

1. *The Los Angeles Times*, June 7, 1970, reported that more than 2.3 million fish, animals, and birds have been killed in California from pollution and pesticides in the last five years, and this figure did not include an accounting of kills from two Santa Barbara oil spills. See also Jacques-Yves Cousteau, "The Oceans: No Time to Lose," *Los Angeles Times*, Oct. 24, 1971; George E. Frakes and Curtis B. Solberg, eds., *Pollution Papers* (New York, 1971), pp. 1–7, 84 ff.; Rachel Carson, *Silent Spring* (Boston, 1962), pp. 129–52; Frank Graham, *Since Silent Spring* (Boston, 1970), pp. 93–108. The latest and most dangerous frontier of nuclear pollution is discussed by Jerold M. Lowenstein in *Sierra Club Bulletin* 56 (July–August 1971):22–23.

2. Frederick Jackson Turner, *The Frontier in American History* (New York, 1921), pp. 14–15. Elsewhere in this important book Turner stresses that frontiersmen's "growing families demanded more land . . ." identifying population growth with development of the West. See p. 21. For a discussion of the frontier as a "garden" and population lure and the tradition of profligacy among frontiersmen guided by the biblical injunction "increase and multiply," see

James H. Cassedy, *Demography in America, Beginnings of the Statistical Mind, 1600–1800* (Cambridge, Mass., 1969), pp. 150–71.

3. For a documented account of the poisoning and grisly torture of coyotes by federal "Wildlife Services," see Harold L. Perry, "Predator Control Notes from Arizona, the Torture of Coyotes and Our Poisoned Land," *Defenders of Wildlife News,* vol 45, no. 1 (January, February, March 1970):31–36; *Ibid.,* (Winter, 1971), 406–32. An early protest against the indiscriminate use of such poisons as 1080 was made by a Department of Interior investigating board headed by Professor A. Starker Leopold of the University of California. This board, the Advisory Board on Wildlife Management, transmitted a penetrating report on "Predator and rodent control in the United States" on March 9, 1964 (a copy of which is in the possession of W. R. Jacobs) to former Secretary of the Interior Stewart Udall, advocating a complete reexamination of existing American frontier policies in which incessant war has been waged against certain animals including "the lowly coyote." The board argued that a basic tenet in government policy should be that "all native animals are resources of inherent interest and value to the people of the United States. Basic government policy therefore should be one of husbandry for all forms of Wildlife" (p. 4). As a result of the Leopold Report and public protests, a Presidential executive order (*Los Angeles Times,* Feb. 9, 1972) banned poisoning of eagles, coyotes, falcons, and other predators on federal lands as of Feb. 8, 1972, but there is skepticism among conservationists that this order will not be fully enforced because governmental officials have had a policy of soaking the land with thousands of tons of poisons to control rabbits and small rodents, the natural food of predators.

A description of the bounty system can be found in *The Audubon Nature Encyclopedia* (Philadelphia, 1965), 2:308–15, in J. Lloyd Cahill, "Puma," *Sierra Club Bulletin* 56 (March 1971):18–22; and in Wade Greene, "Bounties: Airborne Slaughter of Eagles," in the *New York Times,* Aug. 8, 1971.

4. The late Frank G. Speck, distinguished authority on the woodland tribes, maintained that this concept was found among all the agricultural Indians of the Northeast, the Great Lakes, and the Ohio Valley. In a lecture of 1947 Speck pointed out that since the Mother Earth gave the Delaware medicine plants, "neither the earth nor the plants should be defiled by metal tools." (The Shawnee also held such beliefs, as seen in the article on "Big Jim," grandson of Tecumseh, in F. W. Hodge, ed., *Handbook of the American Indians North of Mexico,* Smithsonian Institution, Bureau of American Ethnology Bulletin, no. 30, pt. 1 [Washington, D.C., 1907], p. 146.) See George S. Snyderman, "Concepts of Land Ownership Among the Iroquois and Their Neighbors," in William N. Fenton, ed., Smithsonian Institution, Bureau of American Ethnology Bulletin, no. 146 (Washington, D.C., 1951), p. 17, for additional data on Speck's research. An excellent summary of Thoreau's views on the woodland tribes is in Stewart L. Udall, "The Indians: First Americans, First Ecologists," *The American Way* 4 (May 1, 1971):8–14.

5. For an example of Turner's protest against pollution see W. R. Jacobs, ed., *America's Great Frontiers and Sections, Frederick Jackson Turner's Unpublished Essays* (Lincoln, Neb., 1965), p. 206. Parkman in his correspondence shows he was angered by encroachment of real estate promoters and railroads in the wilderness areas. See his complaints about desecration around the Lake George area in his letter to Abbé Henri-Raymond Casgrain, Oct. 5, 1892. *Letters of Francis Parkman,* ed. W. R. Jacobs (Norman, Okla., 1960), 2:265.

6. This is a basic theme set forth in Walter Prescott Webb's *The Great Frontier* (Boston, 1952). Webb argues that the natural wealth of the land—furs, timber, and minerals—contributed to American prosperity.

7. One of Turner's most valuable essays, "The Development of American Society," is reprinted with his last handwritten revisions (from the original copy in the Huntington Library Collection of his papers) in Jacobs, ed., *America's Great Frontiers and Sections*, pp. 168–91.

8. See for example, William N. Fenton, "The Iroquois in History" (Paper read at the Wenner-Gren Symposium. Burg Wartenstein, Austria, Aug. 7–14, 1967), pp. 4 ff. Copy in possession of W. R. Jacobs. Iroquois agricultural practices are discussed in detail in Fenton, ed., *Parker on the Iroquois, Iroquois Uses of Maize and Other Plants, The Code of Handsome Lake, The Seneca Prophet, The Constitution of the Five Nations* (Syracuse, N.Y., 1968), pp. 5–109. The early eighteenth-century Canadian Jesuit, Joseph-François Lafitau, missionary and ethnologist, wrote about the woodland Indian reverence for plant life, especially tobacco, which was considered sacred and contained medicinal properties. See Joseph-François Lafitau. *Moeurs des Sauvages Ameriquains, Comparées aux Moeurs des Premiers Temps* (Paris, 1724), 3:121. Many of the themes stressed by Lafitau concerning Indian reverence for the land and plant life are echoed by modern Indians. For instance, Henry Old Coyote, Crow Agency, Montana, in a taped interview, Oct. 14, 1967, Duke Tape 148, Western History Center, University of Utah, complained that tobacco had always been sacred to the Crows, but the white man "steps on it, they chew it, spit it out . . . so now they try to fight diseases . . . the Indians never heard of cancer before the white man came." See also, W. R. Jacobs, "Lo the poor Indian!" *A.H.A. Newsletter* 9 (March 1971):38–40.

9. The Huntington Library copy of *The Annual Report of the American Historical Association for the Year 1893* (Washington, 1894), rare book no. 263629, contains his essay, "The Significance of the Frontier in American History" with this comment written in the margin, p. 227.

10. Paul B. Sears, "Commercial Economics, Forest Regions Outside the Tropics, Grasslands, Arid Lands, Humid Tropics, Capital and Surplus," in William L. Thomas, ed., *Man's Role in Changing the Face of the Earth*, papers from the international symposium sponsored by the Wenner-Gren Foundation for Anthropological Research (Chicago, 1965), p. 428. The white man's basic alteration of North America's original biotic communities is described in Victor E. Shelford, *The Ecology of North America* (Urbana, Ill., 1963), pp. 1–3, 17–18, 23–24 ff.

11. A description of the original great northeastern forest of America (contesting a number of Francis Parkman's interpretations), is in Calvin Martin, "The Aboriginal Northeastern Deciduous Forest" (Graduate paper being revised for publication, University of California, Santa Barbara). Roderick Nash discusses the perplexing question of what men *think* the wilderness is in *Wilderness and the American Mind* (New Haven, 1967), pp. 5–7.

12. Francis Parkman to Abbé Henri-Raymond Casgrain, April 13, 1889, in Jacobs, ed., *Letters of Francis Parksman*, 2:232.

13. Australia has been less successful in making a hero out of the "bushman" or "bushranger." See Russel Ward, *Australia* (London, 1965), pp. 9, 58–59, 94–96. Ward develops the bushranger myth more fully in his excellent volume, *The Australian Legend* (Melbourne, 1961). Romantic myths have grown up around the picturesque Brazilian Bandeirantes, jungle pathfinders whose movements are traced in Indian slave-hunting cycles and prospecting cycles. Richard M. Morse, ed., *The Bandeirantes, The Historical Role of the Brazilian Pathfinders* (New York, 1965), pp. 5, 23, 181–90.

14. "A Galaxy of Mountain Men: Biographical Sketches," *The Rocky Moun-*

tain Journals of William Marshall Anderson, The West in 1840, eds. Dale L. Morgan and Eleanor T. Harris (San Marino, Calif., 1967), p. 279. Carson's friend, mountain man Bill Williams, turned to horse stealing. *Ibid.*

15. An excellent summary of the history of "Corporate Responsibility and the Environment" is in the editorial by Philip S. Berry, president of the Sierra Club, in *Sierra Club Bulletin* 55 (May 1970):2. Individual planters of early eighteenth-century Virginia were aware of changing the ecological balance in nature. See comments of Robert Beverley in note 16 following.

16. James (Jay) Monaghan (born 1891), friend of the author and former cowboy, cattle and sheep rancher, and present writer on American frontier history, has heard this comment, or variations of it, many times from rural citizens of Utah and Colorado. Monaghan is convinced it represents a philosophical outlook of pioneers in American history. Among the few nineteenth-century voices of protest against the exploration of the land was that of George Perkins Marsh whose *The Earth as Modified by Human Action* (1874), has been called a "fountainhead of the conservation movement."

One of the earliest criticisms of the pioneers was made by the Virginia planter and historian Robert Beverley; writing in 1705, he argued that the colonial "Alterations" in the woods were certainly not "Improvements" in disrupting the almost idyllic forest life of the native Indians "in that original State of Nature." Robert Beverley, *The History and Present State of Virginia,* ed. Louis Wright (Chapel Hill, N.C., 1947), p. 156.

17. Raymond F. Dasmann, *The Destruction of California* (London, 1969), pp. 48–58. See also Jacobs, "Lo the poor Indian!" pp. 38–40. The distinguished geographer, Carl Sauer, a former teacher of Dasmann's, argues that the richer countries of the western hemisphere are those that have not exploited the land. If modern Americans wish to see what the soil profiles or the flora and fauna of the American Southwest were like before the advent of the destructive white frontier, they must go below the Rio Grande into the northern provinces of Mexico. See Carl Sauer, *Land and Life* (Berkeley, Calif., 1965), p. 148.

18. Henry D. Thoreau, *The Journal of Henry D. Thoreau,* eds. Bradford Torrey and Francis H. Allen (Boston, 1949), 9:437–38.

19. *Ibid.,* p. 438.

20. Willa Cather, *Death Comes for the Archbishop* (New York, 1926), pp. 235–37.

21. *Navajo Wildlands, "As Long as the Rivers Shall Run,"* ed. David Brower (San Francisco, 1967), p. 148, has an appraisal of the significance of the Navajo wilderness for all Americans.

22. Frank G. Speck, "Aboriginal Conservators," *Audubon Magazine* 40 (1938):258–61.

23. The "Good" and "Evil" aspects of the American conquest myth are explored by Francis Jennings in "Virgin Land and Savage People," *American Quarterly* 22 (1971):519–41; See also D'Arcy McNickle, "The Indian and the European . . ." in D. Walker, ed., *The Emergent Native American . . .* (Boston, 1972), pp. 15, 86.

CHAPTER 2

1. See for instance, the *Journal of William Trent* at Pickawillany, June 21, 1752, Public Record Office, Colonial Office, 5:1327, Library of Congress transcript, pp. 431–47.

2. E. B. O'Callaghan *et al.*, eds., *Documents Relative to the Colonial History of the State of New York* . . . (Albany, N.Y., 1853–87), 7 (1856): 574 (hereafter cited as *New York Col. Docs.*).

3. Sir William Johnson to Arthur Lee, Esq., M.D.F.R.S., Johnson Hall, February 28, 1771, E. B. O'Callaghan, ed., *Documentary History of the State of New York* (Albany, N.Y., 1849–51) 4 (1851):430–39.

4. For the above quotations, see Robert Beverley, *The History and Present State of Virginia*, ed. Louis Wright (Chapel Hill, N.C., 1947), p. 227; "Reflections on the fur Trade carried on with the Indian Nations that inhabit the inland Counties of North America . . ." British Museum, Add. MSS, 35915, fo. 322–331ᵇ, Library of Congress transcript (typescript copy), pp. 665–98. This interesting account of the fur trade is undated and unsigned; but it was extracted from a collection of papers of one John Gray of Quebec and was probably written in the late 1760s or early 1770s.

5. "Reflections on the fur Trade carried on with the Indian Nations that inhabit the inland Counties of North America . . ." pp. 665–98.

6. See Conrad Weiser's journal relating to his trip to the Ohio country in August 1748, *Minutes of the Provincial Council of Pennsylvania* (Philadelphia, 1851–53), 5 (1853):348–58.

7. For a discussion of the desirability of restricting Indian commerce to certain fur trading posts, see "An Estimate Of the Furr and Peltry Trade in the District of Michilimakinac according to the Bounds and Limits, assigned to it by the French, when under their Government, with the Names and Situations of it's several Out Posts written by Major Robert Rogers." Robert Rogers to Fowler Walker, May 27, 1767, British Museum Add. MSS, 35915, Hardwicke Papers, fo. 234–46, Library of Congress transcript (typescript copy), pp. 463–89; Edmond Atkin to the Board of Trade, May 10, 1755, Huntington Library Collection of Loudoun Papers, no. 578 (hereafter cited as LO).

8. See James Sullivan *et al.*, eds., *The Papers of Sir William Johnson* (Albany, N.Y., 1921—), 3:209 (hereafter cited as *Papers of Sir William Johnson*).

9. W. R. Jacobs, *Wilderness Politics and Indian Gifts* (Lincoln, Neb., 1966), pp. 11–28; Wilcomb Washburn, "Symbol, Utility, and Aesthetics in the Indian Fur Trade," *Minnesota History* 40 (Winter 1966):198–202. Washburn stresses the point that the Indians made gifts speak as words. See pp. 198–99.

10. See note 22 for sources on this point.

11. Albert T. Volwiler, *George Croghan and the Westward Movement 1741–1782* (Cleveland, 1926), pp. 198–201.

12. Winthrop Sargent, ed., *The History of an Expedition Against Fort Du Quesne in 1755* . . . Historical Society of Pennsylvania, *Memoirs*, 5 (Philadelphia, 1856):372–73; Kenneth P. Bailey, *Thomas Cresap, Maryland Frontiersman* (Boston, 1944), p. 180.

13. *New York Col. Docs.*, 7:989.

14. Johnson found it necessary on several occasions to defend himself from criticism. In 1764 he wrote to the Board of Trade that ". . . the disinterested plan by which, I have hitherto regulated my conduct, has occasioned me to forego many opportunities, which my long residence in this Country afforded of improving my fortune. . . ." See Sir William Johnson to the Lords of Trade, Johnson Hall, January 20, 1764, *ibid.*, 7:599–602.

15. Sir William Johnson, "Review of the Trade and Affairs of the Indians in the Northern District of America" (1767), *ibid.*, 7:953–78.

16. *Ibid.*

17. *Ibid.*

18. See *ibid.*, 7:665.
19. *Ibid.*, 7:953–78.
20. *Ibid.*
21. *Papers of Sir William Johnson*, 3:271.
22. Bouquet Papers, A.4 (Canadian Archives photostat), pp. 313–15. See also Howard H. Peckham, *Pontiac and the Indian Uprising* (Princeton, 1947), p. 70 (this valuable work has been republished in printings of 1961 and 1970); Francis Parkman, *The Conspiracy of Pontiac and the Indian War after the Conquest of Canada* (Boston, 1898) 1:174–75.
23. Edmond Atkin's scheme for setting up the superintendency system in 1755 included a plan for regulating the fur trade. See LO, no. 578.
24. "Plan for the future Management of Indian Affairs (1764)," *New York Col. Docs.*, 7:637–41, 661–66.
25. *Ibid.*
26. See John Richard Alden's comments on the "Plan of 1764" in his *John Stuart and the Southern Colonial Frontier, A Study of Indian Relations, War, Trade, and Land Problems in the Southern Wilderness* (Ann Arbor, Mich., 1944), pp. 241–47; John Stuart's report to John Pownall, Charleston, August 24, 1765, Shelburne Papers, vol. 60, W. L. Clements Library (photostat).
27. Parkman, *Conspiracy of Pontiac*, 2, Appendix B, 343.
28. [Robert Rogers], *Ponteach or the Savages of America. A Tragedy* (London, 1756), pp. 3–5. Allan Nevins has edited the play with an introductory biography of Rogers. See Nevins, ed., *Ponteach: Or the Savages of America, A Tragedy By Robert Rogers* (Chicago, 1914).
29. The cruelty and duplicity of whites in trade and treaties is a basic theme in thousands of pages of Indian oral history tapes, Duke Project, Western History Center, University of Utah. This is brought out particularly in interviews with Ute Chief Jackhouse, tape no. 199; Navajo Clyde Benally, tape no. 36; and Crow Henry Old Coyote, tape no. 148.
30. Francis Parkman in his *Old Régime* (Boston, 1898) stresses this point in detailed descriptions of the operation of the Canadian fur trade.
31. I am indebted to my advanced students who first introduced me to Craig MacAndrew and Robert B. Edgerton's *Drunken Comportment, A Social Explanation* (Chicago, 1969), which stresses the significance of trader patterns of drunken behavior and the influence these had upon the Indian. In other words, these were learned forms of drunkenness that the Indians adopted (pp. 13–36). While accepting MacAndrew and Edgerton's findings, Nancy O. Lurie argues that Indians often drank to become "purposefully drunk to confirm the stereotype of the drunken Indian." Dr. Lurie goes on to argue that "the fact that Indian drinking distresses and disturbs whites and forces them to take notice may well explain why it can so easily become a form of social protest." Her views are contested by Vine Deloria in *We Talk, You Listen, New Tribes, New Turf* (New York, 1970), p. 10. See also Lurie, "The World's Oldest On-Going Protest Demonstration: North American Indian Drinking Patterns." *Pacific Historical Review* 40 (1971):312, 331. For an account of "The Fur Trader As Depictor of Savagery," involving the "philosophy of rum," see Lewis O. Saum, *The Fur Trader and the Indian* (Seattle, Wash., 1965), pp. 3–26, 150–51, 168–69, 190–91, 210–15.
32. Verner W. Crane, *The Southern Frontier, 1670–1732* (Ann Arbor, Mich., 1964), pp. 194–95.
33. W. R. Jacobs, ed., *The Appalachian Indian Frontier* (Lincoln, Neb., 1967), p. 87.

34. *A New Voyage to Carolina by John Lawson*, ed. Hugh H. Lefler (Chapel Hill, N.C., 1967), p. 232.

CHAPTER 3

1. *Containing Roger Williams' Key to the Indian Language* in Rhode Island Historical Society, *Collections*, 1 (Providence, R.I., 1827):128–30 (hereafter cited as Roger Williams, *Key*).
2. Francis Parkman, *The Conspiracy of Pontiac and the Indian War after the Conquest of Canada* (Boston, 1898), 1:194–95.
3. Nicholas B. Wainwright, ed., "George Croghan's Journal 1759–1763," *The Pennsylvania Magazine of History and Biography* 71 (1947):435.
4. See note 1 for the source as to the color of wampum beads. Williams notes that the blue beads were inclined to be black in color. F. W. Hodge, ed., *Handbook of the American Indians North of Mexico*, Smithsonian Institution, Bureau of American Ethnology Bulletin, no. 30, pt. 1 (Washington, D.C., 1907), pp. 446–47, states that the white purplish beads were taken from the quahog. Conrad Weiser's memorandum of wampum contains records of only black and white wampum. See Samuel Hazard, ed., *Pennsylvania Archives*, 1st ser. (Philadelphia, 1852–56), 2:17 (hereafter cited as *Pennsylvania Archives*). Contemporaries have established the fact that white and dark wampum were taken from different types of shell. See Public Record Office, Colonial Office, 5:1328, Library of Congress transcript. This document, dated 1753, states:

> Wampum is of two Sorts, White and Purple: the white is work'd out of the Inside of a Conque [sic] Shell into the Form of a Bead perforated to string on Leather: The purple is work'd out the Inside of the Mussell Shell.

5. *Penn Wampum Belts*, Leaflets of the Museum of the American Indian, no. 4 (New York, 1925), plate IV.
6. Reuben G. Thwaites, ed., *Collections* of the State Historical Society of Wisconsin 18 (Madison, Wis., 1908) 18:465.
7. Hodge, pt. 2, pp. 904–09; Robert Beverley, *The History and Present State of Virginia*, ed. Louis Wright (Chapel Hill, N.C., 1947), p. 227.
8. Roger Williams, *Key*, pp. 128–30.
9. *Ibid.* The archaeologist, William A. Ritchie in the *Archaeology of New York State* (Garden City, N.Y., 1969), p. 270, states that the woodland Indians first made tubular bone beads and, about the time of European contact, shell wampum beads. The original crude shell bead prototypes were refined by use of European tools. "Wampum," Ritchie argues, "was a European-trade-inspired commodity" (*ibid.*).
10. Hodge, pt. 1, pp. 446–47.
11. See the Journal of William Trent, June 21, 1752, enclosed in Robert Dinwiddie's letter to the Board of Trade, December 10, 1752, Public Record Office, Colonial Office, 5:1327, Library of Congress transcript. The Twightwees sometimes wrapped the stem of the sacred calumet pipe with wampum. See *Minutes of the Provincial Council of Pennsylvania* (Philadelphia, Pa., 1851–53), 5 (1851:307–19(hereafter cited as *Pa. Col. Recs.*).
12. Lewis H. Morgan, *League of the HO-DE-NO-SAU-NEE or Iroquois*, ed. Herbert M. Lloyd (New York, 1901), 2:52. This plate shows green, red, and blue beads. In the *Journal of William Trent* (see note II, above), a green belt is mentioned that was used by the Miamis.

13. James Sullivan et al., eds., The Papers of Sir William Johnson (Albany, N.Y., 1921—), 3:159 (hereafter cited as Papers of Sir William Johnson).

14. See George Clinton to William Johnson, September 7, 1749, ibid., 1: 247–48.

15. Ibid., 3:172.

16. Ibid., 2:579.

17. Pennsylvania Archives, 1st ser., 2:17.

18. See Conrad Weiser's journal in Pa. Col. Recs., 5:348–58.

19. William Johnson to Arthur Lee, February 28, 1771, E. B. O'Callaghan, ed., Documentary History of the State of New York (Albany, N.Y., 1849–1851), 4 (1851): 273.

20. Conrad Weiser's journal of his trip to the Ohio country contains perhaps the best example of the chain of friendship legend as told by Thanayieson, speaker for the Senecas. See Pa. Col. Recs., 5:348–58.

21. For lists of presents, see vols., 5, 6, and 7; Papers of Sir William Johnson, vols. 1, 2, 3, and 4.

22. The Historical Society of Pennsylvania also owns one of these belts. See illustration, p. 45.

23. Penn Wampum Belts, pp. 10–11; Treaty with the Indians held by Colonel James Innes [in the absence of Governor Horatio Sharpe, Commander of forces at Wills Creek], December 17, 1754, Public Record Office, Colonial Office, 5:15, Library of Congress transcript.

24. Charles Thompson acted as Teedyuscung's clerk. For Thompson's activities on behalf of the Delaware chief, see Pa. Col. Recs., 7:314–25, 724–25.

25. Papers of Sir William Johnson, 3:209.

26. See the journal of William Fairfax, Indian commissioner at a meeting held with the Ohio Indians and their allies at Carlisle, Pennsylvania, from September 10 to September 17, 1753, Public Record Office, Colonial Office, 5: 1328, Library of Congress transcript. Here the Twightwees are described as taking a belt in their hand as they begin to speak and holding it throughout their talk.

27. E. B. O'Callaghan et al., eds., Documents Relative to the Colonial History of the State of New York . . . (Albany, N.Y., 1853–87), 6:966–67 (hereafter cited as New York Col. Docs.).

28. Papers of Sir William Johnson, 2:126–27.

29. Theodore C. Pease, ed., Illinois on the Eve of the Seven Years' War, Illinois State Historical Library, Collections, 29 (Springfield, Ill., 1940):129.

30. New York Col. Docs., 6:974–75.

31. Colonel James Patton, 1692–1755, was a former naval officer. He was appointed commander-in-chief of all military forces in Augusta County in July 1752, after the Treaty of Logstown. See Draper MSS I QQ 68; I QQ 83 (film), Wisconsin State Historical Society, Madison, Wis.

32. At his home, Old Town, Cresap met the warriors who were traveling north and south during the perpetual feuds between the northern and southern Indians. The house was surrounded by a log fort where Cresap, "the Rattle Snake Colonel and vile rascal," handed out goods to the Indians. See the "Morris Journal" in Winthrop Sargent, ed., History of an Expedition against Fort Du Quesne in 1755 . . . , Historical Society of Pennsylvania, Memoirs, 5 (Philadelphia, 1856): 372–73. General Edward Braddock had a very low opinion of Cresap. See Pa. Col. Recs., 6:400. Despite these references to his character, Cresap enjoyed the confidence of Robert Dinwiddie and George

Washington. For further information on this interesting frontiersman, see Kenneth P. Bailey, *Thomas Cresap, Maryland Frontiersman* (Boston, 1944); Bailey, *The Ohio Company of Virginia and the Westward Movement, 1748–1792, A Chapter in the History of the Colonial Frontier* (Glendale, Calif., 1939), pp. 81, 131–32, 153–54, 191.

33. *Papers of Sir William Johnson,* 1:524; 2:500.

34. *New York Col. Docs.,* 10:141, 206. In this case the Cayugas gave the French their promise of neutrality and friendship.

35. *Papers of Sir William Johnson,* 2:293–97, 298, 500.

36. *Pa. Col. Recs.,* 4:579–81. The Delawares in their war against the whites (1756) declared their independence from the Iroquois.

37. *Ibid.,* 4:362.

38. Harold E. Driver, *Indians of North America,* 2d ed., rev. (Chicago, 1969), pp. 216, 221, 323–24, 563.

39. Cited in Margaret G. Meyers, *A Financial History of the United States* (New York, 1970), p. 3.

40. Edmond Wilson, *Apologies to the Iroquois* (New York, 1960), p. 54.

41. William N. Fenton to W. R. Jacobs, May 22, 1970.

CHAPTER 4

1. Clark Wissler, *Indians of the United States,* rev. ed. (Garden City, N.Y., 1967), pp. 283–97.

2. This estimate revises early figures by James Mooney and A. L. Kroeber. See Henry F. Dobyns, "Estimating Aboriginal American Population, An Appraisal of Techniques with a New Hemisphere Estimate," *Current Anthropology* 7 (October 1966):395–449. See also comments in note 34, Chapter 11.

3. W. R. Jacobs, *Wilderness Politics and Indian Gifts* (Lincoln, Neb., 1966), p. 53.

4. Marquis de Duquesne to Claude Pierre Pécandy, Sieur de Contrecoeur, January 27, 1754, *Papiers Contrecoeur, et autres documents concernant Le Conflit Angli-Français sur L'Ohio de 1745 à 1756,* ed. Ferand Grenier (Québec, 1952), p. 94.

5. *Jean-Bernard Bossu's Travels In the Interior of North America, 1751–1762,* trans. and ed. Seymour Feiler (Norman, Okla., 1962), p. 74.

6. Emma H. Blair, ed. and trans., *The Indian Tribes of the Upper Mississippi Valley and the Region of the Great Lakes . . .* (Cleveland, 1911), 1: 186.

7. Harold Driver, *Indians of North America* 2d ed. rev. (Chicago, 1969), p. 210.

8. Jacobs, pp. 15–17.

9. See the conversation between the French and the Iroquois sachem Half King (Tanacharisson) on this subject in the *Minutes of the Provincial Council of Pennsylvania* (Hereafter cited as *Pa. Col. Recs.*) (Philadelphia, 1851–53), 5: 665–70. For a full explanation of the significance of the hatchet as a gift, see Sir William Johnson's letter to Arthur Lee, Johnson Hall, February 28, 1771, in E. B. O'Callaghan, ed., *Documentary History of the State of New York* (Albany, N.Y., 1849–51) 4 (1851):430–37.

10. "The French Regime in Wisconsin," in Reuben G. Thwaites, ed., *Collec-*

tions of the State Historical Society of Wisconsin (Madison, Wis., 1908), 18: 193.

11. *Ibid.*, pp. 193–94.

12. Dunbar Rowland, ed., *Mississippi Provincial Archives, 1763–1776* (Nashville, Tenn., 1911), 1:28–29.

13. James Sullivan *et al.*, eds., *The Papers of Sir William Johnson* (Albany, N.Y., 1921—), 3:334–35 (hereafter cited as *Papers of Sir William Johnson*).

14. Examples of British gifts are in Proposed Division of Presents for the Northern and Southern Indians by Sir William Johnson, November 1750, Huntington Library Collection of Loudon Papers, no. 2507 (hereafter cited as LO), and in *Papers of Sir William Johnson*, 2:898, 900.

15. Vaudreuil's Letter Book, LO, no. 26.

16. Blair, 2:54n.

17. The Miami were called the Twightwee by the English. For a tabulation of the warrior strength along the northwest frontier in 1763, see Memorandum on the Six Nations and other Confederacies, November 18, 1763, *Papers of Sir William Johnson*, 4:240–46. There is some variation in the warrior strength figures as printed in E. B. O'Callaghan *et al.*, eds., *Documents Relative to the Colonial History of the State of New York . . .* (Albany, N.Y., 1853–87), 7 (1856): 582–84 (hereafter cited as *New York Col. Docs.*). Also see Evarts B. Greene and Virginia D. Harrington, *American Population Before the Federal Census of 1790* (New York, 1932), pp. 194–206.

18. The Abnaki were among those Indians who aided Montcalm in the victory at Fort William Henry in August 1757. For accounts of the voracious appetites of these warriors for plunder, presents, and scalps and their cruelty to British prisoners, see Reuben G. Thwaites, ed., *The Jesuit Relations and Allied Documents* (Cleveland, 1896–1901), 70 (1900): 113–203; M. de Montcalm to Brigadier General Webb, August 14, 1757, and M. de Vaudreuil to M. de Moras, Montreal, September 1757, in *New York Col. Docs.*, 10:618–19, 631–34.

19. *Papers of Sir William Johnson*, 4:240–45. For maps showing the locations of the Iroquois tribes, see the frontispieces of vols. 1 and 2 of Lewis H. Morgan, *League of the HO-DE-NO-SAU-NEE or Iroquois*, ed. Herbert M. Lloyd (New York, 1901).

20. See Weiser's journal in *Pa. Col. Recs.*, 5:351. In 1755 Edmond Atkin, later British Indian superintendent, wrote that the Ohio tribes had only five hundred warriors. Atkin to the Board of Trade, May 30, 1755, LO, no. 578, edited by W. R. Jacobs in *The Appalachian Indian Frontier* (Lincoln, Neb., 1967), pp. 3–95.

21. For a list of the annual French presents given the Choctaw, see Rowland, 1:28–29. These shipments are also mentioned in Theodore C. Pease, ed., *Illinois on the Eve of the Seven Years' War*, Illinois State Historical Library, *Collections*, 29 (Springfield, Ill., 1940): 234–35.

22. See Prologue and Robert A. Goldstein, *French-Iroquois Diplomatic and Military Relations, 1609–1701* (The Hague, The Netherlands, 1969), pp. 182–204.

23. The activities of the Joncaire brothers are difficult to follow because of the fact that both were called Sieur Joncaire or simply Joncaire. Philip Thomas, an ensign, was sent to reside among the Seneca in the 1740s and by 1745 his reports covering the activities of all of the Six Nations were sent to the governor general. See "Military and other Operations in Canada during the years 1745–46," in *New York Col. Docs.*, 10:38–75. The younger brother, Daniel,

Sieur de Chabert et de Clausonne, appears to have taken over the Seneca post in 1748 because of the ill health of Philip Thomas. In 1755 Sir William offered a reward to any Frenchman in New York who could capture Chabert Joncaire. See *Papers of Sir William Johnson*, 2:388–89. For a sketch of this important family see Frank H. Severance, *An Old Frontier of France* (New York, 1917), 1:151–96; 2:442–43; *Illinois on the Eve of the Seven Years' War*, pp. xxxiv–xxxv. Both of these brothers appear to have been captured by Sir William Johnson at Niagara in 1759. An excellent example of Chabert's success with the Seneca is found in a record of a conference between the French and the sachems of that nation. To show his allegiance to the French, one of the chiefs declared, "I forget that there are any English on earth, and to give you proof that I despise them and look on them as dogs, see, I tear off the medal of the King of England which hangs from my neck, and trample it under foot." See M. de Vaudreuil to M. de Machault, Montreal, October 31, 1755, in *New York Col. Docs.*, 10:377–78.

24. Also known as Céleron de Bienville. See his journal in "The French Regime in Wisconsin," 18 pp. 36–58 cited in note 25. For the original journal in French see Pierre Margry, ed., *Découvertes et Etablissements des Français dans l'Ouest et dans le Sud de l'Amérique Septentrionale (1614–1754)*, (Paris, 1879–1888), 6 (1888): 666–726.

25. Reuben G. Thwaites, ed., "The French Regime in Wisconsin 1727–" 1748 in Collections of the State Historical Society of Wisconsin (Madison, Wis., 1906) 17:270. The only autographed letter of Langlade's that has been found has been reproduced in "The British Regime in Wisconsin," in *ibid.*, 18: 462. Charles Langlade was born in 1729 and appears to have died after 1800. He came from a prominent family of voyageurs and Indian traders and is said to have been the first settler in Wisconsin. According to Theodore C. Pease, his full name was Charles-Michel Mouet, Sieur Langlade. See *Illinois on the Eve of the Seven Years' War*, p. xxxvii.

26. For the British land purchases that angered the Indians, see the "Treaty of Logg's Town," in *Virginia Magazine of History and Biography* 13 (1905): 154–74; Robert Dinwiddie to James Glen, July 28, 1755, in R. A. Brock, ed., *The Official Records of Robert Dinwiddie, Lieutenant Governor of the Colony of Virginia, 1751–1758*, in Virginia Historical Society, *Collections*, n. s. (Richmond, Va., 1882–92), 4 (1884):125–26.

27. Jean Marie Shea, ed., *Relations Diverses sur La Bataille de Malangueulé. Gangé le 9 Juillet, 1755, par les François sous m. de Beaujeu, Commandant du Quesne sur les Anglois sous m. Braddock, Général en chef des troupes Angloises* (New York, 1860), p. 20.

28. M. de Vaudreuil to ————, August 5, 1755, Archives Nationales, Ministere des Colonies, F 3, 14, 128–31 (Library of Congress photostat). Had the Indians not been absorbed in plundering, it is doubtful whether any of the British would have escaped. See Journal of the Operations of the Army from July 22 to September 30, 1755, in *New York Col. Docs.*, 10:338.

29. For an account of the problems that the British had in securing Indian auxiliaries for Braddock see Jacobs, *Wilderness Politics and Indian Gifts*, pp. 136–40. The best account of the French side of the conflict is Ronald D. Martin, "Confrontation at the Monongahela: Climax of the French Drive into the Upper Ohio Region," *Pennsylvania History* 37 (April 1970):133–50.

30. Letter from an Officer, Camp at Chouaguen, August 22, 1756, *New York Col. Docs.*, 10:454.

31. Instructions for M. de Vaudreuil, 1755, *ibid.*, 10:295–96.

32. *Illinois on the Eve of the Seven Years' War,* pp. xix–xx; *New York Col. Docs.,* 10:297–99.

33. *New York Col. Docs.,* 10:295–96.

34. Adam Shortt, ed., *Canadian Currency and Exchange During the French Period* (Ottawa, 1925), 2:764–71; *Illinois on the Eve of the Seven Years' War,* p. xxvi; M. Bigot to M. Berryer, April 15, 1759, *New York Col. Docs.,* 10: 685. Norman W. Caldwell's essay, "The French in the Mississippi Valley, 1740–1750," *Illinois Studies in Social Sciences* 26 (1941): 33–34, estimates costs of French gifts in the 1740s.

35. Memoir of Bougainville, 1757, in "The French Regime in Wisconsin," 18: 194–95.

36. M. Doreil to M. de Paulmy, Oct. 25, 1757, *New York Col. Docs.,* 10: 653.

37. M. Bigot to M. Berryer, April 15, 1759, *ibid.,* p. 967.

38. See *ibid.* These posts were usually given as a monopoly to an army officer. As an example, see "Ordonnance de M. de la Jonquière qui permet au Sr Simblin enseign des troupes en Canada de faire construire à ses frais au Lac à la Carpe, un fort, un maison et un magasin avec le pouvoir d'y commander et d'y faire les commerce exclusif pendant le term 6 années, 27 fevrier 1751," Archives Nationales, Ministère des Colonies, F 4, 14 (Library of Congress photostat).

39. J. Berryer to M. Bigot, Versailles, January 19, 1759, in *New York Col. Docs.,* 10:938.

40. M. de Montcalm to M. de Normand, Montreal, April 12, 1759, *ibid.,* pp. 962–66.

41. For selected correspondence on this matter, see the following letters: Jeffery Amherst to Henry Bouquet, April 4, 1762, Bouquet Papers, A. 4, pp. 125–26 (Canadian Archives photostat); same to same, May 2, 1762, Bouquet Papers, A. 4, pp. 128–32 (Canadian Archives photostat); same to same, June 7, 1762, Bouquet Papers, A. 4, pp. 133–35 (Canadian Archives photostat); same to same, July 25, 1762, Bouquet Papers, A. 4, pp. 140–41 (Canadian Archives photostat); George Croghan to Jeffery Amherst, April 30, 1763, Bouquet Papers, A. 4, pp. 227–28 (Canadian Archives photostat); Jeffery Amherst to George Croghan, May 11, 1763, Bouquet Papers, A. 4, pp. 233–35 (Canadian Archives photostat). Also see the "Minutes of the Proceedings of Sir William Johnson Bart with the Indians on his Way to, and at the Détroit in 1761 whither he went by his Excellency Sir Jeff. Amhersts Orders to Establish peace, & settle all affairs between the English, and the several Nations of the Northern and Western Indians," July–September, 1761, *Papers of Sir William Johnson,* 3:428–503.

42. "The British Regime in Wisconsin," in *Collections* of the State Historical Society of Wisconsin 18:228.

43. Sir William Johnson to Cadwallader Colden, Johnson Hall, December 24, 1763, *Papers of Sir William Johnson,* 4:273–77.

CHAPTER 5

1. "Relation du Combat du 9 Juillet, 1755," in Winthrop Sargent, ed., *The History of an Expedition Against Fort du Quesne in 1755 . . . ,* Historical Society of Pennsylvania, *Memoirs* 5 (Philadelphia, 1856): 409.

2. See Sir William Johnson to William Pitt, October 24, 1760, in James Sul-

livan *et al.*, eds., *The Papers of Sir William Johnson* (Albany, N.Y., 1921–   ),
3:269–75 (hereafter cited as *Papers of Sir William Johnson*).

3. At the suggestion of George Washington, Gist was appointed to aid Atkin.
See Washington to Robert Dinwiddie, June 12, 1757, in John C. Fitzpatrick,
ed., *The Writings of George Washington* (Washington, D.C., 1931–1944), 2:
57–59. For Gist's work in aiding Atkin, see Huntington Library Collection of
Loudoun Papers, nos. 4640, 3990, and 4723 (hereafter cited as LO). For
Atkin's work in aiding Forbes, see Alfred P. James, ed., *Writings of John
Forbes Relating to His Service in North America* (Menasha, Wis., 1938), pp.
41, 69, 92, 98, 103, 109, 135–36.

4. Edmond Atkin to William Pitt, March 27, 1760, in Public Record Office,
Colonial Office, 5:64 (Public Record Office photostat).

5. Atkin's quarrel with George Croghan, William Johnson's chief deputy,
is recorded in E. B. O'Callaghan *et al.*, eds., *Documents Relative to the Colonial History of the State of New York . . .* (Albany, N.Y., 1853–87), 7
(1856):281 (hereafter cited as *New York Col. Docs.*).

6. James Adair, *The History of the American Indians . . .* (London, 1775),
p. 274.

7. John R. Alden, *John Stuart and the Southern Colonial Frontier . . .*
(Ann Arbor, Mich., 1944), p. 68. Alden cites Atkin's will, May 22, 1760.

8. "Conference between Edmund Atkin, Esq., and the Six Nations," November 21, 1756, in *New York Col. Docs.*, 7:211.

9. Atkin is listed as a member of the council as early as January 17, 1738.
South Carolina Council Journal, ms., 7:135 (microfilm; original in The Dept.
of Archives and History of S.C., Columbia). See also Atkin to Board of Trade,
May 30, 1755, p. 1. LO 578.

10. *New York Col. Docs.*, 7:211.

11. See the record of Atkin's activities in the year 1749, for example, in
Public Record Office, Colonial Office, 5:374, Library of Congress transcript.

12. Atkin to John Pownall, June 8, 1754, *ibid.*

13. "Historical Account of the Revolt of the Chactaw Indians . . . ," Lans-
downe ms., 809, ff. 1–33 vo. (British Museum photostat).

14. *Ibid.*

15. Atkin to Board of Trade, May 30, 1755, in LO, no. 578.

16. *Ibid.*, p. 1.

17. *Ibid.*, p. 4. After the creation of the superintendencies, both Atkin and
William Johnson employed gunsmiths for powerful interior Indian tribes to
prevent defections to the French. See W. R. Jacobs, *Wilderness Politics and
Indian Gifts* (Lincoln, Neb., 1968), p. 86.

18. Atkin to Board of Trade, May 30, 1755, LO, no. 578, pp. 20–21.

19. John Carl Parish, *The Persistence of the Westward Movement and Other
Essays* (Berkeley, Calif., 1943), p. 149. This book of essays was edited by the
late Louis Knott Koontz following the death of his colleague Parish. No footnotes could be located to accompany the essay on Atkin.

20. Atkin to Board of Trade, May 30, 1755, p. 21. William Johnson also
praised the northern Indians. See the superintendent's famous letter to Arthur
Lee on Indian culture, dated February 28, 1771, in E. B. O'Callaghan, ed.,
Documentary History of the State of New York (Albany, N.Y., 1849–51), 4
(1851):430–37. Johnson's correspondence contains much information on Indian diplomacy and Indian customs.

21. See John Stuart's report, "Total number of Gun Men in the Southern

District," December 1, 1764, an unidentified Public Record Office ms. on file in Illinois Historical Survey (University of Illinois Library); William Johnson, "Enumeration of Indians within the Northern Department," November 18, 1763, in *New York Col. Docs.*, 7:582–84; Evarts B. Greene and Virginia D. Harrington, *American Population before the Federal Census of 1790* (New York, 1932), pp. 194–202, 206.

22. For accounts of Atkin's later travels among his Indian wards after his appointment as southern superintendent, see "The Indian Books of South Carolina" 6 (microfilm; originals in South Carolina Dept. of Archives and History). These have recently been edited and published by the Historical Commission of South Carolina in Columbia.

23. C. H. McIlwain in his introduction to *Wraxall's Abridgement* of Indian affairs, suggested that Peter Wraxall's work was responsible for the new scheme of Indian management. But this is to overrate Wraxall's influence. John Richard Alden maintains that the deliberations of the Albany Conference of 1754 were primarily responsible for creating the Indian superintendency offices. Alden further points out that the recommendations of Sir William Johnson and of the colonial statesman, Thomas Pownall, were enclosed with the Albany Conference journals when they were sent to the Board of Trade. But as early as 1751 a member of the New York council, Archibald Kennedy, had suggested the establishment of the office of the superintendent. See Charles H. McIlwain, ed., *An Abridgement of the Indian Affairs Contained in Four Folio Volumes Transacted in the Colony of New York, from the Year 1678 to the Year 1751 by Peter Wraxall,* Harvard Historical Studies, no. 21 (Cambridge, Mass., 1915); John R. Alden, "The Albany Congress and the Creation of the Indian Superintendencies," in *Mississippi Valley Historical Review* 27 (1940–41): 193–210; Archibald Kennedy, *The Importance of Gaining and Preserving the Friendship of the Indians to the British Interest Considered* (New York, 1751).

24. Parish, p. 160. Atkin's report and plan have been edited by W. R. Jacobs and published by the University of Nebraska Press under the title of *The Appalachian Indian Frontier* (Lincoln, Neb., 1967).

25. See William T. Hagan, *The American Indian* (Chicago, 1961), pp. 66–67; Angie Debo, *A History of the Indians of the United States* (Norman, Okla., 1971), pp. 225 ff.; for Canadian Indian agents and provisions of the Canadian Indian Act, see Robert J. Surtees, *The Original People* (Toronto, 1971), pp. 23, 35, 43, 70. For the Australian Aboriginal "Protector" system, see Chapter 11, note 46.

CHAPTER 6

1. Men from Captain Israel Putnam's Company of Connecticut Rangers as well as from Captain Robert Rogers' Rangers performed messenger service during the siege. See the Huntington Library Collection of Loudoun Papers (hereafter cited as LO) no. 4041, A, B, and C.

2. See LO, no. 4050. The creases in the paper are still visible. The fact that the message was carried in the sergeant's vest is noted in "Journal of the Expedition against Fort William Henry. From 12th of July, to 16th August, 1757," E. B. O'Callaghan *et al.*, eds., *Documents Relative to the Colonial History of the State of New York . . . ,* (Albany, N.Y., 1853–87) 10:603 (hereafter cited as *New York Col. Docs.*).

3. Eyre directed the construction of the fort in 1756, completing it in two months. He was later chief engineer to the British army under Amherst and he

was drowned while on passage to Ireland in 1764. See *New York Col. Docs.*, 10:729; E. B. O'Callaghan, ed., *The Documentary History of the State of New York* (Albany, N.Y., 1849–51), 4 (1851):525.

4. There is a map of Fort William Henry in the Huntington Library Collection of maps and plans supplementing the Loudoun Papers. See also *New York Col. Docs.*, 10:opp. 602; Francis Parkman, *Montcalm and Wolfe* (Boston, 1893), 1:495; Lawrence Henry Gipson, *The British Empire Before the American Revolution, 7, The Great War for the Empire: The Victorious Years, 1758–1760* (New York, 1949): opp. 79.

5. For the French report on this campaign, see M. de Vaudreuil to the Keeper of the Seals, Montreal, April 22, 1757, *New York Col. Docs.*, 10:542–43.

6. *Ibid.*, 10:625.

7. LO, no. 6660.

8. *New York Col. Docs.*, 10:609.

9. "Montcalm à Monsieur le commandant des troupes du fort George," August 3, 1757, LO, no. 4144 A.

10. "Geo[rge] Monro to [General Montcalm]," August 3, 1757, LO, no. 4038.

11. A more decisive commander like James Wolfe undoubtedly would not have waited to send reinforcements. Militiamen converged upon Fort Edward, and by August 7 Webb had approximately four to five thousand men. The French estimated six thousand. See *New York Col. Docs.*, 10:597. E. B. O'Callaghan in a critical note on the general indicates that he had four thousand. In spite of his behavior on this occasion Webb was twice promoted and somehow escaped official censure. *Ibid.*, p. 574. Lawrence H. Gipson declares, however, that Webb was "treated like a dog" by his fellow officers. See Gipson, p. 88. The official journal of the siege takes great pains to protect Webb's reputation: "And as General Webb, never had it in his Power, to send a number sufficient for our relief; he shew'd great wisdom in not sending any." LO, no. 6660. The use of the phrase "in his power," which appeared in the letter to Monro on August 4, makes one suspect that Webb went over the report carefully before it was sent on to his superior, the Earl of Loudoun.

12. LO, nos. 4053, 4081, 4133, 4104, 4031, 4032, and 4034. See also John A. Schutz, *Thomas Pownall, British Defender of American Liberty* . . . (Glendale, Calif., 1951), pp. 92 ff.

13. LO, no. 4050. See also *New York Col. Docs.*, 10:603, 612, 628. The last citation, from "Detail of the Campaign of 1757," states that "One of our Indians intercepted a letter. . . ." Other references merely mention that "the Indians" killed the sergeant, implying that a number of warriors were involved. It is possible that the sergeant had a companion who was taken prisoner.

14. *New York Col. Docs.*, 10:613.

15. Translation of LO, no. 4134, which is the original manuscript, signed in Montcalm's childlike hand.

16. LO, no. 6660. The manuscript is unsigned.

17. "Opinion of the Several Officers Regarding the Defence of Fort William Henry," August 9, 1757, LO, no. 4158 A. For the articles of capitulation see "Articles de la Capitulation accordée au Lt. Colonel Monro pour la Garrison de sa Majesté britannique de fort Guillaume henri," August 9, 1757, LO, no. 4159 A. This is signed by both Monro and Montcalm.

18. *New York Col. Docs.*, 10:615. According to the terms of the capitula-

tion Montcalm was to care for the wounded; but it appears that these unfortunates were quickly killed by the Indians.

19. The Loudoun Collection was then purchased by Henry E. Huntington before the date set for the auction. Norma B. Cuthbert, comp., "American Manuscript Collections in the Huntington Library for the History of the Seventeenth and Eighteenth Centuries," *Huntington Library Lists*, no. 5 (San Marino, Calif., 1941), p. 37. Miss Cuthbert indicated that Loudoun acquired a number of French manuscripts, letters of Pierre François, Marquis de Vaudreuil-Cavagnal, governor-general of Canada, and other papers in 1757. There seems to be a bare possibility that the Fort William Henry material was included here. It appears, however, that these French documents were originally acquired when the governor-general's brother was captured in 1755. See *New York Col. Docs.*, 10:298–99.

20. There are two copies in the Loudoun Papers (nos. 4041, 6660). In addition, the document is summarized in a number of French sources. See *New York Col. Docs.*, 10:603, 612, 642, 649.

21. Parkman, *Montcalm and Wolfe*, 1:502. Parkman based his version of the letter on the journal of Bougainville. He had a number of experienced agents who secured copies of important manuscripts for him in foreign archives. He later had these bound in leather, and today the manuscript volumes are housed at the Massachusetts Historical Society in a large, hand-carved wooden cabinet, designed by Parkman himself. His French documents, like the Public Record Office papers, are arranged chronologically but not indexed. Almost all of these materials are now duplicated in Library of Congress transcripts.

22. See Parkman's review of Cooper's *Works* in the *North American Review* 84 (January 1852):147–61. Parkman may have seen the Webb letter after it was printed, with variations from the original in John Entick, *History of the Late War* . . . (London, 1763), 2:398. Entick, whose account of the events in North America is often muddled, gives a reasonably accurate report of the loss of Fort William Henry.

CHAPTER 7

1. There has been a persistent neglect of Indian peacemaking efforts by historians of American frontier history. Even Francis Parkman, in his efforts to dramatize early frontier history, tended to portray Indians as aggressors when in fact they initiated peace proposals. See Francis P. Jennings, "A Vanishing Indian: Francis Parkman and His Sources," *Pennsylvania Magazine of History and Biography* 47 (1963): 306–23.

2. Confederated Indians to American Indian Commissioners, 1793 quoted in George S. Snyderman, "Concepts of Land Ownership . . ." Smithsonian Institution, Bureau of American Ethnology Bulletin, no. 149 (Washington, D.C., 1951), p. 29.

3. Speech of July 7, 1742, *Minutes of the Provincial Council of Pennsylvania*, (Philadelphia, Pa., 1851–53) 4:570–71

4. T. O. Ranger, "Indian and African Responses to Christianity, A Critique of Salvation and the Savage by Robert F. Berkhofer" (Paper given in the Winter 1971 UCLA Seminar on the Interactions of American Indian and African Historiography).

5. For accounts of Johnson's works as superintendent, see Arthur Pound and Richard E. Day, *Johnson of the Mohawks, A Biography of Sir William Johnson, Irish Immigrant, Mohawk War Chief, American Soldier, Empire Builder* (New

York, 1930); William L. Stone, *The Life and Times of Sir William Johnson, Bart.* (Albany, N.Y., 1865).

6. Many of Weiser's journals and letters are included in Paul Wallace, *Conrad Weiser, 1696–1760, Friend of Colonist and Mohawk* (Philadelphia, 1945).

7. For Croghan's work among the Ohio Indians and the Six Nations, see Albert T. Volwiler, *George Croghan and the Westward Movement, 1741–1782* (Cleveland, 1926); Nicolas B. Wainwright, *George Croghan, Wilderness Diplomat* (Chapel Hill, N.C., 1959).

8. See Jeffery Amherst to William Johnson, October 2, 1759, February 23, 1760, in James Sullivan, *et al.*, eds., *The Papers of Sir William Johnson* (Albany, N.Y., 1921–), 3:141–42, 192–93 (hereafter cited as *Papers of Sir William Johnson*).

9. See, for example, Jeffery Amherst to Henry Bouquet, January 16, 1762, Jeffery Amherst to George Croghan, May 11, 1763, in the Bouquet Papers, A. 4, pp. 83–84, 233–35, Canadian Archives photostat.

10. General Robert Monckton relayed Amherst's orders to Colonel Henry Bouquet. See Robert Monckton to Henry Bouquet, August 23, 1760, Bouquet Papers, A. 8, pp. 157–60, Canadian Archives photostat.

11. *Papers of Sir William Johnson*, 3:345.

12. "Indian Trade Regulations at Fort Pitt," in *ibid.*, 3:530–32.

13. Robert Monckton to Henry Bouquet, April 5, 1761. Bouquet Papers, A. 8, pp. 260–63, Canadian Archives photostat.

14. "Minutes of the Proceedings of Sir William Johnson Bart with the Indians on his Way to, and at the Detroit in 1761 whither he went by his Excellency Sir Jeff. Amherst's Orders to Establish peace, & settle all affairs between the English, and the several Nations of Northern and Western Indians," July–September 1761, in *Papers of Sir William Johnson*, 3:428–503; Stone, *Sir William Johnson*, Appendix, 2:429–77.

15. *Papers of Sir William Johnson*, 3:472.

16. Henry Bouquet to Robert Monckton, February 24, 1761, Bouquet Papers, A. 8, pp. 250–51, Canadian Archives photostat.

17. George Croghan to William Johnson, May 10, 1762, in *Papers of Sir William Johnson*, 3:732–34.

18. "Order of the King in Council on a Report of the Lords of Trade," November 23, 1761, in E. B. O'Callaghan *et al.*, *Documents Relative to the Colonial History of the State of New York* . . . (Albany, N.Y., 1853–87), 6 (1855):473 (hereafter cited as *New York Col. Docs.*).

19. Clarence W. Alvord, *The Mississippi Valley in British Politics* (Cleveland, 1917), 1:122. Alvord cites *Canadian Archives Report* (1889), pp. 73 ff.

20. See Bouquet to Amherst, April 1, 1762, and Francis Fauquier to Bouquet, January 17, 1762, in Bouquet Papers (British Museum photostats). Fauquier later supported the British policy of limiting settlement in the West. See, for example, Fauquier to the Board of Trade, September 4, 1766, in Chalmers Papers, Virginia, vol. 2, no. 11 (New York Public Library film).

21. *Papers of Sir William Johnson*, 4:62–63.

22. George Croghan to Jeffery Amherst, April 30, 1763, Bouquet Papers, A. 4, pp. 227–28, Canadian Archives photostat.

23. The Mortar, grim and seasoned diplomat of the Upper Creeks, had long recognized the land hunger of the English, and he bitterly complained in May 1763 that "the White People intend to stop all their [the Indians'] breath by settling around them." See Allen D. Candler, ed., *Colonial Records of the State*

of Georgia (Atlanta, 1904–16), 9:72–73. He was also known as Yahya-Tustanage or Great Mortar. See James Adair, *History of the American Indians* (London, 1775), p. 254. For more detailed information about this remarkable Indian, see John R. Alden, *John Stuart and the Southern Colonial Frontier* (Ann Arbor, Mich., 1944), pp. 199–200, 204–07, 310.

24. *Journal of the Congress of the Four Southern Governors and the Superintendent of that District with the Five Nations of the Indians at Augusta,* 1763 (Charles Town, 1764). A microfilm copy of an original in the New York Public Library has been used. Of the fifty copies of this rare work printed by Peter Timothy, only two others have been located, one in the De Renne Library in Georgia, and the other in the William L. Clements Library at Ann Arbor, Mich.

25. Sir Charles Wyndham, the second Earl of Egremont (1710–63), approved of Amherst's shortsighted policy of cutting expenses, but he expressed astonishment at the news of Pontiac's Uprising, which he termed an "unlucky incident." See *New York Col. Docs.,* 7: 538–40. Johnson blamed Amherst's policy of "oeconomy" for the Indian war of 1763. See *Papers of Sir William Johnson,* 4: 273–77. Egremont's instructions regarding the Augusta congress are mentioned in his letter to the Board of Trade, May 5, 1763, in *New York Col. Docs.,* 7:519–22.

26. For accounts of the Indian policies of Henry Ellis, see Alden, pp. 76, 94–95, 97–100, 108–110; Alvord, 1:159, the citation here being to the "Knox Manuscripts," in Historical Manuscripts Commission, *Reports on Manuscripts in Various Collections,* 6:192 ff.

27. Distribution of Presents at the Congress of Augusta, Nov. 19, 1763, North Carolina Historical Commission, Transcripts of English Records, C.O. 5, Bdl. 65, p. 324.

28. "A Map of the Southern District of North America Compiled under the Direction of John Stuart, Esq. . . . [London, 1776]," Newberry Library, Chicago. Another copy of this rare map is in the Public Record Office, London.

29. Henry Bouquet to Jeffery Amherst, May 19, 1763, Bouquet Papers, A. 4, pp. 249–51, Canadian Archives photostat.

30. After news of the native outbreak, Amherst's Indian policy became more severe. He wrote to Colonel Henry Bouquet on June 16, 1763, declaring "I am fully convinced the only Method of Treating those Savages is to Keep them in proper Subjection, & punish without Exception, the Transgressors." See Bouquet Papers, A. 4, pp. 262–64, Canadian Archives photostat.

31. Extract of a letter from William Johnson to Jeffery Amherst, July 11, 1763, Bouquet Papers, A. 4, pp. 313–15, Canadian Archives photostat.

32. This point is documented in an unpublished paper by Harry Kelsey, Director of the Los Angeles Museum of Natural History.

33. Francis Parkman, *The Conspiracy of Pontiac and the Indian War after the Conquest of Canada* (Boston, 1898), 1:184.

34. Parkman, 2:173–74. Colonel Henry Bouquet's answer to Amherst's request is found in a letter from Bouquet to Amherst dated July 13, 1763. Bouquet wrote: "I will try to inoculate the . . . . with Some Blankets that may fall in their Hands, and take Care not to get the Disease myself." Pennsylvania Historical Survey, *The Papers of Col. Henry Bouquet* (Harrisburg, Pa., 1940–43), ser. 21634, pp. 214–15. Captain Simeon Ecuyer, commander at Fort Pitt during the siege, did give the Indians some blankets from the smallpox hospital. See A. T. Volwiler, ed., "William Trent's Journal at Fort Pitt, 1763," *Mississippi Valley Historical Review* 11 (1924): 400.

35. Milton W. Hamilton, "Myths and Legends of Sir William Johnson," *New York History* 34 (1953): 15; Richard Dorson, "Comic Indian Anecdotes," *Southern Folklore Quarterly* 10 (1946):113–28. Leo Lemay, early American literature specialist at U.C.L.A., has located the Johnson-Indian dream story in two eighteenth-century accounts: *Funny Stories, or, The American Jester* (Worcester, Mass., 1795), Evans 28720, p. 34; *The Merry Fellow's Companion; being the Second Part of the American Jest Book* (Philadelphia, 1789), p. 89.

36. Statement by William L. Stone in Hamilton, p. 15.

CHAPTER 8

1. Francis Parkman, *The Conspiracy of Pontiac and the Indian War after the Conquest of Canada* (Boston, 1898), 1:194–95. Although Parkman had reservations about the use of "conspiracy" he concluded that "Johnson's dictionary will bear me out in the use of the word. . . ." Parkman to [G. E. Ellis], July 16 [1850], W. R. Jacobs, ed., *Letters of Francis Parkman* (Norman, Okla., 1960), 1:73. In spite of making a number of revisions in various editions of *Pontiac,* Parkman never seems to have considered revising the title or changing his interpretation of Pontiac's role in the uprising. When in 1879 Edward Eggleston approached him on the use of the book for a juvenile-type biography of Pontiac, Parkman declined to give permission: "I would rather that another book on Pontiac should not be published. . . . You have full appreciation of the time & labor employed in gathering obscure & widely scattered material, visiting and studying localities, & becoming personally familiar with Indians in their primitive conditions." *Ibid.,* 2:127–28.

2. See Kerlerec to Minister, July 4, 1763, Archives Nationales, Colonies, C 13, 43:206. Also see sketch in Reuben G. Thwaites, ed., "The French Regime in Wisconsin—," *Collections* of the State Historical Society of Wisconsin, 18 (Madison, Wis., 1908):221n.

General Thomas Gage, who succeeded Amherst as commander-in-chief of British forces consistently praised Pontiac's abilities, and like Parkman, seems to have based his opinion on letters written by d'Abbadie. Writing to the Earl of Halifax, April 14, 1764, Gage wrote that according to "a paragraph in M. d'Abbadie's letter [no date given], there is reason to judge of Pontiac, not only as a Savage, possessed of the most refined cunning and treachery natural to Indians, but as a person of extra abilities . . . Pontiac keeps two Secretaries, one to write for him, and the other to read the letters he receives, & he manages them so, as to keep each of them ignorant of what is transacted by the other. I proposed to send advice to Major Gladwin [at Detroit] of Pontiac's designs, that he may be on his guard. . . ." E. B. O'Callaghan, ed., *Documents Relative to the Colonial History of the State of New York* . . . (Albany, N.Y., 1853–87), 7:619–20 (hereafter cited as *New York Col. Docs.*).

3. Howard H. Peckham, *Pontiac and the Indian Uprising* (Princeton, N. J., 1947), p. 111.

4. Parkman soon found in his researches that sources on Pontiac himself were scarce. He wrote of his plans to Lyman C. Draper, Dec. 23, 1834: "My first idea was to make something like a biography of him; but you know how meagre is the information that one gets concerning the life of an Indian chief, —and I resolved to embrace the whole war in my design, and to give a minute and complete account of its causes, progress, and results, chiefly with the view of exhibiting the traits of the Indian character." Jacobs, ed., 1:31.

5. Parkman, 1:215n.

6. Peckham, as noted above, relied primarily upon Robert Navarre's *Journal of the Conspiracy of Pontiac*, 1763, trans. by R. Clyde Ford (Detroit, 1910), for most of the material in his book relating to the immediate origin of the war. R. Clyde Ford states that Robert Navarre, the scrivener, was probably the author. C. M. Burton, who wrote the preface to the translation, states that the writing proves that no priest was the author of the manuscript. For a description of the General Thomas Gage Papers in the William L. Clements Library, also consulted by Peckham, see *Guide to the Manuscript Collections in the William L. Clements Library*, comp. Howard H. Peckham (Ann Arbor, Mich., 1942). Selections from these papers were published by Clarence E. Carter in *The Correspondence of General Thomas Gage with the Secretaries of State, 1763–1775* (New Haven, Conn., 1931–33). Peckham also used the Sir Jeffery Amherst Papers, Public Record Office, War Office 34. A summarized index covering volumes 1–250 and a detailed index covering part of the papers are available in the division of manuscripts of the Library of Congress. The University of Michigan General Library has a microfilm copy of the Amherst Papers.

7. See manuscript and printed works relating to Robert Rogers, George Croghan, Sir William Johnson, Sir Jeffery Amherst, General Thomas Gage, General Robert Monckton, Colonel Henry Bouquet, Major Henry Gladwin, and Captain Donald Campbell. Much of the source material relating to the Indian war is in the Bouquet Papers in the British Museum. The Bouquet correspondence has been made available in mimeographed form by the Pennsylvania Historical Commission. See also the transcripts of the Bouquet Papers, Series A., in the Canadian Archives. A calendar begun by Douglas Brymer, archivist, to be found in the *Reports* of the Canadian Archives is very useful.

8. Nicolas B. Wainwright, ed., "George Croghan's Journal, 1759–1763," *Pennsylvania Magazine of History and Biography* 62 (1947): 411. The Seneca plan is mentioned in other sources, but Croghan gives details of the secret plan of attack.

9. Parkman, 1:194–96.

10. James Sullivan *et al.*, eds., *The Papers of Sir William Johnson* (Albany, N.Y., 1921—), 3:27–30, 271 (hereafter cited as *Papers of Sir William Johnson*).

11. Daniel Claus to William Johnson, August 6, 1763, in *Collections* of the State Historical Society of Wisconsin 18 (1908): 256–58; Wainwright, p. 435. The Seneca chief Kaiaghshota (spelled Keyashuta in the document) later denied responsibility for the uprising stating that it was the fault of the western Indians and "our foolish young men." See speeches of Seneca and Delaware chiefs, Oct. 17, 1764, in Pennsylvania Historical Survey, *The Papers of Col. Henry Bouquet*, series 21655, pp. 235–36, mimeographed (Harrisburg, Pa., 1940–43).

12. *The Annual Register or A View of History, Politics, and Literature for the Year 1763* (London, 1796), p. 31.

13. Thomas Gage, who succeeded Jeffery Amherst as commander-in-chief, thought the only way to make peace with the Indians was to "win over Pontiac." Thomas Gage to Henry Bouquet, Dec. 20, 1764, Bouquet Papers, A. 8, pp. 491–92, Canadian Archives photostat.

14. Sir William Johnson criticized the Delaware sachem, Teedyuscung, for claiming to represent in 1756, "all the Indian Nations from the Sunrise . . . beyond the Lakes, as far as the Sun setts" (*Papers of Sir William Johnson*, 2: 826; *Pennsylvania Colonial Records* [Harrisburg, Pa., 1851–1853], 7:33), but Johnson did not accuse Pontiac of misrepresenting his authority.

15. R. Clyde Ford translation of the Pontiac Manuscript in Milo M. Quaife, ed., *Journal of Pontiac's Conspiracy, 1763* (Chicago, 1958), pp. 14–15. An older, and in some respects a better, translation of the Pontiac Manuscript is in the Pioneer Society of the State of Michigan, *Collections* (Lansing, Mich., 1907), 7:266–339. The original French version together with the Ford translation is published as Michigan Society of Colonial Wars, *Journal of Pontiac's Conspiracy*, ed., M. Agnes Burton (Detroit, 1942).

It was through Lewis Cass that Francis Parkman was able to get a copy of the document. Jacobs, ed., 1:36–37n. The entertaining story about the history of the document itself is told by Helen M. Ellis in "A Mystery of Old Detroit," Detroit Historical Society, *Bulletin*, 9 (October 1952): 11–12.

16. Quaife, ed., p. 144.

17. *New York Col. Docs.*, 7:862; Lawrence H. Gipson, *The Triumphant Empire* (New York, 1956), p. 96n.

18. Anthony F. C. Wallace, *The Death and Rebirth of the Seneca . . .* (New York, 1970), p. 121. See also pp. 114–21, 347. Wallace seems to have accepted the "conspiracy" theory of Parkman, however, without clearly characterizing the Indian war as war of native self-determination.

19. Quaife, ed., pp. 14–15.

20. Wallace, p. 120.

21. *Ibid.*, p. 117.

22. As Bernard Bailyn has argued, there is also considerable evidence to show that the American leaders of the Revolution were convinced that they were faced with "a deliberate conspiracy to destroy the balance of the constitution and eliminate the freedom . . . ." Bernard Bailyn, *The Ideological Origins of the American Revolution* (Cambridge, Mass., 1967), p. 144.

23. A similar conclusion was reached by Howard H. Peckham in his searching study, *Pontiac and the Indian Uprising*, p. 322.

24. Parkman, 1:217.

25. *Ibid.*, 1: 225.

26. *Ibid.*, 1: 238, 237, 218, 237.

27. *Ibid.*, 1: 210–11, 238, 267.

28. Describing the atrocious murders of Indians by a provincial, David Owens, Parkman wrote: "His example is one of the many in which the worst acts of Indian ferocity have been thrown into shade by the enormities of the white barbarians." Parkman, 2:217. Parkman also gave his reader a vivid account of the massacre of Conestoga mission Indians by the Paxton boys. *Ibid.*, 2: 125–44.

29. See Melville's review of the *Oregon Trail* in the *Literary World* 4, no. 113 (March 31, 1849): 291–93. Parker's critique of *Pontiac* was included in a letter to Parkman, December 22, 1851, Parkman Papers, Massachusetts Historical Society. The letter is printed in the appendix of deluxe editions of C. H. Farnham's *Life of Francis Parkman* (Frontenac and Champlain editions of Parkman's works).

30. Father Joseph-François Lafitau. See Jacobs, ed., 1:xxxvi, 23, 23n.

31. This statement represents a change of mind on my part. After some twenty years of off and on study of Parkman and his work I have concluded that he did indeed sometimes distort the facts for "dramatic interest." I am also convinced that such distortion was an outgrowth of Parkman's mental illness. See *ibid.*, pp. xliii–xlvii, lviii; Louis Casamajor, "The Illness of Francis Parkman," *American Journal of Psychiatry* 107 (1951):749–52.

32. In a readable, provocative essay, "Parkman's Indians and American

Violence," *Massachusetts Review* 12 (1971):221–39, Robert Shulman argues that the *Conspiracy of Pontiac* provides insight into white violence since the book exhibits ideas Americans have had to justify in their brutality toward the Indians. Here is background for understanding later American violence against the Indians, Vietnamese, and other non-white peoples.

33. Jacobs, ed., 1:35.

CHAPTER 9

1. See "An Accurate Map of North America Describing and Distinguishing the British, Spanish and French Dominions on this great Continent According to the Definitive Treaty Conducted at Paris 10th Feby. 1763—Also the West India Islands Belonging to and possessed by the several European Princes and States. The Whole laid down according to the latest and Most authentick Improvements by Eman Bowen Geogr. to His Majesty and John Gibson Engraver," London, 1763 (photostatic copy; original in John Carter Brown Library, Providence); "A Map of the British and French Dominions in North America with the Roads, Distances, Lands, and Extent of Settlements, Humbly Inscribed to the Right Honourable The Lord of Halifax, And the other Right Honourable The Lords Commissioners for Trade and Plantations, By their Lordships—Most Obliged and very humble Servant Jno. Mitchell," London, 1755 (photostatic copy; a duplicate of the original is in the William L. Clements Library, Ann Arbor, Mich.). Of the two, the Mitchell map is the more faithful to its title.

2. The late John Carl Parish noted the parallel Indian and white frontiers; it was logical, he wrote, "that there should arise the idea of an Indian boundary line forming a third parallel within the intervening zone." See John Carl Parish, *The Persistence of the Westward Movement and Other Essays*, Louis Knott Koontz, ed. (Berkeley, Calif., 1943), p. 131.

3. William Johnson to the Board of Trade, November 13, 1763, in E. B. O'Callaghan et al., eds., *Documents Relative to the Colonial History of the State of New York . . .* (Albany, N.Y., 1853–87), 7:534 (hereafter cited as *New York Col. Docs.*).

4. The tragic siege and final surrender of Fort Loudoun in the Overhill country of the Cherokee in August 1760 during the Cherokee War went unobserved by Amherst. Had he been alert Sir Jeffery might have realized that a parallel situation existed in the North, and that the Indians might prolong the war by seizing ammunition from the isolated forts. John Richard Alden makes this point in his *John Stuart and the Southern Colonial Frontier* (Ann Arbor, Mich., 1944), p. 117. George Croghan and his superior, Sir William Johnson, both declared that during Pontiac's Uprising the warriors prolonged the war by looting forts and trading posts of their valuable military supplies. See George Croghan to the Board of Trade (January 1764), *New York Col. Docs.*, 7:602–07; William Johnson to the Board of Trade, September 25, 1763, *ibid.*, 7:560.

5. Sir William Johnson, "Memorandum on Six Nations and Other Confederacies," in James Sullivan *et al.*, eds., *The Papers of Sir William Johnson*, (Albany, N.Y., 1921—), 4:240–46 (hereafter cited as *Papers of Sir William Johnson*). These figures are also printed with some variation in *New York Col. Docs.*, 7:582–84. By 1790 the Mohawk were reduced, according to one source, to one lone family. See W. A. Rossiter, ed., *A Century of Population Growth, from the First Census of the United States to the Twelfth, 1790–1900*

(Washington, D.C., 1909), p. 39. This table should be used with caution, however. For more reliable accounts of Indian population, see Evarts B. Greene and Virginia D. Harrington, *American Population before the Federal Census of 1790* (New York, 1932), pp. 194–202, 206.

6. Reuben G. Thwaites, ed., *Collections* of the State Historical Society of Wisconsin 18 (Madison, Wis., 1908): 240–41n.

7. Robert Dinwiddie, lieutenant governor of Virginia, 1751–58, argued that the southern Indians should be courted by the English because these tribes could muster more warriors than the northern confederacies.

8. "Total number of Gun Men in the Southern District," December 1, 1764, an unidentified Public Record Office manuscript on file in the Illinois Historical Survey, University of Illinois. Indian populations are very difficult to ascertain with exactness. John R. Swanton who carried on intensive research into Indian populations complained of this fact in his *Early History of the Creek Indians and Their Neighbors,* Smithsonian Institution, Bureau of American Ethnology Bulletin, no. 73 (Washington, D.C., 1922), p. 421.

9. Johnson lists 11,980 warriors. *Papers of Sir William Johnson,* 4:246. Population estimates on warrior strength are summarized in the early chapters in James H. Cassedy, *Demography in Early America; Beginnings of the Statistical Mind, 1600–1800* (Cambridge, Mass., 1969), pp. 78–82, 108, 112. Iroquois population decline about 1698 from some 2,800 to an estimated 1,324 was attributed to King William's War. *Ibid.,* p. 81. Epidemic diseases were another cause for Iroquois depopulation. *Ibid.*

10. For accounts of the "barbarous outrages" that followed see W. R. Jacobs, ed., *The Paxton Riots and the Frontier Theory* (Chicago, 1967), pp. 3–14. The role of Franklin and that of the Quakers in the riots is analyzed in David Sloan, "The Paxton Riots" (Ph.D. diss., University of California, Santa Barbara, 1969).

11. Reproduced in Howard H. Peckham, *Pontiac and the Indian Uprising* (Princeton, N.J., 1947), pp. 236–37.

12. General Thomas Gage to Henry Bouquet, Dec. 7, 1764, Gage Papers, cited in *ibid.,* p. 263.

13. *Ibid.*

14. *Ibid.,* pp. 310–11.

15. Peckham gives Parkman's version of Pontiac's death, based upon recollections of old St. Louis traders, but Peckham's evidence from the Gage Papers makes it probable that a Peoria chief killed Pontiac. See *ibid.* and Francis Parkman, *The Conspiracy of Pontiac and the Indian War after the Conquest of Canada* (Boston, 1898), 2:328–29.

The factionalism among Indian chiefs, often resulting in fierce rivalries, was particularly strong among the Iroquois who had three kinds of leaders: sachems, or peace chiefs; pinetree orators, known for their wisdom; and war chiefs, often young men who might later become sachems or orators. See William N. Fenton, "Factionalism in American Indian Society," *Tirage à part: Actes du IVe Congrès International des Sciences Anthropologiques et Ethnologiques* (Vienna, 1952), 2:330–40.

16. Parkman, 2:248.

17. *Ibid.,* 2:251.

18. See the discussion of Indian-white intermarriage in Chapter 10.

19. This map is reproduced in Louis DeVorsey, Jr., *The Indian Boundary in the Southern Colonies, 1763–1775* (Chapel Hill, N.C., 1966), p. 37.

20. *New York Col. Docs.,* 7:637–41.

21. DeVorsey, p. 232.

22. I am indebted to one of my advanced students, Dan Reddell, for calling my attention to maps concerning the Fort Stanwix treaty in this series. See "Map of the Frontiers of the Northern Colonies . . . Ft. Stanwix in Novr. 1768," *New York Col. Docs.*, 7:136–37 for the line Johnson negotiated. The Board of Trade line, which Johnson seems to have ignored, is in *ibid*, 8:30–31.

23. Dan Reddell, in a paper being revised for publication, "The Fort Stanwix Treaty Re-examined," argues that the treaty line was partly responsible for Indian attacks during the Revolution. See also Ray A. Billington, "The Fort Stanwix Treaty of 1768," *New York History* 25 (April 1944): 182–94 and Jack M. Sosin, *The Revolutionary Frontier, 1763–1783* (New York, 1967), pp. 14–19, for land speculation schemes relating to the treaty.

24. See DeVorsey, p. 234.

25. Quoted in Reginald Horsman, *Expansion and American Indian Policy, 1783–1812* (East Lansing, Mich., 1967), p. 8.

26. *Ibid.*, p. 9.

27. Angie Debo, *A History of the Indians of the United States* (Norman, Okla., 1971), p. 101; Georgiana C. Nammack, *Fraud, Politics, and the Dispossession of the Indians, The Iroquois Land Frontier in the Colonial Period* (Norman, Okla., 1969), pp. 153 ff.

28. Nammack, pp. 153 ff.

29. William Hagan stresses the ironic fact that today the reservation has "become the last stronghold of Indian culture and of an emerging Indian nationalism." Francis Paul Prucha, William T. Hagan, and Alvin M. Josephy, Jr., *Indiana Historical Society Lectures, 1970–1971, American Indian Policy* (Indianapolis, Ind., 1971), p. 36.

30. See the Prologue of this volume and Winthrop D. Jordan, *White Over Black, American Attitudes Toward the Negro, 1550–1812* (Chapel Hill, N.C., 1968), pp. 12–14, 162–63, 216–17, 391, 477–81, for analyses of the origins of prejudice against the Indian.

31. For a description of the seventeenth- and eighteenth-century New England Indian reservations and the legal network of argumentation setting up these areas, see Yasu Kawashima, "Legal Origins of the Indian Reservation in Colonial Massachusetts," *New England Quarterly* 13 (1969): 42–56. The subsequent legal rationale for the occupation of Indian lands is set forth in Wilcomb E. Washburn, *Red Man's Land, White Man's Law: A Study of the Past and Present Status of the American Indian* (New York, 1971), pp. 27 ff.

CHAPTER 10

1. "Indeitsy" [Indians], *Bol'shaia Sovetskaia Entsiklopediia* (Moscow, 1949–58), 17:630.

2. W. R. Jacobs and Edmond E. Masson, "History and Propaganda: Soviet Image of the American Past," *Mid-America* 46 (April 1964): 75–91.

3. G. B. Nash, "Red, White, and Black, the Origins of Racism in America," in G. B. Nash and Richard Weiss, eds., *The Great Fear, Race in the Mind of America* (New York, 1970), pp. 4–6; Maurice Marc Wasserman, "The American Indian as Seen by the Seventeenth-Century Chroniclers" (Ph.D. diss., University of Pennsylvania, 1954), pp. 2, 4, 9, 407, 408, 409, 415. See also two well-documented essays: Wilcomb Washburn, "The Moral and Legal Justifications for dispossessing the Indians," and Nancy O. Lurie, "Indian Cultural

Adjustment to European Civilization," in James Morton Smith, ed., *Seventeenth-Century America, Essays in Colonial History* (Chapel Hill, N.C., 1959), pp. 15–32, 33–60.

4. W. R. Jacobs, *Wilderness Politics and Indian Gifts* (Lincoln, Neb., 1966), pp. 90–114.

5. M. Eugene Sirmans, *Colonial South Carolina, A Political History, 1663–1763* (Chapel Hill, N.C., 1966), pp. 17, 23, 40–43, 53–54, 60; Verner W. Crane, *The Southern Frontier, 1670–1732* (Ann Arbor, Mich., 1964), pp. 19, 31, 80–81, 112–14.

6. Louis DeVorsey, Jr., *The Indian Boundary in the Southern Colonies, 1763–1775* (Chapel Hill, N.C., 1966), pp. 27 ff., 48 ff., 93 ff.; William Brandon, *The American Heritage Book of Indians* (New York, 1961), pp. 199–202.

7. William Christie MacLeod, *The American Indian Frontier* (New York, 1928), pp. 422–23; Francis Paul Prucha, *American Indian Policy in the Formative Years, The Indian Trade and Intercourse Acts, 1790–1834* (Cambridge, Mass., 1962), pp. 3, 26–40, 143 ff.; David H. Corkran, *The Creek Frontier, 1540–1783* (Norman, Okla., 1967), 309–25. Alvin M. Josephy Jr., *The Indian Heritage of America* (New York, 1968), pp. 314–16. Reginald Horsman's provocative volume, *Expansion and American Indian Policy, 1783–1812* (East Lansing, Mich., 1967), p. 61, develops the startling thesis that a policy of bringing civilization to the benighted Indian evolved in the first years of the Republic partly because the founding fathers decided that the alternative of exterminating the Indian would probably besmirch the national honor. One of the most valuable essays ever written to explain Indian behavior is William N. Fenton's "Factionalism in American Indian Society," *Tirage à part: Actes du IVᵉ Congrès International des Sciences Anthropologiques et Ethnologiques* (Vienna, 1952), 2:330–40. Much of the literature on early American Indian history is summarized in Bernard W. Sheehan's "Indian-White Relations in Early America, A Review Essay," *William and Mary Quarterly* 36 (April 1969): 267–86.

8. Lurie, p. 39. Lurie stresses that the specific points that made the European feel superior had little meaning for the seventeenth-century Indians.

9. Wasserman, pp. 2, 3, 4, 210, 406; William Brandon, "American Indians and American History," *The American West* 2 (Spring 1965): 91. In a brilliant article, N. Scott Momaday, a modern scholar of Kiowa Indian ancestry, analyzes Puritan aggressiveness toward the Pequots and the resulting interpretations of the Pequot War. See N. Scott Momaday, "The Morality of Indian Hating," *Ramparts* 3 (Summer 1964): 29–40. An eloquent defense of Puritan Indian policy is in Alden T. Vaughan's *New England Frontier, Puritans, 1620–1675* (Boston, 1965), pp. 134, 309 ff.; a modified point of view is in Douglas E. Leach's scholarly volumes, *Flintlock and Tomahawk, New England in King Philip's War* (New York, 1958), pp. 50 ff., and *The Northern Colonial Frontier, 1607–1763* (New York, 1966), pp. 36–37, 55–61.

10. For a discussion of Parkman's views on the Indian, see W. R. Jacobs, "Some Social Ideas of Francis Parkman," *The American Quarterly* 9 (Winter 1957): 387–96.

11. Washburn, p. 20. Washburn stresses the modern interpretation of colonial history, envisioning the English invasion of the North American continent as a kind of military beachhead against hostile Indians (*ibid.*, p. 19); Wilcomb Washburn, *Red Man's Land, White Man's Law, A Study of the Past and Present Status of the American Indian* (New York, 1971), p. 33.

12. Washburn, *Red Man's Land, White Man's Law,* pp. 34–35. Washburn quotes Alexander Brown, *The First Republic of America* (Boston, 1898), pp. 41–42.

13. Washburn, *Red Man's Land, White Man's Law,* pp. 33–34. Washburn cites Roger Clap's "Memoirs" (London, 1731), in Alexander Young, ed., *Chronicles of the First Planters of the Colony of Massachusetts, From 1623 to 1636* (Boston, 1846), p. 350. See also Wasserman, pp. 3–4 ff.

14. James Adair's, *History of the American Indians* (London, 1775) is largely an extended essay comparing the Indians and the ten lost tribes. This theory had been a favorite of European writers. See Lee Eldridge Huddleston, *Origins of the American Indians, European Concepts, 1492–1729* (Austin, Tex., 1967), pp. 33–47.

15. *Minutes of the Provincial Council of Pennsylvania* (Philadelphia, 1851–53), 9:138–42, contains the complete text of the "Remonstrance" made by the Paxton rioters. Franklin, in an unsigned pamphlet, criticized the rioters for murdering peaceful natives: "The only Crime of these poor Wretches seems to have been that they had reddish brown Skin, and black hair." *A Narrative of the Late Massacres, in Lancaster County, of a Number of Indians . . .* (Philadelphia, 1764). See also W. R. Jacobs, ed., *The Paxton Riots and the Frontier Theory* (Chicago, 1967), pp. 8–29.

16. An interesting discussion of this question appears in Bernard W. Sheehan, "Civilization and the American Indian in the Thought of the Jeffersonian Era" (Ph.D. diss., University of Virginia, 1965), pp. 251 ff. Sheehan, in tracing the origins of European attitudes toward the land, points out that John Locke, in his *Second Treatise on Civil Government,* associated ownership of property with cultivation. Theodore Roosevelt later referred to Indian lands as a "game preserve." *Ibid.* See Georgiana C. Nammack, *Fraud, Politics, and the Dispossession of the Indians, The Iroquois Land Frontier in the Colonial Period* (Norman, Okla., 1969), pp. xiii–21 for an excellent discussion of the European and Indian concepts of land ownership. Washburn, *Red Man's Land, White Man's Law,* pp. 6 ff., also deals with the historic background of conflicting Indian-white claims to the land.

17. Lurie, pp. 39–40.

18. References to Indian generosity and kindness are detailed in Brandon, "American Indians and American History," p. 17; in Washburn, *Red Man's Land, White Man's Law,* pp. 34 ff.; and in Edmund S. Morgan, "The American Indian: Incorrigible Individualist," *Mirror of the Indian,* Booklet published by the Associates of the John Carter Brown Library (Providence, R.I., 1963), pp. 10 ff.

19. Brandon, p. 25, quoting Robert Rogers, *A Concise Account of North America* (London, 1765).

20. Johnson to Arthur Lee, February 28, 1771, E. B. O'Callaghan, ed., *Documentary History of the State of New York* (Albany, N.Y., 1849–51), 4 (1851): 430–39.

21. *Ibid.*

22. Charles Lee to Miss Sidney Lee, June 18, 1756, New York Historical Society, *Collections* for the year 1871 (New York, 1872), 1:3.

23. *Ibid.*

24. W. R. Jacobs, ed., *The Appalachian Indian Frontier* (Lincoln, Neb., 1967), p. 68.

25. *Ibid.,* p. 38.

26. There has been a tendency among modern scholars to belittle the
noble savage image of the American Indian as it is found in American history
and literature. Roy Harvey Pearce, writing in his book *The Savages of America*,
exemplifies this tendency when he writes:

> The discovery of America furnished savages in abundance. The question
> was: How noble were they? . . . the forces which informed the idea
> of savagism at one and the same time destroyed the idea of the noble sav-
> age and made isolated radicals of those who would believe in it.

The Savages of America, A Study of the Indian and the Idea of Civilization,
rev. ed. (Baltimore, 1965), p. 136. Bernard W. Sheehan, in a chapter on "Violence," concludes that "the Indian's penchant for the most exotic brands of
violence . . . commanded a realistic appraisal of his savage character." "Civilization and the Indian," p. 325.

27. Robert Beverley, *The History and Present State of Virginia*, ed. Louis B.
Wright (Chapel Hill, N.C., 1947), pp. xix, 11.

28. *Ibid.*, p. 159.

29. *Ibid.*, p. 171.

30. Governor Alexander Spotswood of Virginia in a long letter to the Board
of Trade, April 5, 1717, R. A. Brock, ed., *The Official Letters of Alexander
Spotswood* (Richmond, Va., 1885), 2:227, comments on this point.

31. Prucha, pp. 215, 217; William T. Hagan, *American Indians* (Chicago,
1961), p. 54.

32. Excerpts from sources on early educational contacts between Europeans
and Indians are in Robert H. Bremner, *et al.*, eds., *Children and Youth in
America, A Documentary History, 1600–1865* (Cambridge, Mass., 1970),
1:74–78.

33. Anthony F. C. Wallace, *The Death and Rebirth of the Seneca* . . .
(New York, 1970), p. 200.

34. Wright, ed., p. 189.

35. William C. Reichel, ed., *Memorials of the Moravian Church* (Philadelphia, 1870), 1:95–96.

36. Francis Parkman, *The Conspiracy of Pontiac and the Indian War After
the Conquest of Canada* (Boston, 1898), 2:246–49.

37. MacLeod, pp. 359–60. See also documentary accounts of tobacco brides
of early Virginia in Bremner, 1:30–32.

38. Wright, ed., pp. 38–39.

39. *Ibid.*

40. *William Byrd's Histories of the Dividing Line Betwixt Virginia and
North Carolina*, ed. William K. Boyd (Raleigh, N.C., 1929), pp. 3–4.

41. *Ibid.*

42. Governor Spotswood to the Board of Trade, April 5, 1717, *Letters of
Alexander Spotswood*, 2:227. Gary B. Nash, in an excellent analysis of "The
Image of the Indian in the Southern Colonial Mind" (Paper given at the Winter
1971 U.C.L.A. Seminar on the Interactions of the American Indian and African
Historiography), also stresses the almost complete absence of white intermarriage with Indians despite frequent comments on their physical attractiveness and cleanliness of body and mind. John Lawson, who visited the southern
Indian frontier in 1700, gave glowing accounts of the attractiveness of the
southern Indians almost in the language of Robert Beverley, of their "very
hale Constitution; their Breaths are as sweet as the Air they breathe in, and

the woman seems to be of that tender composition . . . their Love is never that of Force . . . when slighted are as ready to untie the Knot at one end, as you are at the other." Lawson implies here that there was more interracial mating than such writers as Beverley, Byrd, or Spotswood acknowledged. In one instance Lawson reported, "I knew an *European* Man that had a Child or two by one of these *Indian* Women, and afterwards married a Christian." The Indian woman later "fell a crying . . . in great Disorder." John Lawson, *A New Voyage to Carolina*, ed. Hugh T. Lefler (Chapel Hill, N.C., 1967), p. 195.

43. "CONSIDERATIONS *For Securing Improving & Enlarging your Majesty's Dominions in America*," Sept. 8, 1721, E. B. O'Callaghan *et al.*, eds., *Documents Relative to the Colonial History of the State of New York* . . . (Albany, N.Y., 1853–87), 5 (1855):627.

44. Jacobs, *Wilderness Politics*, p. 170. Lieutenant Governor Robert H. Morris declared war on the Delawares in April 14, 1756. *Minutes of the Provincial Council of Pennsylvania* (Philadelphia, 1851–53), 7:88.

45. Jacobs, ed., *The Appalachian Indian Frontier*, p. 40.

46. George Edward Reed, ed., *Pennsylvania Archives*, 4th ser. (Harrisburg, Pa., 1900), 3:292–93; Jacobs, ed., *The Paxton Riots*, pp. 33–34.

47. Edmund Atkin to Horatio Sharpe, June 30, 1757, Samuel Hazard, ed., *Pennsylvania Archives*, 1st ser. (Philadelphia, 1852), 3:199.

48. Jacobs, *Wilderness Politics*, pp. 138–39n.

49. John Fitzpatrick, ed., *The Writings of George Washington* . . . (Washington, D.C., 1931), 1:97, 115.

50. See Douglas E. Leach's free transcription of the treaty in his edition of *A Rhode Islander Reports on King Philip's War, The Second Harris Letter of August, 1676* (Providence, R.I., 1963), pp. 89–95.

51. *Ibid.*, pp. 6–7. Leach suggests that the attack was based upon "the theory of preventive war and . . . the potential market value of Narragansett land. . . ." *The Northern Colonial Frontier, 1607–1763*, pp. 66–67. In his earlier work, *Flintlock and Tomahawk*, Leach stresses the Narragansetts' treachery as a justification for the Massachusetts' attack (pp. 112 ff.).

52. "Treaty of Logg's Town," *Virginia Magazine of History and Biography* 13 (October 1905):154–74.

53. "Indian Proceedings at Mount Johnson," June 17–21, 1755, James Sullivan *et al.*, eds., *The Papers of Sir William Johnson* (Albany, N.Y., 1921—), 1:640–42.

54. For a partial list of other important Indian treaties of the colonial era, see Henry F. DePuy, *A Bibliography of English Colonial Treaties with the American Indians Including a Synopsis of Each Treaty* (New York, 1917). A number of significant treaties are discussed by the editors in their introduction in Carl Van Doren and Julian P. Boyd, eds., *Indian Treaties Printed by Benjamin Franklin, 1736–1762: Their Literary, Historical, and Bibliographical Significance* (Philadelphia, 1938).

55. Crane, pp. 80 ff. A description of the Carolina Indian slave trade appears in Sirmans, pp. 33, 38, 40–43, 47, 53–54, 60. The remarkable series of South Carolina Commons House committees devoted to all phases of Indian affairs is described and analyzed in George E. Frakes, *Laboratory for Liberty, the South Carolina Legislative Committee System, 1719–1776* (Lexington, Ken., 1970), pp. 31–32, 94–96.

56. Yasuhide Kawashima, "Indians and the Law in Colonial Massachusetts,

1689–1763" (Ph.D. diss., University of California, Santa Barbara, 1967), pp. 28, 281.

57. *Ibid.*, pp. 280 ff. See also Winthrop D. Jordan, *White Over Black, American Attitudes Toward the Negro, 1550–1812* (Chapel Hill, N.C., 1968), pp. 66–69, for a brief discussion of enslavement of the Indians in New England.

58. Crane, pp. 80 ff.

59. George Milligen, *A Short Description of the Province of South Carolina, with an Account of The Air, Weather, and Diseases, at Charles-Town* [written in 1763] (London, 1770), p. 26, quoted in James H. Cassedy, *Demography in Early America, Beginnings of the Statistical Mind, 1600–1800* (Cambridge, Mass., 1969), p. 86. Dr. Milligen in later life assumed the name of Milligen-Johnston.

60. Nammack, pp. 86–89.

61. Brandon, pp. 187–202, includes an excellent analysis of Indian-white conflict in the colonial era. See also MacLeod, pp. 209–92; William T. Hagan, pp. 1–30; Francis Paul Prucha, ed., *The Indian in American History* (New York, 1971), pp. 7 ff. Denton R. Bedford's "The Great Swamp War" of 1675, stressing the heroism of Narragansett leaders Canonchet and Pometacomet as seen from the modern Indian point of view, is published in *The Indian Historian* 4 (Summer 1971): 27–41, 58.

62. Dale Van Every, *Disinherited: The Lost Birthright of the American Indian* (New York, 1966), pp. 239 ff.; Thurman Wilkins, *Cherokee Tragedy, The Story of the Ridge Family and the Decimation of a People* (New York, 1970), pp. 304–29.

63. Wright, ed., p. 233.

CHAPTER 11

1. Douglas L. Oliver in his *The Pacific Islands*, 3rd ed. (New York, 1961), pp. xii, 1–80, stresses the extreme importance of ecological factors in shaping the cultures of native peoples of the Pacific Islands, New Guinea, and Australia. Similarly, Alfred L. Kroeber, Frank G. Speck, John M. Cooper, and William N. Fenton have described Indian cultures that maintained an ecological balance with wilderness areas. Speck, for example, in *The Penobscot Man* (Philadelphia, 1940), pp. 207 ff., analyzes the family hunting ground system of the northeastern Indians, a method of conserving beaver supply. Debate on Speck's theories and discussion of the impact of the fur trade on the northeastern Indians is in Rolf Knight, "A Re-examination of Hunting, Trapping, and Territoriality among the Northeastern Indians," in Anthony Leeds and Andrew P. Vayda, eds., *Man, Culture, and Animals* (Washington, D.C., 1965), pp. 27–41. Calvin Martin, "The Algonquin Family Hunting Territory Revisited" (Paper, University of California, Santa Barbara), shows that evidence in the *Jesuit Relations* supports Speck's theories on Indian conservationist techniques. Further discussion on this point is in Eleanor Leacock, *The Montagnais "Hunting Territory" and the Fur Trade*, The American Anthropological Association, memoir no. 78 (Beloit, Wis., 1954), pp. 24–40. The remarkable agricultural techniques of the Hurons who successfully maintained productive corn fields for a dozen years or more are analyzed in Conrad E. Heidenreich, "The Geography of Huronia in the First Half of the 17th Century" (Ph.D. diss., McMaster University, 1970), pp. 267–73.

2. See Douglas Oliver's essay on "The Dispossessed" in *The Pacific Islands*, pp. 157–73.

3. Edward H. Spicer in *Cycles of Conquest: The Impact of Spain, Mexico, and the United States on the Indians of the Southwest, 1533–1960* (Tucson, Ariz., 1962), pp. 581–82, discusses, for example, H. H. Bancroft's idea that "savages cannot be civilized under the tuition of superior races," a point of view found in the sources Bancroft used.

4. The literature published by anthropologists on these native peoples is immense. See Note on Sources.

5. J. C. Beaglehole, ed., *The Journals of Captain James Cook on His Voyage of Discovery, The Voyage of the Endeavor* (Cambridge, Eng., 1955), p. 508. Cook and other writers stressed that the Aborigines seemed happy living on only the bare necessities, yet Europeans were unhappy. There was an undercurrent of dissatisfaction with civilization because it had abandoned nature. Alan Moorehead in his perceptive book, *The Fatal Impact, An Account of the Invasion of the South Pacific, 1767–1840* (Ringwood, Victoria, 1966), pp. 150–51, comments on this attitude of certain Pacific explorers.

6. Donald Craigie Gordon, *The Australian Frontier in New Guinea, 1870–1885* (New York, 1951), pp. 19–42, summarizes the activities of the first explorers in New Guinea. See also Andrew Sharp, *The Discovery of Australia* (London, 1963), pp. 21 ff.

7. A. P. Elkin's chapter, "The Land and the Aborigines," in his *The Australian Aborigines* (Sydney, 1954), pp. 24–48; essay on Aboriginal land rights dated Nov. 15, 1839, possibly written by John D. Lang (1799–1878), clergyman and early anthropologist, in manuscript volume labeled "Aborigines," A 610, Mitchell Library, Sydney; *Indian Place Names, Their Origin, Evolution, and Meaning*, by John Rydjord (Norman, Okla., 1968); Erwin G. Gudde, *California Placenames, The Origin and Etymology of Current Geographical Names*, 2d ed. (Berkeley, Calif. 1960), and the linguistic and ethnographic criticism of this book by William Bright in *The American Journal of Folklore* 75 (1962): 78–82; A. L. Kroeber, *California Placenames of Indian Origin* (Berkeley, Calif., 1916); diagram 2, "Religious Beliefs and Change of Land Rights," in Ian Hogbin and Peter Lawrence, *Studies in New Guinea Land Tenure* (Sydney, 1967), p. 117.

8. Elkin, pp. 132–55; R. M. and C. H. Berndt, *The First Australians* (Sydney, 1969), pp. 74–78; A. L. Kroeber, *Anthropology, Race, Language, Culture, Psychology, Prehistory* (New York, 1948), p. 396; William N. Fenton, "The Iroquois in History" (Paper read at the Wenner-Gren Symposium, Burg Wartenstein, Austria, August 7–14, 1967); F. W. Hodge, ed., *Handbook of the Indians*, Smithsonian Institution Bureau of American Ethnology Bulletin, no. 30, pt. 2 (Washington, D.C., 1910), pp. 787–95. New Guinea natives' shamanism, magic, and animistic ritual is described in Roy A. Rappaport, *Pigs For Ancestors* New Haven, 1967), see especially "Pigs, Eels, and Fertility," pp. 210–13.

9. Leonard W. Labaree, ed., *The Papers of Benjamin Franklin* (New Haven, Conn., 1969) 13:351. For a modern appraisal of this method of limiting population growth, see Christopher Tietze, "The Effect of Breastfeeding on the Rate of Conception," *Proceedings of the International Population Conference* (New York, 1961), 2:129–36. Among Dr. Tietze's conclusions are: "Since . . . breastfeeding tends to prolong the interval between pregnancies, it seems worthwhile to evaluate it as a method of child spacing" (p. 133).

10. C. D. Rowley, *The New Guinea Villager* (Melbourne, 1965), pp. 32–52; P. Biskup, B. Jinks, and H. Nelson, *A Short History of New Guinea* (Syd-

ney, 1968), pp. 1–28. The variety of modern primitive life is described by a former patrol officer, J. P. Sinclair, in his *Behind the Ranges, Patrolling New Guinea* (Melbourne, 1966).

11. The specific new diseases that caused depopulation among Pacific islanders and Australian Aborigines after contacts with Europeans are discussed in Felix M. Keesing, *The South Seas in the Modern World* (New York, 1941), pp. 57 ff., 367; Kroeber, *Anthropology*, pp. 182 ff. Kroeber makes the point that epidemics once so deadly to islanders and American Indians are reduced to the level of mild virulence after a generation or two. Edward Spicer stresses a cycle theory of the conquest and withdrawal of Europeans who may leave behind newly invigorated native societies much enriched by cultural exchange. Spicer, p. 568.

12. Rowley, p. 115.

13. Theodore F. Bevan, *Toil, Travel, and Discovery in British Guinea* (London, 1890), p. 276.

14. Hogbin and Lawrence, pp. xiii, 32–33, 100–34.

15. Statement by John Douglas, "Her Majesty's Special Commissioner to New Guinea," Dec. 31, 1886, *British New Guinea, Report for the Year 1886* (Victoria, 1887), p. 8. A collection of early British reports on the protectorate is preserved in the New Guinea History Collection, Library of the University of Papua-New Guinea, Port Moresby.

16. *British New Guinea Annual Report, Her Majesty's Administrator of Government from 4th of September, 1888 to 30th June 1889* (Melbourne, 1890), p. 6.

17. Biskup *et al.*, p. 25; Rowley, p. 58.

18. *British New Guinea Report for the Year 1886*, pp. 8–9.

19. *The Papuan Courier*, June 16, 1931.

20. *Ibid.* Perceptive comments on native sorcery are in Beatrice Grimshaw, *The New Guinea* (Philadelphia, 1911), p. 200; Jan Hogbin, *Transformation Scene: The Changing Culture of a New Guinea Village* (London, 1951), pp. 136, 142–47, 222–26.

21. D. A. M. Lea and P. G. Irwin, *New Guinea: The Territory and Its People* (Melbourne, 1967), pp. 18–19, chart rainfall up to 250 inches per year in parts of New Guinea and New Britain.

22. The gradual changes of the "salubrius" native village of eight hundred native people located at the site of Port Moresby is described in Élisée Recus, *Australasia*, ed. A. H. Keane (London [1889]), pp. 313–14.

23. Brian Essai, *Papua and New Guinea: A Contemporary Survey* (Melbourne, 1961), pp. 237–38; Albert Maori Kiki, *Kiki, Ten Thousand Years in a Lifetime, A New Guinea Autobiography* (Melbourne, 1968), pp. 161–87, gives the viewpoint of an elected leader of the New Guinea native people. See also John Wilkes, ed., *New Guinea . . . Future Indefinite?* (Sydney, 1968), 139–67.

24. Elkin's strictures are in *The Australian Aborigines*, pp. 29, 44, 156–62 ff., and are echoed in A. Grenfell Price, *White Settlers and Native Peoples . . .* (Melbourne, 1949), pp. 194–95; see also S. F. Cook, *The Conflict Between the California Indian and White Civilization: The Indian Versus the Spanish Mission* (Berkeley, Calif., 1943), pp. 3–12, 15, 113–28. A similar discussion is in Felix M. Keesing, *The South Seas in the Modern World* (New York, 1941), pp. 79–80. Keesing's study of *The Menomini Indians of Wisconsin: A Study of Three Centuries of Cultural Contact and Change* (Phila-

delphia, 1939) reveals a recognizable tribal identity among these Indians, but only fragments of their aboriginal culture have survived.

25. A. P. Elkin, "The Reaction of Primitive Races to the White Man's Culture," *Hibbert Journal* 35 (1937):537–45, cited in Price, pp. 196, 225.

26. William N. Fenton, ed., *Parker on the Iroquois,* . . . (Syracuse, N.Y., 1968), intro., pp. 25–47; bk. 1, pp. 5–113; bk. 3, pp. 7–132.

27. W. R. Jacobs, *Wilderness Politics and Indian Gifts* (Lincoln, Neb., 1966), pp. 5, 159 ff. An excellent documented account of the dispossession of Iroquois tribal communities is in Georgiana C. Nammack, *Fraud, Politics and the Dispossession of the Indians,* . . . (Norman, Okla., 1969), pp. 22–106.

28. Fenton, ed., bk. 2, pp. 5–138; Anthony F. C. Wallace, *The Death and Rebirth of the Seneca* . . . (New York, 1969), pp. 239 ff.

29. Elkin, *The Australian Aborigines,* pp. 328–38. For the relationship between the Delaware Prophet and Pontiac, mentioned above, see Chapter 9.

30. Kroeber, *Anthropology,* p. 431. Kroeber makes the interesting point that, if by a miracle a major Indian tribe had conquered the whites, our culture would be perhaps only slightly modified (p. 430).

31. Kroeber, *Cultural and Natural Areas of Native North America* (Berkeley, Calif., 1947), pp. 46, 52, 206–28.

32. Australian Department of Territories, *The Australian Aborigines* (Sydney, 1967), p. 6.

33. *Ibid.,* p. 3.

34. See Harold E. Driver, *Indians of North America,* 2d ed., rev. (Chicago, 1969), pp. 63–65, for an additional critique of Dobyns' estimates and methodology. Driver cuts Dobyns' population figures by about 50 percent. Dobyns' stress on epidemic diseases as a cause for Indian depopulation is admirably set forth in his "An Outline of Andean Epidemic History to 1720," *Bulletin of the History of Medicine,* XXXVII (Nov.–Dec., 1963), pp. 493–515.

35. Biskup *et al.,* p. 8, a Chimbu area estimate.

36. The deplorable condition of many of the California Indians after American occupation is described in *The Indians of Southern California in 1852* . . . , ed. John W. Caughey (San Marino, Calif., 1952); Cook, pp. 5–95.

37. A. L. Kroeber, "The Nature of Land-Holding Groups in Aboriginal California," in *Aboriginal California: Three Studies in Culture History* (Berkeley, Calif., 1963), pp. 81–120.

38. *Ibid.;* William Brandon, "The California Indian World," *The Indian Historian* 2 (Summer 1969): 4–7.

39. Elkin, *The Australian Aborigines,* pp. 1–23.

40. "I confess myself at a loss to comprehend how a few strolling savages, entirely ignorant . . . [and] averse to cultivating the land[,] . . . may be said to possess a small portion of it today by erecting their crude huts, [since they] will abandon it tomorrow. . . ." Diary of Mary Thomas, p. 185, quoted in Ralph M. Hague, typescript ms, "The Law in South Australia, 1836–67," chap. 11, p. 3, State Library of South Australia, Archives Dept., accession no. 1051.

41. [John D.] Lang, essay on Aboriginal land rights in manuscript volume labeled "Aborigines," A 610, Mitchell Library, Sydney. A portion of the signature on this document is obscured.

42. *Ibid.* See also note 7.

43. Lang, "Aborigines."

44. See, for example, [George Augustus] "Robinson's Reports on the Tas-

manian Aborigines," A 612, pp. 76–77, Mitchell Library, Sydney; see especially the letter dated Sept. 9, 1839, from Robinson to Governor George
Arthur, in which Robinson comments on "the mortality" that "has pervaded the
whole Aboriginal population." Robinson wrote that after contact with "white
men" the Aborigines were "imbibed [with] similar debauched habits and vicious propensities."

On the creation of the "Protectorate" system by the British government in
1838–42, see Box 3, "Aboriginal Protectorate," State Library of Victoria Archives, Melbourne. A "Chief Protector" was appointed with four assistant protectors, each officer to have "a district." He was to induce natives "to assume
more settled habits of life . . . and watch over the rights and interests of the
natives. . . ." These officers had duties somewhat similar to those of the
Indian superintendents in the British colonies. See W. R. Jacobs, ed., *The Appalachian Indian Frontier* (Lincoln, Neb., 1967), pp. xviff .; Samuel C. Mc-
Culloch, "Sir George Gipps and Eastern Australia's Policy Toward the Ab-
origine," *Journal of Modern History* 33 (1961):261–69.

45. Comment by Thomas Henry Braim (1814–91), Anglican clergyman of
Hobart and Sydney in a handwritten essay, "The Aborigines," pp. 3–4, A 614,
Mitchell Library, Sydney.

46. Dampier is quoted at length in C. M. H. Clark, *A History of Australia,
From the Earliest Times to the Age of Macquarie* (Melbourne, 1962), pp.
39–40.

47. Anthony Trollope, *Australia,* ed. P. D. Edwards and R. B. Joyce (St.
Lucia, Queensland, 1967), pp. 113, 475.

48. *Ibid.,* p. 475.

49. Clark, p. 169.

50. Quoted from A. T. Yarwood's penetrating essay on Marsden in *Australian Dictionary of Biography* (Melbourne, 1967), 2:209.

51. Geoffrey Blainey, *The Tyranny of Distance, How Distance Shaped Australia's History* (Melbourne, 1969), p. 132.

52. Aboriginese were often referred to as "blacks" or "savages" in newspaper
accounts of disturbances and occasional murders of settlers. See, for example,
The Melbourne Argus, Nov. 20, 1846, p. 2, for an account of troopers cap-
turing three natives, Bobby, Tolmey, and Bullet-eye, all charged with murder.
"Poisoning" Aborigines, "was fairly widespread" according to Bryan W. Harrison, "The Myall Creek Massacre and Its Significance in the Controversy over
the Aborigines During Australia's Early Squatting Period" (B.A. Honours
thesis, New England University, Armidale, 1966), pp. 101–02. On page 102n.,
Harrison cites the following publications as evidence of poisoning: *The Colonist,* July 4, 1838; *Sydney Gazette,* December 20, 1838; *Sydney Monitor,*
December 24, 1838. The Myall Creek massacre and white use of poisons are
briefly covered in Clark, p. 87. See also Kathleen Hassel, *The Relations Between the Settlers and Aborigines in South Australia, 1836–60* (Adelaide,
1966), pp. 2 ff.

Whites were reluctant to acknowledge use of poisons against Indians, but
according to Jim Mike, an Ute Indian, in an interview on June 20, 1968, the Ute
Chief Posey, "was poisoned with flour" in 1923. Duke Project, Western History
Center, University of Utah, tape no. 550. Forbes Parkhill, *The Last of the Indian
Wars* (New York, 1961), pp. 28–29, 47–48, 70–77, 116, gives the generally
accepted interpretation of the last "Ute War" and Posey's death resulting from
body wounds. Other Duke tapes deal with a variety of subjects, many neglected or ignored by white historians: Spanish slavery of Acoma Indians, tape

no. 70; outrages committed by Spanish priests, tape no. 73; the white man's treaties, tape no. 9; reservation outrages, tape no. 36; the Indian's hostility to the white man's culture, tape no. 65; white encroachment on Indian lands and sacred places, tapes no. 148, 102, 198, 82; tobacco as a sacred plant and the white man's desecration of it, tape no. 148. An excellent new tribal history, *Ute People: An Historical Study,* comp. June Lyman and Norma Denver and ed. Floyd A. O'Neil and John D. Sylvester (Salt Lake City, Utah, 1970), incorporates much of the Indian oral history material from the Duke tapes.

53. On Queensland punitive raids against Aboriginese, see Price, p. 138; Elkin, *The Australian Aborigines,* p. 323, states that "pacification" by force continued until the 1930s.

54. See note 53, above.

55. A. Barrie Pittock, *Toward a Multi-Racial Society: The 1969 James Backhouse Lecture* (Pymble, New South Wales, 1969), p. 5.

56. *Ibid.,* p. 12.

57. Francis Paul Prucha, *American Indian Policy in the Formative Years, The Indian Trade and Intercourse Acts, 1790–1834* (Lincoln, Neb., 1970), pp. 226–27, 229; Louis DeVorsey, Jr., *The Indian Boundary in the Southern Colonies, 1763–1775* (Chapel Hill, N.C., 1966), pp. 27 ff.

58. Wilcomb Washburn, "The Moral and Legal Justifications for Dispossessing the Indians," in James M. Smith, ed., *Seventeenth-Century America: Essays in Colonial History* (Chapel Hill, N.C., 1959), pp. 15–32.

59. Quoted in *ibid.,* p. 23.

60. See Albert K. Weinberg's well-documented chapter, "The Destined Use of the Soil," in *Manifest Destiny, A Study of Nationalist Expansionism in American History* (Baltimore, 1935), pp. 72–99.

61. Statement by Senator Thomas H. Benton. Quoted in *ibid.,* p. 73.

62. Washburn, p. 23.

63. Nancy Lurie, "Indian Cultural Adjustment to European Civilization," in Smith, pp. 38–60.

64. *Ibid.,* pp. 56–60.

65. *Ibid.,* p. 57.

66. *Ibid.,* pp. 38–39.

67. See Chapter 10.

68. John D. Cross of the Mitchell Library staff in Sydney has called my attention to eighteenth-century drawings of Aborigines as exemplified by artists who were with Captain Cook. Here we have heroic, masculine figures. Later portrayals of the Aborigines, especially in the 1840s, depict them almost as monkeys with thin legs and pot bellies. Examples of both kinds of drawings are in Moorehead, pp. 144–45. Perhaps the best overall study on noble savage imagery in the South Pacific is Bernard Smith, *European Vision of the South Pacific, 1768–1850* (New York, 1960).

69. Lurie, pp. 38–39.

70. *Ibid.* Little Carpenter, the Cherokee chief who visited England, remembered only "kind Promises" that were made to him. William L. McDowell, Jr., ed., *Documents relating to Indian Affairs, 1754–1765 in Colonial Records of South Carolina* (Columbia, S.C., 1970), p. 138.

71. Quoted in Weinberg, pp. 86–87.

72. *Ibid.* The relatively unknown but similar story of the later dispossession of the Indians of the Far West during the Mexican War era is told in Robert Anthony Trennert, "The Far Western Indian Frontier and the Beginnings of the Reservation System, 1846–1851" (Ph.D. diss., University of California,

Santa Barbara, 1969). Trennert discusses "the policy of extermination long advocated by many Texans" (p. 152) and the bitterly fought Texas Indian wars of 1846–51 (pp. 113–54, 320–64).

73. George Simpson, Hudson's Bay Company executive, repeatedly emphasizes in his journals the importance of the Indian in the company's fur trade enterprises. He even goes so far as to consider "the effect the conversion of Indians might have on the trade," concluding that it would not be "injurious," and indeed might be "highly beneficial" causing the Indians to be "more industrious, more seriously . . . [concerned with] the Chase." Frederick Merk, ed., *Fur Trade and Empire, George Simpson's Journal . . . 1824–1825* (Cambridge, Mass., 1968), pp. 108–09. On the company's price wars that resulted from American trading ships contacting Indians, see John S. Galbraith, *The Hudson's Bay Company as an Imperial Factor, 1821–69* (Berkeley, Calif., 1957), pp. 138–40. A House of Commons report of 1857 strongly supported the company's desire to maintain a monopoly for the "protection of the natives against the evils of openly competitive bidding and for conservation of fur-bearing animals." Quoted in Douglas MacKay, *The Honourable Company, A History of the Hudson's Bay Company* (New York, 1936), p. 274. However, as Simpson's journal demonstrates, the company's concern with profits was such that it would not follow a policy of conservation of fur-bearing animals, even when the supply was near exhaustion in areas where they were "unremittingly hunted." See Merk, pp. 151–52.

74. H. C. Allen, *Bush and Backwoods: A Comparison of the Frontier in Australia and the United States* (Sydney, 1959), pp. 24–25; John Wesley Powell, "From Warpath to Reservation," in Wilcomb E. Washburn, ed., *The Indian and the White Man* (New York, 1964), pp. 377–91; R. M. W. Reece, "The Aborigines and Colonial Society in New South Wales Before 1850, With Special Reference to the Period of the Gipps Administration, 1838–1846" (M.A. thesis, University of Queensland, 1969), pp. 10–143.

75. See Chapter 1 and notes.

76. *Ibid.*

77. Australian writers have perhaps been less successful in making a hero out of the "bushman" or "bushranger." See Russell Ward, *Australia* (London, 1965), pp. 9, 58–59, 94–96. Ward develops the bushranger myth more fully in his readable volume, *The Australian Legend* (Melbourne, 1961). Romantic myths have also grown up around the picturesque Brazilian Bandeirantes, jungle pathfinders whose movements were governed by Indian slave hunting and mining prospecting cycles. Richard M. Morse, ed., *The Bandeirantes: The Historical Role of the Brazilian Pathfinders* (New York, 1965), pp. 5, 23, 181–90.

78. Ward, *Australia* p. 27.

79. There is a substantial body of literature on present Aboriginal problems. See, for example, *We the Australians: What Is to Follow the Referendum? Proceedings of the Inter-Racial Seminar Held at Townsville, December, 1967* (Townsville, Queensland, 1968); Frank Stevens, *Equal Wages for Aborigines, The Background to Industrial Discrimination in the Northern Territory of Australia* (Sydney, 1968); T. G. H. Strehlow, *Assimilation Problems: The Aboriginal Viewpoint* (Adelaide, 1964); Fay Gale, *A Study of Assimilation, Part-Aborigines in South Australia* (Adelaide, 1964); Tom Roper, *Aboriginal Education, The Teacher's Role* (Melbourne, 1969); Jack Kelly, *Human Rights for Aborigines, Pre-requisite for Northern Development* (Sydney, 1966–67); Frank G. Engel, *Turning Land into Hope, Toward a New Aboriginal Policy*

for Australia (An address delivered at the Annual Conference of the Federal
Council for the Advancement of Aborigines, Parkville, Victoria, April 1968);
Daisy Bates, *The Passing of the Aborigines, A Lifetime Spent among the Natives of Australia* (Melbourne, 1966), pp. 190–243; Frank Hardy, *The Unlucky Australians* (Sydney, 1968), pp. 175–209.

80. Douglas Oliver in his searching study of natives of the Pacific also makes
this point. See Oliver, pp. 425–26. O. Mannoni, *Prospero and Caliban, The
Psychology of Colonization* (N.Y., 1964), pp. 83–84, 100–01, 160–61, throws
considerable light on special relationships between native people and resident
Europeans.

EPILOGUE

1. W. R. Jacobs, ed., *The Paxton Riots and the Frontier Theory* (Chicago,
1967), pp. 1–5.
2. Francis Parkman, *The Conspiracy of Pontiac and the Indian War after
the Conquest of Canada* (Boston, 1898), 2:93.
3. David Sloan, "The Paxton Riots" (Ph.D. diss., University of California,
Santa Barbara, 1968), devotes several chapters to discussion of the perplexing
moral dilemma faced by the Quakers during the riots.
4. A bibliographical essay discussing the controversies surrounding Turner's
work is in W. R. Jacobs, *The Historical World of Frederick Jackson Turner*
(New Haven, Conn., 1968), pp. 256–74.
5. W. J. Eccles, *The Canadian Frontier, 1534–1760* (New York, 1969),
pp. 103–31; Harold A. Innis, *The Fur Trade of Canada* (Toronto, 1956),
pp. 16–22.
6. An eloquent account of Spanish-Indian policy is in Philip W. Powell, *Tree
of Hate* . . . (N.Y., 1971) pp. 14 ff. See essays by Lewis Hanke, Dauril Alden,
and Edward H. Spicer in Howard Peckham and Charles Gipson, eds., *Attitudes
of Colonial Powers Toward the American Indian* (Salt Lake City, Utah, 1969),
pp. 1–45, 107–35. Mason Wade's excellent article on French policy toward
the Indians is also in this volume, pp. 61–80.
7. Erik H. Erikson makes the same point in writing about British colonialism
in India. By exploiting colonial peoples the British advanced the very people
they damaged because some leaders among the exploited saw clearly the damage and permanent harm done them. Erik H. Erikson, *Gandhi's Truth* . . .
(New York, 1969), p. 266.
8. Seventeenth-century Indian villages that were destroyed by colonists in
this type of campaign were also quite vulnerable to epidemics. Stuart Levine
and Nancy O. Lurie, *The American Indian Today* (Baltimore, 1968), p. 51.
9. Francis Parkman, *The Oregon Trail* (Boston, 1892), pp. 21–23.
10. Lawrence A. Cremin, *American Education, The Colonial Experience,
1607–1783* (New York, 1970), p. 328; Anthony F. C. Wallace, *The Death and
Rebirth of the Seneca* . . . (New York, 1970), p. 137.
11. Wallace, p. 137.
12. Quoted in Fred Eggan, *The American Indian, Perspectives for Study of
Social Change* (Chicago, 1966), p. 149.
13. Quoted in William N. Fenton, "The Iroquois Confederacy in the Twentieth Century: A Case Study of the Theory of Lewis H. Morgan in 'Ancient
Society,'" *Ethnology* 4 (July 1965): 263.
14. That Jackson "consistently directed an anti-Indian policy" is the judgment of Angie Debo as well as most other scholars who have studied the

Jackson administration. See Angie Debo, *A History of the Indians of the United States* (Norman, Okla., 1970), p. 284. This is also my opinion after investigations in preparation for an article on John Ross for the *Encyclopaedia Britannica*. A refutation of this interpretation, however, is in Francis Paul Prucha, "Andrew Jackson's Indian Policy, A Reassessment," *Journal of American History* 55 (December 1969): 527–39. Prucha's interpretation of American Indian policy is discussed by Wilcomb E. Washburn in "The Writing of American Indian History, A Status Report," *Pacific Historical Review* 40 (August 1971): 264–65.

15. Quoted in Arthur H. DeRosier, Jr., *The Removal of the Choctaw Indians* (Knoxville, Tenn., 1970), p. 27.

16. Quoted in Georgiana C. Nammack, *Fraud, Politics, and the Dispossession of the Indians* . . . (Norman, Okla., 1969), p. xv.

17. Margaret Mead's dialogue with James Baldwin on race, Dick Cavett show, ABC-TV, June 1, 1971. The idea is set forth several times in Margaret Mead and James Baldwin, *A Rap on Race* (New York, 1971). See for example, pp. 17–18, 27–28.

18. Harold Driver, *Indians of North America*, 2d ed., rev. (Chicago, Ill., 1969), p. 564.

19. Confidential communication.

20. Confidential communication.

21. Vine Deloria, Jr., *We Talk, You Listen, New Tribes, New Turf, New Tribes, New Turf* (New York, 1970), pp. 189–90.

22. *Ibid.*, p. 196.

23. Driver, p. 554; Kenneth MacGowan and Joseph A. Hester, Jr., *Early Man in the New World* (Garden City, N.Y., 1962), pp. 261–76; James C. Malin, "The Grassland of North America," in William L. Thomas, ed., *Man's Role in Changing the Face of the Earth* (Chicago, 1965), p. 359.

24. Eric Ross, *Beyond the River and the Bay* . . . (Toronto, 1970), pp. 82 ff.; Driver, pp. 559 ff.; Robert E. and Pat Ritzenthaler, *The Woodland Indians* . . . (Garden City, N.Y., 1970), pp. 60 ff.

25. Anthony F. C. Wallace, "Dreams and Wishes of the Soul: A Type of Psychoanalytic Theory among the Seventeenth Century Iroquois," *American Anthropologist* 60 (1958):234–38.

26. Virgil J. Vogel, *American Indian Medicine* (Norman, Okla., 1971), pp. 316–17.

27. *Ibid.*, pp. 6 ff.; Driver, p. 557.

28. Vogel, pp. 38–39.

29. Driver, p. 418.

30. Quoted in Vogel, p. 233.

31. *Ibid.*, p. 240; Hugh T. Lefler, ed., *A Voyage to Carolina by John Lawson* (Chapel Hill, N.C.), p. 194.

32. See, for example, Carlos Castaneda's account of his experiences with a Yaqui medicine man in *The Teachings of Don Juan* . . . (New York, 1968), pp. 9 ff.

33. Stephen J. Kunitz, "Benjamin Rush on Savagism and Progress," *Ethnohistory* 17 (Winter–Spring 1970): 38.

34. *Ibid.*

35. H. L. Mencken, *The American Language* (New York, 1936), pp. 104–07. See William Brandon, ed., *Magic World, American Indian Songs and Poems* (New York, 1971), pp. 96–130 for unique contributions the woodland Indians have made to American literature.

36. Parkman, *The Oregon Trail*, p. 373.
37. W. R. Jacobs, ed., *The Appalachian Indian Frontier* (Lincoln, Neb., 1967), p. 38.
38. William N. Fenton, ed., *Parker on the Iroquois* . . . (Syracuse, N.Y., 1968), bk. 1, pp. 76–77.
39. Quoted in Wallace, *Death and Rebirth of Seneca*, p. 48.
40. W. L. McDowell, Jr., ed., *Documents Relating to Indian Affairs, 1754–1765, Colonial Records of South Carolina*, 2d ser. (Columbia, S.C., 1970), p. 441.
41. Norman O. Brown, *Life Against Death, The Psychoanalytical Meaning of History* (Middletown, Conn., 1959), p. 37.
42. *Ibid.*, pp. 265, 269, 278–79.
43. "Proceedings of the Colonial Congress Held at Albany," 1754, E. B. O'Callaghan *et al.*, eds., *Documents Relative to the Colonial History of the State of New York* . . . (Albany, N.Y., 1853–87), 6 (1855):853–91.
44. William Brandon, *The American Heritage Book of Indians* (New York, 1969), pp. 127–39.
45. Fenton, "The Iroquois Confederacy in the Twentieth Century," pp. 256–57.
46. *Ibid.*
47. Brandon, pp. 244–45.
48. "Subsistence Economies," a discussion, in Thomas, ed., pp. 420–21.
49. *Ibid.*
50. Nancy O. Lurie makes this point in Levine and Lurie, p. 130. Of course seventeenth-century Indian leaders, whose people first confronted whites, saw the dangers posed by European society a century before the inland tribes had to fight for their territories. Powhatan and King Philip, for example, were well aware of the land hunger of the whites as seventeenth-century sources reveal.
51. See Lynn T. White, Jr., on "Christian Values Blamed in Part for Ecological Crisis," *Los Angeles Times*, Nov. 1, 1971; W. R. Jacobs, Reply to Carl Landauer, *A.H.A. Newsletter*, Sept. 1971, pp. 33–34.
52. Lynn I. White, Jr., "The Historical Roots of our Ecologic Crisis," *Science*, 155:1203–06.
53. The tendency of historians, particularly economists who write economic history, to disregard exploitation costs in giving unquestioning praise to economic growth is discussed in W. R. Jacobs, Reply to Carl Landauer, *A.H.A. Newsletter*, pp. 33–34.
54. Vine Deloria, "An Indian's Plea to Churches" (*Los Angeles Times*, Feb. 6, 1972). *The American Indian Quarterly*, 7 (Summer, 1983), under the guest editorship of Christopher Vecsey, is entitled "American Indian Religions" and therein are some of the best essays published on Indian religion: "Water Sprites: Elders of the Fish in Aboriginal North America," pp. 1-22, by A. Hultkrantz; "The Emergence of the Hopi People," pp. 69-92, by Christopher Vecsey; "'We also have a Religion,' The Free Exercise of Religion Among Native Americans," by Robert Michaelson, pp. 111-42. Although there is disagreement about the exact role of Indians as conservationists, there is agreement that Indians regarded nature as the manifestation of the supreme being. See discussion of A. Hultkrantz's views, in the same issue, pp. 150-51.

A number of key manuscript collections have been consulted for these essays. Especially significant in the study of British imperial administration of Indian affairs is the collection of British transcripts, copies of original documents from British archives, housed in the Library of Congress. Among these are the Public Record Office papers in class 5 that include voluminous correspondence on Indian affairs between British officials in England and in colonial America. Much of this documentary material is complemented by the Additional Manuscripts papers in the British Museum, which include documents on the origins of the southern colonial Indian superintendency. I have used British documentary material from Library of Congress transcripts as well as documentary material that I had filmed while working in London at the Public Record Office and the British Museum. I have also used Library of Congress transcripts of French documents as well as original manuscripts from the Archives Nationales, Ministre des Colonies in Paris. In addition, I have consulted early American documentary material on Indians from British and French repositories (microfilm, photostats, typescript copies of documents), in the Louis Knott Koontz and John Carl Parish Collections housed in the Library of the University of California, Santa Barbara.

To supplement my investigations of British and French official papers I have made extensive use of the Loudoun Collection at the Henry E. Huntington Library, San Marino, California. This large private collection, including a substantial body of French materials, is one of the best documentary sources on eighteenth-century Indian frontier history. Close examination of my notes to individual chapters will show that the trail of my investigations led me to various other manuscript collections includ-

ing the Bouquet Papers at the Canadian Archives in Ottawa; the Draper
Collection of the Wisconsin State Historical Society in Madison (now
available in microfilm); the Shelburne Papers at the William L. Clements
Library, Ann Arbor, Michigan; and the Council and Commons House
records concerning Indian affairs at the South Carolina Archives Department in Columbia. Since these original documents are, in some cases, in
a state of physical disintegration, it is fortunate that the South Carolina
Archives Department has sponsored publication of a portion of them under the able editorship of the late J. H. Easterby and W. H. McDowell.

My conclusions on the historical interpretations concerning Indians by
Frederick Jackson Turner and Francis Parkman are based on their printed
works as well as their preserved papers, which include correspondence
as well as research materials. Turner's papers, together with annotated
volumes from his personal library, are at the Huntington Library; the
main collection of Parkman's correspondence and research notes and
documents are at the Massachusetts Historical Society.

For the comparative study of native-white relations in Chapter 11, I
used rare book, newspaper, and manuscript collections at the Mitchell
Library in Sydney, Australia; the National Library in Canberra; the Victoria State Library in Melbourne; the State Library of South Australia in
Adelaide; and the Library of the University of Papua-New Guinea in
Port Moresby. One of the unique sources of Indian history that has
helped me to appreciate the Indian point of view is the typescript record
of the Duke Oral Indian History Collection at the Western History Center, University of Utah, made available to me by Professors C. Gregory
Crampton and David Miller.

The range of my studies has also included a wide variety of published
archival material dealing with native-white relations in Australia, New
Guinea, and in North America. Particularly valuable for the history of
the woodland Indians and their relations with the French and Anglo-
Americans are the published legislative records of the colonies, particularly those of New York and Pennsylvania. These are complemented by
the published *Collections* of the State Historical Society of Wisconsin
and other printed sources. Citations to published documents such as
these, as well as published correspondence of leading white figures who
participated in Indian affairs, are in my notes. I have also cited key source
materials quoted in authoritative secondary works.

Although the footnotes and endnotes identify my sources of fact and
interpretation, it is useful for the critical reader to have an appraisal of
the value of significant secondary works in the field of Indian-white relations, particularly those that concern early American history and the
woodland tribes. A provocative older book (now unfortunately out of

print) that has led me to question established interpretations is William Christy MacLeod, *The American Indian Frontier* (New York, 1928). Published as part of a *History of Civilization* series by Alfred Knopf, the book sweeps over a mass of early twentieth-century anthropological and ethnohistorical data concerning native-white contacts in the western hemisphere. Francis Parkman's classic work, *The Conspiracy of Pontiac and the Indian War After the Conquest of Canada* (2 vols., Boston, 1898) appears in its most complete form in the Frontenac or Champlain editions that contain his last revisions. Parkman's *Pontiac* (which I regard as the most important single historical work on the woodland tribes despite its shortcomings) has sparked my thinking, though some of my conclusions differ from his. Other Parkman volumes, especially *The Oregon Trail,* the *Jesuits,* the *Pioneers, Frontenac,* and *La Salle* provide a wealth of history on the woodland tribes, much of it provocative, all of it vivid and fascinating to read. Part of my interest in Parkman's Indians stems from labor on the manuscript of an unfinished book, "Parkman's Oregon Trail, the Making of a Book and a Historian." Much of the background for Parkman's thinking about Indians, black people, and social questions is revealed in his published correspondence, *Letters of Francis Parkman,* ed. W. R. Jacobs (2 vols., Norman, Okla., 1960). Volume one of these Parkman *Letters,* pp. xli–xlix contains my analysis of Parkman's neurosis, which influenced his interpretations and his portrayal of personages in his volumes, including Pontiac. An important critical appraisal of Parkman's *Pontiac* is in Howard H. Peckham's carefully documented study, *Pontiac and the Indian Uprising* (Princeton, N.J., 1947).

The modern authors of Indian history may even exceed the number of Indian orators in the first two centuries of our history. In my judgment, one of the most eloquent and persuasive of these is William Brandon, whose *American Heritage Book of Indians* (New York, 1961) has superb illustrations as well as text. An inexpensive paperback edition published by Dell (New York, 1969), is available, and I have used it as one of my required readings in teaching an undergraduate course on "The Indian and the Frontier, Ideas and Interpretations." Anyone familiar with Brandon's writings on Indians must recognize that I am heavily indebted to him. A high-water mark in the historiography of the woodland Indians was the printing of *Seventeenth-Century America, Essays in Colonial History,* ed. James M. Smith (Chapel Hill, N.C., 1959), which contains two very significant essays on Indians: Wilcomb Washburn's "The Moral and Legal Justifications for Dispossessing the Indians" * and Nancy O. Lurie's "Indian Cultural Adjustment to European Civilization," pp. 15–32, 33–62. Those interested in the origins of prejudice toward

---

* An extended discussion of this topic is in Washburn, *Red Man's Land—White Man's Law* (New York, 1971), pp. 27–58.

the Indian should begin with these penetrating studies, which silhouette basic white misconceptions about Indian stereotypes. Though I have not accepted all of the findings of Washburn and Lurie, their influence upon me has been significant, especially in connection with their two most recent publications in the *Pacific Historical Review* 50 (August, 1971) devoted to the American Indian. Washburn's stimulating piece, "The Writing of American Indian History: A Status Report," pp. 261–81, supplements Bernard Sheehan's excellent earlier appraisal of historiographical literature "Indian-White Relations in Early America, A Review Essay," in *William and Mary Quarterly* 26 (1969):267–86. Nancy Lurie's remarkable essay on Indian drinking in the August 1971 issue of the *Pacific Historical Review*, "The World's Oldest On-Going Protest Demonstration: North American Indian Drinking Patterns," pp. 311–32, has profound implications for the study of all historic Indian-white relations. Her conclusions are vigorously refuted by Vine Deloria in *We Talk, You Listen* (New York, 1970), pp. 10 ff. and in *Custer Died For Your Sins* (New York, 1970), pp. 86 ff., two strong, far-ranging critiques of white Indian policy, and white anthropological-historical research on Indian societies. A book that Nancy Lurie, as well as all others who study Indian drinking patterns must acknowledge as a key source is Craig MacAndrew and Robert B. Edgerton, *Drunken Compartment, A Social Explanation* (Chicago, 1969).

For the general reader, a readable brief history of the American Indians is William T. Hagan, *American Indians* (Chicago, 1961). Hagan has evaluated trends of Indian historiography in *The Indian in American History* (New York, 1963), vol. 50 of the A.H.A.'s pamphlets for teachers and students of history. The volume that best incorporates a detailed account of major tribes and their experiences during and after the great removal is Angie Debo, *A History of the Indians of the United States* (Norman, Okla., 1970). Although Debo's *History* is extremely valuable for nineteenth-century Indian history, the first portions of the book, particularly the chapters dealing with early native-white contacts, do not include results of the anthropological investigations. But few, indeed, are the histories of Indians written by historians that pay much attention to the findings of nonhistorians.

Two well-researched volumes, based upon extensive use of historical documentary sources are Alden T. Vaughan's *New England Frontier, Puritans and Indians, 1620–1675* (Boston, 1965) and Francis Paul Prucha's *American Indian Policy in the Formative Years: The Indian Trade and Intercourse Acts, 1790–1834* (Cambridge, Mass., 1962), paperback Bison series edition (Lincoln, Neb., 1970). Vaughan's approval of Puritan Indian policy and Father Prucha's almost total defense of Andrew Jackson in "Andrew Jackson's Indian Policy: A Reassessment," *Journal of Ameri-*

can History 56 (1969): 527–39 (reproduced without notes in Prucha, ed., *The Indian in American History* [New York, 1971], a problems study booklet), should be mentioned here because their sympathetic interpretation of white Indian policy produced an almost opposite reaction in me after having examined some of the same sources they used. My general interpretations of American Indian history tend to agree more with the findings of William Brandon, Wilcomb Washburn, William T. Hagan, and William C. MacLeod. However, I found stimulating a broader framework of American history incorporating a resume of native-white contacts in Albert K. Weinberg, *Manifest Destiny, A Study of Nationalist Expansionism in American History,* first published by the Johns Hopkins University Press (Baltimore, 1935) and reprinted in paperback by the Quadrangle Press (Chicago, 1963).

Two compilations of documents that support Weinberg's charges of white exploitation of native people are Wilcomb Washburn, ed., *The Indian and the White Man* (Garden City, N.Y., 1964) and Jack D. Forbes, ed., *The Indian in America's Past* (Englewood Cliffs, N.J., 1964). Additional documentary material can also be found in Edward H. Spicer's *A Short History of Indians of the United States* (New York, 1969). Spicer, like a number of other anthropologists, is now making inroads in American Indian history to explain the origins of attitudes and conflicts in early native-white relations. A work of genuine significance in all Indian history (though it deals primarily with the Indians of the American Southwest), is Spicer's *Cycles of Conquest* (Tucson, Ariz., 1964). If I ever doubted the contributions of anthropologists to the history of Indian-white relations, it was dispelled by reading Harold E. Driver's learned and authoritative *Indians of North America,* 2d ed., rev. (Chicago, 1969). My interpretation of North American Indian population data came partly from Driver, who in turn takes a conservative view of Henry Dobyns' population estimates set forth in a carefully documented (and widely criticized) essay, "Estimating Aboriginal American Population," in *Current Anthropology* 7 (1966): 395–449, Dobyns' argument and evidence to support the estimates of a nine to ten million Indian population in North America and some ninety to one hundred million Indians for the western hemisphere at the time of discovery is largely based upon research in the history of epidemic diseases and other factors that brought about Indian depopulation. After conversations with Dobyns and after rereading his publications I am converted to his point of view and am convinced that historians have tended to neglect the key factors of Indian depopulation and disease (mainly smallpox) in writing about frontier history, Indian history, or native-white relations.

My great indebtedness to anthropologists comes from their writings about the culture of the Indians, especially the woodland tribes. Dean of scholars on the forest Indians (particularly those of the Northeast) was the late Frank G. Speck, whose concept of the Indian as a conservationist was set forth in *The Penobscot Man* (Philadelphia, 1940) and in a number of articles in the *American Anthropologist* and other scholarly publications now listed in Driver, pp. 588–89 (bibliography). The most persuasive of Speck's publications for me was a little known essay, "Aboriginal Conservators," *Audubon Magazine* 40 (1938): 258–61. Here Speck condensed a lifetime of research to bring his findings to a wider, non-scientific audience. For my interpretation of Indian culture areas I am also indebted to A. L. Kroeber's magnificent volume, *Anthropology, Race Language, Culture, Psychology, Prehistory* (New York, 1948), which digests a large mass of data published before 1948.

Basic for the study of the North American Indians are also F. W. Hodge, ed., *Handbook of the American Indians* (2 vols., Washington, D.C., 1907, 1910); Hodge, ed., *Handbook of the Indians of Canada* (Ottawa, 1913); A. L. Kroeber, *Handbook of the Indians of California* (Washington, 1925); Kroeber, *Cultural and Natural Areas of Native North America* (Berkeley, Calif., 1945); John R. Swanton, *Indian Tribes of North America* (Washington, D.C., 1953); and S. F. Cook's statistical studies on *The Conflict Between the California Indian and White Civilization* (4 vols., Berkeley, Calif., 1943), supplemented by the excellent bibliographical notes in Wendell H. Oswalt, *This Land Was Theirs: A Study of the North American Indian* (New York, 1966). William Brandon's *The American Heritage Book of Indians* incorporates a large mass of anthropological data into a readable historical narrative. Valuable surveys of prehistory Indian societies are in Alvin M. Josephy, Jr., *The Indian Heritage in America* (New York, 1968) and Peter Farb, *Man's Rise to Civilization as Shown by the Indians of North America . . .* (New York, 1968).

A. L. Kroeber's *Anthropology* is useful for studying early native-white contacts in almost all areas where Europeans spread their frontiers, but the best work in print on Aboriginal Australians is A. P. Elkin's classic volume, *The Australian Aborigines, How to Understand Them*, 3rd ed. (Sydney, 1954). This is supplemented by a series of research studies by Elkin's former students and admirers, *Aboriginal Man in Australia, Essays in Honor of Emeritus Professor A. P. Elkin*, ed. Ronald M. Berndt and Catherine H. Berndt (Sydney, 1969). *The Australian Aborigines*, a short illustrated volume published by the Department of Territories (Sydney, 1967), tends to give a favorable coloration to government policies. D. J. Mulvaney, ed., *Australian Archaeology, A Guide to Field Techniques*, Australian Institute of Aboriginal Studies, manual no. 4 (Canberra, 1969), pp. 119–30, has a classification of aboriginal stone implements. Mulvaney's comprehensive *Ancient Peoples and Places, The*

Prehistory of Australia (London, 1969) argues, with considerable evidence, that Aboriginal life was in a constant state of technological change. A basic reference volume is Felix M. Keesing's comprehensive *Culture Change, An Analysis of Bibliography of Anthropological Sources to 1952* (Stanford, Calif., 1953).

One of the most illuminating studies on the native people of New Guinea is by a political scientist, C. D. Rowley, whose *The New Guinea Villager* (Melbourne, 1965) is based upon interdisciplinary research and first-hand experience. *Pigs For Ancestors: Ritual in the Ecology of a New Guinea People,* by Roy A. Rappaport (New Haven, Conn., 1967), is a technical study showing how the ritual cycle of Tsembaga native people governed their adjustment to their environment (see especially pp. 224–42). The Tsembaga keep four kinds of animals: pigs, chickens, dogs, and cassowaries, which are captured young and provide meat and feathers. Other useful volumes on the New Guinea villagers are: Ian Hogbin, *Transformation Scene: the Changing Culture of a New Guinea Village* (London, 1951); Gavin Souter, *New Guinea: The Last Unknown* (London, 1963); Brian Essai, *Papua and New Guinea: A Contemporary Survey* (London, 1961); and *Studies in New Guinea Land Tenure: Three Papers* by Ian Hogbin and Peter Lawrence (Sydney, 1967). An excellent survey of the island and its native people by two geographers is *New Guinea: The Territory and its People,* by D.A.M. Lea and P. G. Irwin (Melbourne, 1967). A book which, in my judgment, tends to oversimplify New Guinea native life by stressing Aboriginal warfare is Robert Gardner and Karl G. Heider, *Gardens of War, Life and Death in the New Guinea Stone Age* (New York, 1968).

Though historians, anthropologists, geographers, and ecologists have been taking sides for some time on the underlying implications and consequences of European contacts among Indians and other native people in previously unexplored areas, factual detailed investigations upon which judgment can be based are few. The area of study is so vast and so many interdisciplinary points of research are involved that no one scholar has been able to master the field. A starting point for the investigation of the fate of Pacific native people in the wake of the European invasion is Douglas L. Oliver's *The Pacific Islands* (Garden City, N.Y., 1961), a learned work encompassing several disciplines with a classified bibliography on anthropology, colonial history, sociology, and geography. A. Grenfell Price, *White Settlers and Native Peoples, An Historical Study of Racial Contacts between English-speaking Whites and Aboriginal Peoples in the United States, Canada, Australia and New Zealand* (Melbourne, 1949) is a pioneering study by a geographer. Though based upon dated sources, the book is full of insights. A volume that shows the backwash of native culture and the land on the Australian national character is

Russell Ward's thoughtful study, *The Australian Legend* (Melbourne, 2d ed., 1965). In many respects, the most complete appraisal of the native people's rise from village jungle life to self-government throughout their long association with Europeans in Papua-New Guinea is a secondary school textbook, *A Short History of New Guinea* (Sydney, 1968), by P. Biskup, B. Jinks, and H. Nelson.

To study the impact of European culture upon the land and on the American Indian, a good beginning can be made with Victor E. Shelford, *The Ecology of North America* (Urbana, Ill., 1963), which contains a readable description of major North American biomes and ecosystems, together with brief descriptions of prehistoric Indian communities mentioning their hunting, agricultural, and burning practices. Most of Carl O. Sauer's *Seventeenth Century in North America, The Land and the People as Seen by Europeans* (Berkeley, Calif., 1971) a study of the Indians and the land before massive changes took place and Sauer's *Land and Life, A Selection of the Writings of Carl Ortwin Sauer*, ed. with an introduction by John Leighly (Berkeley, Calif., 1969) point to the significance of ecological shifts on the North American continent, a theme that is further explored in most of the chapters in William L. Thomas, ed., *Man's Role in Changing the Face of the Earth* (Chicago, 1965), a series of papers read at the international symposium sponsored by the Wenner-Gren Foundation for Anthropological Research. The anthropologist who has stimulated me most in the study of perhaps the greatest of the woodland peoples, the Iroquois, is William N. Fenton whose mastery of his subject is demonstrated by his brilliant introduction to *Parker on the Iroquois, Iroquois Uses of Maize and Other Food Plants, the Code of Handsome Lake, the Seneca Prophet, the Constitution of the Five Nations* (Syracuse, N.Y., 1968). Anthropologist Anthony F. C. Wallace, who like William Fenton combines historical and anthropological research in the study of the Indian, has given Americans one of the finest examples of minority history in his *Death and Rebirth of the Seneca* . . . (New York, 1970).

Two historians who have contributed much to the understanding of the significance of racial prejudice in American history have also contributed to my understanding of the origins of the morality of Indian-hating. One of these is Winthrop Jordan, whose prize-winning volume, *White Over Black, American Attitudes Toward the Negro, 1550–1812* (Chapel Hill, N.C., 1968) explores the origins of white attitudes toward Indians as well as toward blacks. Peter Loewenberg's "The Psychology of Racism," in Gary B. Nash and Richard Weiss, ed., *The Great Fear, Race in the Mind of America* (New York, 1970) does much to supplement arguments brought forth by Jordan and to place them within the context of Freudian thought. Three additional volumes should be mentioned here because they also provide insights into the American mind: James H. Cassedy, *Demography in America, Beginnings of the Statistical Mind, 1600-1800* (Cambridge, Mass., 1969) reveals the concern Anglo-Americans had about numbers of Indians, particularly warriors; Roderick Nash, *Wilderness and the American Mind* (3d. ed., New Haven, Conn., 1982) reveals the grand heights of thought scaled by Americans of vision who had an appreciation of the wilderness heritage the Indian preserved for us. Patterns of white exploitation of that heritage are clearly seen in Leo E. Oliva, "Our Frontier Heritage and the Environment," *The American West*, 9 (January, 1972), pp. 44-47, 61-63, and in Donald Worster, *Nature's Economy* (San Francisco, 1977). The kind of thinking that led to the assault on Indians and their homelands is discussed in a series of published lectures edited by Howard Peckham and Charles Gibson, *Attitudes of the Colonial Powers Toward the American Indian* (Salt Lake City, 1969).

Serious scholars in American Indian History are indebted to Francis Paul Prucha for his two comprehensive bibliographical aids, *A Bibliographical Guide to the History of Indian-White Relations in the United States* (Chicago, 1977), and a supplementary work, *Indian-White Relations in the United States: A Bibliography of Works Published, 1975-1980* (Lincoln, Nebr., 1982). No scholar who makes an investigation of Indian history or Indian-white relations can overlook ABC Clio Press's well-organized and up-to-date volumes of historical abstracts. These are easily available because of detailed author and subject index volumes. The whole of this mass of reference material is now available through computers available in most libraries which subscribe to the ABC Clio data bank. As an example, volume 21, no. 2, *America: History and Life* (Santa Barbara, Calif., 1984), has article abstracts and citations to recent Indian studies on pp. 36ff.

Of great importance for reference is the series of bibliographies annotated by individual editors and published by the Newberry Library Center for the History of the American Indian. The series, edited by Francis Jennings and William Swaggerty, is published by the Indiana University Press. Individual volumes that have proved useful to me are Henry Dobyns, *Native American Historical Demography* (1976); Michael D. Green, *The Creeks* (1979); Clara Sue Kidwell and Charles Roberts, *The Choctaws* (1980); and Raymond D. Fogelson, *The Cherokees* (1978).

In recent years a number of articles and books have influenced my thinking about frontier history and Indian-white relations. Jack D. Forbes, a prolific writer and Turnerean critic, crystalizes his main ideas in a convincing essay, "Frontiers in American History and the Role of the Frontier Historian," in *Ethnohistory*, 15 (Spring, 1968), pp. 203-205. Some of Forbes's arguments are echoed and documented in David A. Nichols, "Civilization over Savage: Frederick Jackson Turner and the Indian," in *South Dakota History* 11 (Fall, 1972): 383-405.

Stimulated by research discussions at the national meetings of the American Society for Ethnohistory and teaching programs in Native American studies, there has been an outpouring of significant books and articles, many of them by graduates of the Newberry Library Center. Calvin Martin's prize-winning *Keepers of the Game: Indian-Animal Relationship and the Fur Trade* (Berkeley, 1978), challenging ecological and cultural studies by generations of anthropologists, provoked a vigorous response from leading scholars in *Indians, Animals, and the Fur Trade, A Critique of Keepers of the Game*, edited by Shepard Krech (Athens, Georgia, 1981). Another pathbreaking study, by Neal Salisbury, *Manitou and Providence, Indians, Europeans, and the Making of New England, 1500-1643* (New York, 1982) is a model volume of ethnohistorical research showing the clash of cultures of the whites and the Indians. It provides new insights on historic racial discrimination and on the dispossession of Indians by the onslaught of smallpox and other diseases.

Salisbury's book supports themes set forth in Francis Jennings's influential study *The Invasion of America, Indians, Colonialism, and Cant of Conquest* (Chapel Hill, N.C., 1975) and Alfred W. Crosby's *The Columbian Exchange, Biological and Cultural Consequences of 1492* (Westport, Conn., 1972). Sherburne F. Cook's continuing researches on disease, especially his article "The Significance of Disease in the Extinction of the New England Indians" in *Human Biology* 45 (1973): 485-508. W. R. Jacobs, "The Tip of an Iceberg, Pre-Columbian Indian Demography and Some Implications for Revisionism, *William and Mary Quarterly*, 3d series, 31 (1974): 123-32, and Henry F. Dobyns, *Their Number Become Thinned, Native American Population Dynamics in Eastern North America* (Knoxville, Tenn., 1983), analyze the debate on Indian population dynamics and make understandable the impact of massive Indian dislocations caused by continental pandemics. William H. McNeill's global overview, *Plagues and Peoples* (Garden City, N.Y., 1976), is largely based upon demographic works of other scholars. His lectures on *The Great Frontier: Freedom and Hierarchy in Modern Times* (Princeton, N.J., 1983) survey worldwide impacts of disease and make the argument that Frederick Jackson Turner's freedom-loving frontier was confined to the frontiersmen themselves who enslaved non-Europeans whenever they could to exploit their labor. Criticisms of Turner, and Francis Parkman as well, are set forth in Francis Jennings formidable new volume, *The Ambiguous Iroquois Empire, The Convenant Chain Confederation of Indian Tribes with English Colonies from Its Beginnings to the Lancaster Treaty of 1744* (New York, 1984). The Iroquois covenant chain or "chain of friendship" is also discussed in an older work, W. R. Jacobs' *Diplomacy and Indian Gifts* (Stanford, Calif., 1949), republished as *Wilderness Politics and Indian Gifts* (Lincoln, Nebr., 1966); and in an authoritative study, Richard Aguila's *The Iroquois Res-*

toration, Iroquois Diplomacy on the Colonial Frontier, 1701-1754 (Detroit, 1982). Dorothy V. Jones, in *License for Empire, Colonialism by Treaty in Early America* (Chicago, 1982), documents white land grabs by treaty from the Iroquois and other tribes.

If we take the view that early American history should not follow the Frederick Jackson Turner geographical frontier strategy of interpretation, moving forward from the east to the west, the new *Handbook of North American Indians* volumes, edited by William Sturtevant, show ethnohistorical beginnings of early frontier history all over the northern hemisphere. One of Turner's disciples, Herbert Eugene Bolton, some years ago set the pattern for hemispheric studies in Indian-white relations and exploration with such volumes as the *Rim of Christendom: A Biography of Eusebio Francisco Kino, Pacific Coast Pioneer* (New York, 1936). With a similar perspective, the new *Handbook* volumes in ethnohistorical settings are invaluable for seeing the hemispheric impact of the European invader on Native Americans. Volume 8 of the series, *California* (Washington, D.C., 1978), edited by Robert F. Heizer, has given me a new appreciation of California Indians' cultures, their languages, their territories, and their life-styles as tuned to environmental conditions. This work is closely related to a most persuasively written and sympathetically understanding volume, *The Natural World of the California Indians*, by R. F. Heizer and Albert B. Elsasser (Berkeley, 1980). Editors Christopher Vecsey and Robert W. Venables brought together a symposium of papers that gives a sharp appraisal of Indian environmental factors in *American Indian Environments, Ecological Issues in Native American History* (Syracuse, N.Y., 1980). In this volume there are worthy statements on Navajo and Iroquois ecological perspectives by Native American spokesmen Peter MacDonald and Oren Lyons.

Other volumes already published in the *Handbook* series are equally valuable in giving the hemispheric view of early American native-white relations: volume 15, *Northeast* (Washington, D.C., 1978), edited by Bruce G. Trigger; volume 9, *Southwest* (Washington, D.C., 1979), edited by Alfonso Ortiz; volume 6, *Subarctic* (Washington, D.C., 1981), edited by June Helm. Twenty volumes are planned in this series sponsored by the Smithsonian Institution. Another useful volume soon to be published is on the *History Of Indian-White Relations*, edited by Wilcomb E. Washburn. Washburn's *The Indian in America* (New York, 1975) gives readers a comprehensive ethnohistorical portrait of Indians and Indian-white relations and is especially valuable insight on Christian Indian missionary activity. This latter subject unusually controversial, is one that Henry W. Bowden has undertaken in *American Indians and Christian Missions* (Chicago, 1981). Bowden sympathetically looks over the shoulders of historic missionaries as they went about their work. A more critical and more ethnohistorical approach is in Brian W. Dippie, *The Vanishing American, White Attitudes and U.S. Indian Policy* (Middletown, Conn., 1982), a work that enlarges on themes set forth in Robert F. Berkhofer's admirable, carefully researched volume *The White Man's Indian: Images of American Indians from Columbus to the Present* (New York, 1978). It is ironic that the most respected study of *The Religions of the American Indians* (Berkeley, 1979), is by a Swedish scholar, Ake Hultkrantz. In Hultkrantz's writing we can, with the oral and written accounts preserved by Native American religious leaders themselves, begin to appreciate the complexity of Indian religious beliefs.

The late Sherburne F. Cook reconstructed population dynamics of the California Indians by ethnohistorical approaches in two heavily documented volumes, *The Conflict Between the California Indian and White Civilization* (Berkeley, 1976) and *The Population of the California Indians, 1769-1970* (Berkeley, 1976), which cause an uneasy burden of guilt to be felt by some Franciscan historians (e.g., for the frequent and heavy disciplinary flogging of missionary Indians). The leader among the order today in stating and in arguing justifications for missionary behavior is Francis M. Guest, O.F.M. In two essays, "An Examination of the Thesis of S. F. Cook on the Forced Conversion of Indians in California Missions," *Southern California Quarterly* 61 (Spring, 1979): 1-77, and "Cultural Perspectives on California Mission Life," *Southern California Quarterly* 65 (Spring, 1983): 1-65, Guest attempts to answer the question "whether or not the mission administration was brutal." Controversy, the lifeblood of Indian History and Indian-white relations, runs the gamut of topics, from religion, land, and slavery to racism. The role of Indians themselves in enslaving other Indians—a provocative issue—is shown to be one of the evils of white contact in Theda Perdue's *Slavery and the Evolution of Cherokee Society* (Knoxville, Tenn., 1979), Richard Haan's essay, "The 'Trade do's Not Flourish as Formerly': The Ecological Origins of the Yamassee War of 1715," *Ethnohistory*, 28 (1981): 341-58; and in John Phillip Reid's penetrating legal study, *A Better Kind of Hatchet: Law, Trade, and Diplomacy in the Cherokee Nation during the Early Years of European Contact* (University Park, Pa., 1976). The controversial ecological impact of white traders who looted wildlife reserves of Indian people is objectively analyzed in David J. Wishard's *The Fur Trade of the American West, 1807-1840* (Lincoln, Nebr., 1979). In a prize-winning tribal history, R. David Edmunds, *The Potawatomis: Keepers of the Fire* (Norman, Okla., 1978), details the history of the impact of whites, disease, traders, missionaries, and chiefs bribed with gifts at treaties to sign away a landed heritage. What has particularly impressed me is that the new ethnohistorical work, such as that done by Edmunds, portrays Indians as native American people with complex and fascinating cultures. Such themes, which are aspects of the chronicle of dispossession, are in a superb account by Arrell M. Gibson, *The American Indian, Prehistory to the Present* (Lexington, Mass., 1980), and in a valuable frontier history series volume, Robert M. Utley, *The Indian Frontier of the American West, 1846-1890* (Albuquerque, 1984). That Howard Lamar, distinguished historian of the frontier and an ethnohistorian, is an editor in that series, Histories of the American Frontier, has undoubtedly encouraged publication of volumes so outstanding as Utley's. Lamar's edition of a comprehensive *Reader's Encyclopedia of the American West* (New York, 1977) has dozens of pages on Indians and disease, on Indian leaders, and on Indian cultures, art, tribes, policies, and languages (see especially pp. 539-69). Here is an indication that Indian people are to be reckoned with in any future history of the frontier. Lamar shows that the old simplistic explanations of Indian-white relations are a thing of the past. The research behind the history itself is ever more challenging. One glance at *Extending the Rafters, Interdisciplinary Approaches to Iroquoian Studies*, essays in honor of William F. Fenton, edited by Michael K. Foster et al. (Albany, N.Y., 1984), serves warning that such techniques as "upstreaming" are complex indeed. This ethnohistorical technique of revitalizing Indian studies, pioneered by Francis Parkman and refined by William Fenton, involves utilizing perspectives from ethnohistorical sources to evaluate documentary sources. We will, with the benefit of "upstreaming," more and more be able to understand why Indians did what they did and why white sources were skewed by racism and passed on to posterity those unfortunate Indian stereotypes. In a similar way, new research is bringing about a gradual disappearance of wild-predatory-varmint stereotypes, as even coyotes are viewed as necessary wilderness animals (Thomas Dunlap, "Values for Varmints . . . ," *Pacific Historical Review*, 53 [May, 1984]: 141-61). What is fascinating about much of the modern research is that it tells us things that Indians have known for a long, long time.

The widespread impact of Europeans on many global frontiers shows that other native peoples besides Indians struggled to avoid dispossession. There were violent and often fatal confrontations in Papua New Guinea, in Australia, and in Southern Africa. A report from the World Bank on *Papua New Guinea, Its Economic Situation and Prospects for Development* (Washington, D.C., 1978), describes how native indigenous people, surviving such an ordeal after achieving political independence in 1975, have taken over 97 percent of their nation's land base and have moved rapidly toward developing their resources under a parliamentary system of government. Australians should have world recognition for their tutorial work as trustees in preparing Papua New Guinea peoples for nationhood. A paradox is that historic Australian actions directed toward their own Aborigines brought about dispossession, depopulation from disease, detribalization, and policies resulting in deculturation. This harrowing episode of harsh Anglo-Australian colonialism, duplicated in part by Spaniards in California, is described in a comparative study by Diane Kirkby, "Colonial Policy and

Native Depopulation in California and in New South Wales, 1770-1840,"
Ethnohistory 31 (1984): 1-13, one of a series of carefully researched
articles coming out of her comprehensive master's thesis on the same subject from University of California, Santa Barbara, 1980. A comparative
analysis of the global results of exploration is in Richard Van Orman's
*The Explorers, Nineteenth-Century Expeditions in Africa and the American
West* (Albuquerque, 1984), showing the emergence of Anglo hero figures
opening a wedge in the wilderness. Howard Lamar and Leonard Thompson
have edited papers from a consequential symposium on *The Frontier in
History: North America and Southern Africa Compared* (New Haven, Conn.,
1981). The editors and their associates stress Frederick Jackson Turner's
role as a catalyst in frontier history, although he did overlook the exploitation of native peoples. When the collision of peoples took place on
American and southern African frontiers, those native peoples, such as the
Bantu, with better resistance to disease and varied patterns of subsistence
had the best chances for remaining alive and keeping a land base.

Although controversy remains, among the ethnohistorians as well as
among the traditional historians of frontier Indian history, the new ap-
proaches to Indian studies tend to prevail. Books such as James T. Axtell's
*The European and the Indian: Essays in the Ethnohistory of Colonial North
America* (New York, 1981) have been generally accepted as advocating
Indian history based upon interdisciplinary sources, especially those used
by anthropologists. Behind the renascence in the history of the American
Indian are many eminent scholars, headed by physiologist Sherburne F.
Cook and anthropologists Henry F. Dobyns, William F. Fenton, Robert F.
Heizer, Anthony F. C. Wallace, Bruce Trigger, Elisabeth Tooker, and Al-
phonso Ortiz. Historians Woodrow Borah, Francis Jennings, Wilcomb Wash-
burn, William Brandon, Alvin Josephy, Arrell M. Gibson, Paul Prucha, and
William T. Hagan should be added to the list. Books by these writers
can be found in any large library.

It gives me particular pleasure to note that the renascence in American
Indian history, blending with the reinterpretation of black history, Mexican-
American history, and womens' history, has helped to bring about a more
enlightened, pluralistic general American history. This new approach, sometimes identified as the new social history, is finding its way into our best
textbooks, particularly those surveys of American history written by Mary
Beth Norton, Elliott Brownlee, and John W. Caughey.

And American Indians themselves, as demonstrated by a 1984 conference
on "Indian Self-Determination" held at Sun Valley, Idaho, under the spon-
sorship of the Institute of the American West, led by Richard Hart and
Alvin Josephy, will no longer passively tolerate distorted versions of their
history. We know this because of articulate conference statements and
publications by Indian spokespeople such as Rupert Costo, Jeannette Henry,

Alphonso Ortiz, Sam Deloria, Oren Lyons, and Ada Deere. A sign of things to come is the 1985 appearance of two brilliant new books. The first, Yasu Kawashima's monumental legal history, "Puritan Justice and the American Indians," will be under the imprint of the Wesleyan University Press. The second volume, Christopher Miller's reevaluation of missionary-Indian confrontation in the Pacific Northwest, *When Prophets Meet, Converging Millennia and the Plateau Indian Apocalypse*, will be published by the Rutgers University Press.

A number of books by Indian authors have influenced my thinking in the last decade about Indian History. Donald Grinde's *The Iroquois and the American Nation* (San Francisco, 1979); Vine Deloria's *The Trail of Broken Treaties* (New York, 1980); and M. Scott Momaday's *The Way to Rainy Mountain* (New York, 1975) have significant messages and interpretations on America's Indian heritage.